EXCAVATIONS AT WICKLIFFE MOUNDS

Excavations
at
Wickliffe Mounds

KIT W. WESLER

Foreword by Victoria G. Fortner

CONTRIBUTIONS BY
Kristin Brown
Richard B. Edging
Rebecca L. Fye
Brad T. Koldehoff and Philip J. Carr
Paul P. Kreisa and Jacqueline M. McDowell
Jenna Tedrick Kuttruff and Penelope Ballard Drooker
Hugh B. Matternes
John Pafford
James M. Phillips
Mark R. Schurr and Margaret J. Schoeninger

THE UNIVERSITY OF ALABAMA PRESS

Tuscaloosa and London

1 2 3 4 5 6 7 8 9 • 09 08 07 06 05 04 03 02 01

Typeface: AGarmond
Credits for cover photographs: top, Fain and Blanche King and associates, from *Under Your Feet* by Blanche Busey King, copyright 1971 by Ayer Company Publishers; bottom, courtesy of the Office of Archaeological Services, University of Alabama Museums, Moundville, Alabama.

∞

The paper on which this book is printed meets the minimum requirements of American National Standard for Information Science–Permanence of Paper for Printed Library Materials, ANSI Z39.48-1984.

Library of Congress Cataloging-in-Publication Data

Wesler, Kit W.
    Excavations at Wickliffe Mounds / Kit W. Wesler; foreword by Victoria G. Fortner; contributions by Kristin Brown . . . [et al.].
        p. cm.
    Includes bibliographical references and index.
    ISBN 0-8173-1064-9
    1. Wickliffe Mounds (Ky.) 2. Mississippian culture—Kentucky—Ballard County.
3. Excavations (Archaeology)—Kentucky—Ballard County. 4. Ballard County
(Ky.)—Antiquities. I. Title.
E99.M6815 W47 2001
976.9'96—dc21   2001001662

British Library Cataloguing-in-Publication Data available

Contents

Figures

(suffix CD indicates that the figure is found on the CD-ROM; the suffix is not used for chapters contained entirely on the CD-ROM)

Additional artifact photographs are found on the CD-ROM.

The list of figures for Chapter 18 may be found on the CD-ROM.

Tables

Foreword

It seems to be part of the human condition that we view places and events through our own personal experience. My good friend Ric TallEagle always said, "If you had fifteen Indians in one room, you would have sixteen opinions." That too is a personal perception. I am only one indigenous person and cannot speak for all Native Nations. I can, however, offer you the views of a person whose involvement with Wickliffe Mounds has been part of a personal journey and vision.

Archaeology has been a very devastating science among the aboriginal population of the Americas. Where there have been federal, state, and local laws protecting Euro-American, African-American, and Asian-American graves and their contents, until most recently finding the grave site of an indigenous American would get you offers of grants for excavation. Pot hunting, too, has been a lucrative profession. There are laws now, protecting the remains of the aboriginal people of Turtle Island, and laws that allow for the repatriation of the remains held in public and private collections. That is where my journey began.

The excavations at Wickliffe Mounds began as an amateur archaeological attempt and roadside attraction: not too dignified for the tribal people who once populated this unique site. Through site ownership by different parties, the ancestral remains lay on public display, although their loved ones had followed the prescribed funerary ceremonies, grieved, and committed their bodies back to the Mother.

It was not until my first visit to Wickliffe Mounds and the beginning of an important personal and professional friendship with the site director, Dr. Kit Wesler, that the desecration at the mounds site started to be repaired. We are still in process with the repatriation and reinterment of the remains of the indigenous people of Wickliffe. It has often been slow and frustrating for all persons concerned, but it has also been a process that has brought about a better understanding between cultures.

There have always been two sides to the issue of repatriation. Not everyone agrees with the events at Wickliffe Mounds. However, Dr. Wesler and his staff and interns have been people of exceptional quality who have stretched themselves and gone the extra distance to help and support in this difficult task. The site has gone from being one of questionable technique and study in the days of Fain King, to one of broad education, supporting the indigenous tribal people, both past and present, of Turtle Island. Today, there are no human remains on display. The repatriation efforts have brought many different Native Nations to the site to lend guidance and support. The aboriginal people of Wickliffe's past are remembered and honored. The conch trumpet has been sounded again on the main mound, this time by a new generation of indigenous Americans. Tribal songs, dances, games, and stories have returned too as Wickliffe sponsors several events during the year, linking past and present and acknowledging indigenous traditions. As an educational site, Wickliffe Mounds is moving forward into a future in which Euro-Americans and Native Americans work together for a better understanding of Turtle Island and Her First Nations.

Victoria G. Fortner (Shawnee)
Peatohah-Nape Tamsah
St. Louis, Missouri

Preface and Acknowledgments

The original manuscript for this volume was over 1000 pages long, including figures, tables, and references. Publishers balked. In order to reduce the paper volume to a reasonable (and affordable) length, most of the field data, the contributed analyses, the artifact photographs and many of the other figures, many of the detailed tables, and the full list of references have been placed on a CD-ROM that accompanies this text.

Doing this required some tactical decisions but also provided some opportunities. The greatest opportunity is to allow publication of extensive field data, including descriptions of each test unit, and also of database files. Researchers who are interested in the data may review them in excruciating detail, while readers who are interested primarily in the interpretations may be satisfied with the printed volume. Another opportunity is to include color photographs of artifacts instead of black-and-white prints.

The CD-ROM includes many more illustrations and tables than could comfortably be accommodated in print. However, shifting figures and tables onto the CD-ROM posed a problem for numbering them. Normally figures and tables are numbered in sequence as they are first mentioned in the discussion, and they are printed in that order. This method is a convention, not a law. The convention runs afoul of the needs of the CD-ROM when the discussion refers first to a print table, next to a CD-ROM table, next to a print table, etc. The solution adopted here is to number the tables (and figures) in sequence as discussed in the text, but to add the suffix CD to those placed on the CD-ROM. Here again, the reader interested primarily in interpretation will be able to follow the discussion and consult the summary tables, while the researcher interested in the nitty-gritty can find more details as needed. Tables and figures are numbered in the context of their principal discussion, even if occasional references to them are scattered elsewhere.

This collaboration of print and CD-ROM is an experiment, and reviewers undoubtedly will offer opinions as to how effective it is.

My choice of Asymetrix ToolBook II for programming the CD-ROM, and also some of the organization of the program, were inspired by Davis et al. (1998), and I thank Steve Davis for several discussions as I was getting started.

An archaeological field project is a team effort, especially one that lasts for thirteen years. If everyone who has participated in the project buys a copy of this book, it will be a runaway best-seller. The Wickliffe project, more than most excavations, includes more than the field and lab work: the public education program is inextricably mixed with the research. Crew members in the various projects are too numerous to list here, but their names are included on the CD-ROM. I hope that those who are not named will forgive me my failed memory.

For dedicated volunteer effort and friendship for many years, Kathy Lyons, Susan Hughes, Kay Harbison, Bryce Owens, and Joe Don Curtis stand out.

Staff members over the years have been Bryan Kwapil, Louella Weaver, Kelly Lawson, Rie Engen, Becky Fye, Carla Hildebrand, and longest-lasting Karen Owens. Sarah Neusius, Jim Phillips, Randy Corse, Cathy David, Dana Wrinkle, Nancy Walker, and Beatrice Gilliam served as temporary staff members.

My Middle Mississippi Survey colleagues Carol Morrow and Patrice Teltser, and visiting co-instructors in various field schools Hugh Matternes (several summers), Kelli Carmean, Jeannette Stephens, and Sarah C. Sherwood, have made invaluable contributions. I sincerely thank my colleagues who have contributed analyses, at no benefit to themselves except the advancement of our mutual understanding of the Wickliffe site and its place in Mississippian archaeology, and especially the contributors of the chapters on the accompanying CD-ROM: Kristin Brown, Philip J. Carr, Penelope B. Drooker, Richard B. Edging, Rebecca L. Fye, Brad Koldehoff, Jenna T. Kuttruff, Paul P. Kreisa, Hugh B. Matternes, Jacqueline M. McDowell, John Pafford, James M. Phillips, Margaret J. Schoeninger, and Mark Schurr. My use of their data and conclusions is entirely my own.

I cannot even begin to remember all of the colleagues who have offered consultations and conversations, but those who most helped get me started in Mississippian archaeology include Stephen Williams, Berle Clay, Joseph Granger, Barry Lewis, James Price, Bruce Smith, Dan Morse, James B. Griffin, Chuck Stout, Tom Sussenbach, Richard Edging, Paul Kreisa, and Lynn Mackin Wolforth.

I thank Victoria Fortner, and her community of Native Americans, who have collectively taught me a new way to think about the Wickliffe site and brought new spirit to the old village; I thank her also for her friendship.

At Murray State University, through the years, I have appreciated various support from James Booth, Kenneth Harrell, Joseph Cartwright, Kenneth Wolf, the late Dennis Poplin, Frank Elwell, and Ken Carstens. President Constantine W. Curris recognized the potential of the Wickliffe site to contribute to education and scholarship, and Presidents Kala Stroup, Ronald Kurth, and Kern Alexander have allowed it to continue to do so. Dean Martin Jones and Chair Peter Hirschberg at Southeast Missouri State University were instrumental in creating the Middle Mississippi Survey consortium and keeping it going.

The topographic map that forms the basis of Figure 1.2 and the various permutations of it that follow throughout the volume was digitized, revised, and updated to depict excavation locations by Kristin Brown, from an original base map by Charles B. Stout, used by permission of the Western Kentucky Project, University of Illinois at Urbana-Champaign.

The Wickliffe program has survived also because of the interest and generosity of several granting agencies.

I am grateful for the long-term interest and repeated support of the Kentucky Heritage Council, Director David Morgan, staff Tom Sanders, Dave Pollack, and Charles Hockensmith. Research and programming at the Wickliffe Mounds have been financed in part by several grants from the National Park Service, U.S. Department of the Interior, and administered by the Kentucky Heritage Council. The use of federal funds does not imply endorsement of the content by the National Park Service or the Kentucky Heritage Council. All programs receiving federal funding are operated free from discrimination on the basis of race, color, national origin, age, or handicap. Any person who believes he or she has been discriminated against should write to: Office of Equal Opportunity, U.S. Department of the Interior, P.O. Box 37127, Washington D.C. 20013-7127.

The Wickliffe project has received repeated grant support from the Kentucky Humanities Council for exhibits and programming (my thanks to Virginia Smith and Raenell Schroering for aid and encouragement); support for curation from the National Science Foundation, grants BNS 850699 (1985) and SBR-9307001 (1993) (my thanks to John Yellen for personal attention); research support from the Murray State University Committee on Institutional Studies and Research (CISR); and support for interpretive and visitor facilities from the U.S. Department of Transportation, Great River Road Project and Intermodal Surface Transportation Efficiency Act program (ISTEA), the Southern Foundation, the Kentucky Bicentennial Committee, and an anonymous donor for help with exhibit replicas. I am particularly grateful for the CISR Presidential Research Fellowship that allowed me time to put together this volume.

I am thankful to Judith Knight of the University of Alabama Press for her faith that we could get this "monster" published somehow and for seeing me through the process.

Last but far from least, I thank Renae for making me appreciate life in western Kentucky.

1 Background to the Wickliffe Mounds Projects

The Wickliffe Mounds site (15BA4) overlooks the Mississippi River in Ballard County, Kentucky, about three miles south of the mouth of the Ohio River (Figure 1.1). During the past thousand years, it has been the location of a Native American village, ceremonial center, and cemetery; a patch of woods; a farmed field; a wood lot and office for a lumber company; a site of archaeological excavations; a tourist attraction; and a university research center and public education program, the latter two incarnations (and perhaps earlier ones) including staff residences. The Wickliffe Mounds have a complicated history, and their transformations continue.

The Native American story begins with the establishment of a village belonging to what archaeologists call the Mississippian culture. Mississippian people, farmers and traders with a culture closely ancestral to the historic cultures of the Southeast—Chickasaw, Choctaw, Creek, and others—created a settlement about A.D. 1100, in which they lived for about 250 years. Eventually they moved on, and nature reclaimed the bluff.

After A.D. 1800, American settlers moved into the area. They farmed, hunted, and fished and used the river for transport, much as the Native Americans had before them. Over the next century steamboats, railroads, and roads promoted the development of extractive industries such as lumbering and clay mining. These activities have all left traces on or near the Wickliffe Mounds.

In 1930, the construction of Highway 51/60/62 from Kentucky to Illinois cut a channel through the southern end of the site, revealing archaeological deposits. Fain W. King, a lumberman and entrepreneur from Paducah, Kentucky, bought the site with the hope of making an attraction for the education and entertainment of the public, and not incidentally for his own profit. He excavated in several areas of the site, sometimes with the help and advice of academic archaeologists, sometimes without, and built exhibit shelters and other structures over the excavations and around the site. He marketed the site under several names, including the Wickliffe Mounds, the King Mounds, and the Ancient Buried City, which sobriquet it may never live down. Tiring of the project, ailing, without the respect he thought he should have gotten from academics whom he wanted to consider his colleagues in archaeology, and probably without the profits he had anticipated, King tried to sell the

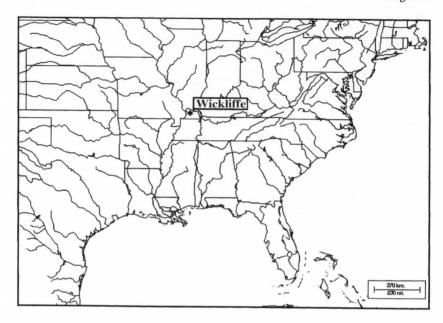

1.1. Location of Wickliffe Mounds site.

site. He never wrote a report of the excavations, and his field notes have disappeared.

In 1946, he turned the site over to the Western Baptist Hospital in Paducah. Western Baptist Hospital agreed to pay King and his wife, Blanche Busey King, an annuity for the rest of their lives. Presumably Western Baptist Hospital was led to expect that the tourist income would pay for the annuity and the upkeep and staffing of the site, with some left over for the benefit of the hospital. It is unlikely that revenues were ever so abundant. Western Baptist Hospital administrators tore down and rebuilt the site's office, built a staff residence, bulldozed out a wide double driveway from the highway (although this may have been a King innovation), staffed the site with persons of fair intentions but no background in archaeology or museum studies, presented high school students as "expert archaeological guides," and did little to upgrade or update exhibits or interpretation.

In the early 1980s, Blanche King died, her husband having predeceased her by some years. Western Baptist Hospital then was able to dispose of the Wickliffe Mounds site. A team of consultants from the University of Louisville Archaeological Survey (DiBlasi and Granger 1982) found that the site had been "all but loved to death" and recommended several options including turning the site over to a university for redevelopment as a research center and museum, or removing the buildings, backfilling the excavations, and creating a passively interpreted city park.

Western Baptist Hospital elected to donate the site and collections to Murray State University in 1983. Murray State University embarked on a long-term project to create the Wickliffe Mounds Research Center (WMRC) as an academic facility dedicated to research, student training, public education, and preservation of the site and collections. WMRC personnel have made progress toward creating an up-to-date museum and educational program.

The research program has also proceeded steadily. When the WMRC was created, it stored some 85,000 artifacts from the Fain King collection, plus numerous artifacts left on display in sheltered King excavation areas. Most of the artifacts—more than 90 percent, as it turned out—had labels inked on them that related to the excavation grids used in the 1930s. As the WMRC staff sorted and recataloged the collection, they also began excavations, employing the Murray State University summer field school, which later was expanded into the Middle Mississippi Survey, a training and research consortium with Southeast Missouri State University and guest institutions.

The excavations had the initial goal of documenting the contexts, as much as possible, from which the King excavations had removed artifacts. Over the thirteen years from 1984 through 1996, excavators reinvestigated five of the six King excavations, formed a process-of-elimination judgment of where the sixth must have been, and expanded the testing program into previously unstudied areas of the site, so that all major site areas were represented (Figure 1.2). The investigations show that areas of the village deposits are still well preserved, even though the mounds were extensively disturbed before 1983.

The results of the project are reported in this volume. The archaeological contexts can be described comprehensively. Analyses of faunal and floral materials, so far only sampled, and of many specialized artifacts—ceramic effigies, tools, ornaments, gaming pieces, and personal items—continue, and even those artifacts given the most attention may be analyzed further. However, it is now possible to reconstruct the culture history of the Wickliffe site in some detail. Parts of the discussion in this volume follow earlier publications closely (see Wesler references), but often with revision, and interpretations offered here supersede those previously published.

Other results cannot be so easily graphed, quantified, or described. Dozens of students were trained in archaeological methods, some of whom have gone into professional archaeology or related fields. Numerous volunteers gained an understanding of what is required to conduct an archaeological excavation, and they will be better able to understand reports of archaeological discoveries in the popular media or to appreciate preservation efforts in their communities. Thousands of visitors saw excavations in progress, and many asked questions; thousands more have seen, and will continue to see, the results of the research as translated into museum exhibits. And, far from least, a few archaeologists and a few Native Americans have made some tentative steps toward mutual understanding, shared with students, volunteers, and visitors along the way.

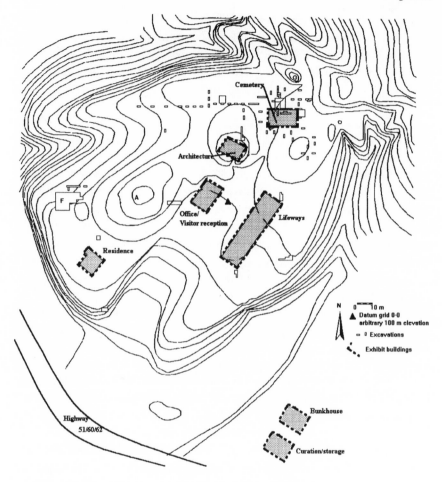

1.2. The Wickliffe site and excavations, 1984–1996.

GEOLOGICAL SETTING

The Wickliffe Mounds site is located on the bluffs of the Mississippi River in the southwest corner of Ballard County, Kentucky (Figure 1.1). Ballard County is part of the Jackson Purchase geological province of western Kentucky. It is a relatively rugged coastal plain, the bluffs rising to 40 to 50 feet above the adjacent floodplain and deeply dissected by a complex drainage system. The Mississippi River floodplain directly west of the site is narrow, the river bank lying less than a quarter mile from the base of the bluff. To the north, however, the floodplain widens dramatically, merging with the broad Ohio River bottoms. The confluence of the two great rivers is only about three miles north of the Wickliffe site and is visible when the leaves are down.

The Jackson Purchase region is the northernmost extension of the Gulf Coastal Plain, underlain by ocean deposits of Cretaceous, Tertiary, and Quaternary age (Humphrey 1976:76). Ravines cutting through these deposits reveal gravels, sands, and silts. These beds contain stone useful to prehistoric tool makers: angular to well-rounded cherts and rounded quartz and quartzite cobbles. The cherts are predominantly brown and yellowish brown (Olive 1974) and coarse, but were utilized as raw materials by the inhabitants of Wickliffe Mounds.

The coastal plain deposits also contain clays of the Claiborne deposits. Olive (1974) notes that clay was mined in the early twentieth century in an area half a mile northeast of the town of Wickliffe. Franklin (1974:10) shows this area as a source of ball clay, a fine-grained, plastic clay of high quality for ceramics (Gildersleeve and Roberts 1945:92). Where the local Mississippian potters obtained their clay is not yet known, but it is clear that raw material was available nearby.

Capping the coastal plain deposits is a loess layer, the Peoria formation. The formation is an unstratified deposit consisting of angular particles of uniform texture, with inclusions of small chert and quartz pebbles and some "ferro-magnesian minerals" (Gildersleeve and Roberts 1945:88; Olive 1974). The loess is the parent material for the loamy bluff-top soils of the area. The soil on the Wickliffe site is a heavily organic midden, but the adjacent areas are characterized by silt loams and silty clay loams. These soils are moderately to highly fertile and typified by a "deep root zone" and "moderate permeability." On ridge tops, as on the Wickliffe Mounds site, these soils are eroded and have a high capacity for moisture (Humphrey 1976:28–30).

From the archaeological perspective, the loess forms the subsoil, a yellow-tan clayey soil that predates human occupation. In color, texture, and lack of cultural remains it is distinguishable from overlying middens or mound soils, and excavations are complete when they penetrate this zone. Usually, intrusive features are easily visible as darker or mottled stains against a clean exposure of the loess.

The natural vegetation of the upland areas is an oak-hickory forest, with a particular presence of the southern red oak. The river bottoms would support a southern floodplain forest, with various oaks, cottonwood, pecan, gum, and cypress among the dominant tree species (Wharton and Barbour 1973).

MISSISSIPPIAN CULTURE

The people who lived at the Wickliffe Mounds between about A.D. 1100 and 1350 were Native Americans bearing a culture known to archaeologists as Mississippian. A brief definition of the Mississippian culture usually relies on three characteristics: shell-tempered pottery, flat-topped mounds built as

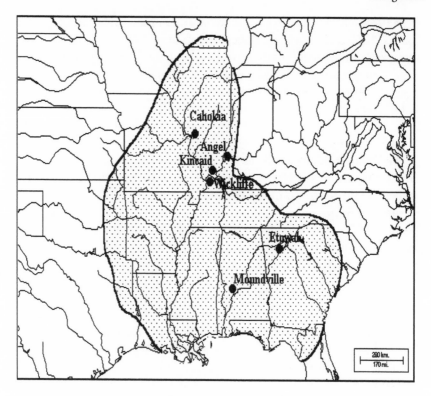

1.3. The Mississippian culture area and some key sites.

platforms for important buildings, and maize agriculture. Such an elementary definition is practical for identifying sites in the field, for drawing a broad outline around the Mississippian culture area as in Figure 1.3, and for applying rough chronological limits of circa A.D. 900 to 1500 (the latter date an arbitrary round figure for European arrival in the Americas).

The simple definition, however handy, understates the sophistication of Mississippian culture and disguises considerable complexity in regional variation, in archaeologists' views of the key elements of the culture, and in historical changes in the definition. It is important to understand the development of the concept of a Mississippian culture, because the term carries nuances and echoes of past conceptions even as each archaeologist attempts a "current" or "new" definition. The conceptual development is important also in understanding a project like the Wickliffe investigations, because the King project in the 1930s occurred during a critical period in the systematization of archaeological data in the Mississippi Valley, while the WMRC project in the 1980s and 1990s inherited a much more detailed conception as a starting point.

James B. Griffin's (1985) account of the development of the Mississippian concept offers a useful backdrop to the Wickliffe project. He notes that investigators in Tennessee made the first steps to an awareness of a regional manifestation now called Mississippian. F. W. Putnam (1878) remarked upon relationships of stone box grave sites in the Nashville area to similar sites in southern Illinois and Missouri. A few years later, G. P. Thruston (1890) widened the region of cultural connections to the fortified agricultural town sites of the Nashville basin, Arkansas, southeast Missouri, southern Illinois, and southwest Indiana. At this time, there was no particular terminology in use, but the slowly accumulating database was beginning to show similarities over a wide area.

W. H. Holmes is a key figure in the recognition of regional classifications. His studies of pottery (Holmes 1886, 1903) created geographic provinces of ceramics, introducing, among other ideas, the terms *Upper, Middle,* and *Lower Mississippi.* His Middle Mississippi area encompassed much of Missouri, Arkansas, and Tennessee and portions of Kentucky, Illinois, Indiana, Alabama, Mississippi, Louisiana, Iowa, and Texas. He noted links to mound sites and suggested that the pottery was made from later prehistoric to historic times. With adjustments (primarily reductions), this area is recognizably the Mississippian culture area as currently accepted.

Holmes (1914) also attempted to define archaeological culture areas in North America, distinguishing a Lower Mississippi Valley from Upper Mississippi Valley–Great Lakes and Georgia-Florida areas, among others. He described the Lower Mississippi Valley as the home of a "remarkable group of peoples whose culture, all things considered, stands higher than that of any other characterization north of Mexico," typified by "sedentary life, extensive practice of agricultural pursuits, and construction of permanent works—domiciliary, religious, civic, defensive, and mortuary, of great magnitude and much diversity of form" (Holmes 1914:424). Holmes noted building styles related to those of the Natchez and other historic tribes, stockaded villages, chipped stone "sword-like blades of Tennessee . . . and agricultural implements of the Illinois region," and incised, painted, and effigy ceramics that "evince excellent taste and great skill" (Holmes 1914:426). It is clear that most of his data came from Mississippian sites, although he also mixed in artifacts of earlier periods, having no method to sort out chronology. Holmes's Lower Mississippi Valley was purely a geographic grouping of mixed assemblages, but Stoltman (1973:132) describes Holmes's ceramic and cultural regions as the "first serious effort at constructing an interpretive framework for the study of Southeastern prehistory."

Holmes's (1914) attempt to move from ceramic provinces to culture area seems not to have been widely followed, and although his pottery illustrations were often cited, the term *Middle Mississippi* does not appear very often in the first three decades of the twentieth century. Participants in an influential conference in Birmingham in 1932 used the term sparingly (Griffin 1985; National Research Council 1932).

Griffin (1985:48–49) recalls that *Middle Mississippi* became a hot term among the University of Chicago field researchers in the early 1930s, especially during the Fulton County project of 1930–1932, when a number of Mississippian sites were investigated (Cole and Deuel 1937). The 1930s saw crucial development of systematic classification of archaeological cultures in eastern North America, and the King project at Wickliffe is most significant when seen against this backdrop.

It is difficult for younger researchers to trace these developments closely, because the ideas and concepts were widely discussed well before they appeared in print (Fisher 1997; Griffin 1985; McKern 1939). The Midwestern Taxonomic System apparently was developed during the period of the Fulton County project and elaborated and codified during the subsequent years of the 1930s, even though not formally published until 1939 (McKern 1939). The system was a hierarchical classification, building up from single sites (components) to ever larger and more broadly defined units relating similar sites. Levels of similarity were evaluated on the basis of lists of traits, ranging from very specific artifact types to broad subsistence patterns, the number of traits in common determining the degree of similarity.

W. C. McKern (1939) described the nature of the classificatory system. He did not provide extended definitions of the various units, but used as an example the distinction between the Mississippi pattern and the Woodland pattern. The Mississippi pattern, briefly described, included extended inhumations; "prevailingly" shell-tempered pottery of a variety of vessel forms and with incised, trailed, and modeled decoration; triangular chipped stone projectile points; ungrooved axes; bone, antler, and shell artifacts; and "sedentary territorial adjustment" (McKern 1939:309). McKern did not extend the definition in part because he intended his article only to explain the system and also because the specifics of the pattern already were widely known.

Thorne Deuel, in several publications, developed the details of the classification for the Mississippi Valley (Cole and Deuel 1937; Deuel 1935, 1937). Cole and Deuel (1937:19) could summarize the characteristics of Middle Mississippi fairly briefly, listing villages; rectangular houses in "bowl-shaped depressions" and containing internal features; small triangular chipped stone projectile points; stone, bone, and shell tools; "doubtless" agriculture; and "highly developed" pottery—a description very similar to McKern's summary. Deuel's (1935:433ff.) more extensive description is considerably more specific. From a turn-of-the-millennium perspective, it is clear that the "Mississippi Basic Culture" glosses over a great deal of geographic and temporal variation. The problem in the early 1930s, however, was not to characterize fully the nuances of Mississippian cultures, but to distinguish Mississippian from Woodland, and both from the as-yet ill-defined preceramic Archaic complexes. By 1937, the term *Basic Culture* had been replaced by *Pattern,* and researchers could subdivide regional expressions such as the Spoon River focus (Cole and Deuel 1937; Deuel 1937).

It is interesting, if difficult, to discern the impact of the King project at Wickliffe on these definitional processes. King attended, uninvited, the Birmingham conference of 1932 (National Research Council 1932; U.K.: Webb to King, 12 January 1933; King to Webb, 4 February 1933), having just completed his initial foray into the Wickliffe site. Cole (1951) credits King with introducing the University of Chicago to the Kincaid site, beginning in 1934. As will be seen in Chapter 2 (cf. Wesler 1988), King and his excavations were widely discussed and closely observed, but the subject was touchy, aggravated by King's insistence in the later 1930s that the Wickliffe data not be published by anyone but himself and his wife; he even forbade mention of the site.

Neither McKern's (1939) explication of the Midwestern Taxonomic System nor Deuel's (1935) application of it specifies sites, except as sources of illustrated items in the latter article. Deuel (1937), nonetheless, mentions Wickliffe among Tolu in Kentucky, Kincaid in southern Illinois, Gordon in Tennessee, Etowah in Georgia, and Moundville in Alabama as closely related sites forming a separate group from the Monk's Mound aspect that incorporated several foci in Illinois. Griffin (1985:53) recalls that Wickliffe was among the sites included in Middle Mississippi at an Indianapolis conference in 1935, when Deuel was refining his 1935 paper toward the 1937 formulation.

The most explicit treatment of Lower Ohio Valley sites in reference to Midwestern taxonomics probably was J. W. Bennett's (1940) thesis. Bennett stated that a Tennessee-Cumberland group of sites, "usually considered as having aspect status," had been recognized "for the past five years." (M. W. Stirling, for example, had called the Tennessee-Cumberland area "one of the most interesting and complex of all the sub-culture areas under discussion" in 1932 [National Research Council 1932:24].) Most of the relevant sites had been "fairly thoroughly excavated, and with the exception of Wickliffe, can be represented by adequate trait lists" (Bennett 1940:108). Bennett's analysis, based on the comparisons of mind-numbing lists, established a sixty-trait inventory of the Tennessee-Cumberland aspect and subdivided the aspect into the Kincaid and Gordon foci, each with distinguishing twenty-six–trait inventories (Bennett 1940:115–19). His Kincaid focus included the Kincaid, Angel, Tolu, Page, and Wickliffe sites. He stated, "Wickliffe, although not represented here by a trait list, has been visited and studied by the author. On the overwhelming similarity to Kincaid pottery and implement complexes, it can be tentatively included in the Kincaid focus" (Bennett 1940:117). It is clear that Bennett was trying hard to comply with King's proscription of any use of Wickliffe data, but could not keep from acknowledging them.

Bennett's formulation evidently held the stage until after the slowdown in American archaeology during World War II, with Wickliffe a shadowy yet immanent player. Cole's (1951:19, 27, 151, 153, 161ff.) Kincaid report is sprinkled with passing references to Wickliffe, citing Bennett's thesis. Maxwell (1952:189) likewise refers to the King site at Wickliffe and the Angel site as Kincaid's "sister cities." Given the close association of Bennett and other Chicago students with King's project in the mid-1930s and Cole's clear intent to draw comparisons between Kincaid and Wickliffe (see Chapter 2), it is impossible to escape the conclusion that Wickliffe data helped to define Middle Mississippian.

McKern (1939:313) concluded that the Midwestern Taxonomic System had "contributed materially towards introducing order into the previously existing chaotic status of general culture concepts throughout the greater Mississippi Valley," which was a fair assessment. However, even as the method was finally codified in print (McKern 1939), its limitations were becoming apparent. The system did not discriminate adequately among major and minor traits in measuring similarity and, even more problematic, it took no account of time. In 1930, chronology was beyond the pale of the database. By 1937, the Chicago researchers could already suggest a tentative and partial cultural sequence in the Spoon River area, Middle Mississippi being the most recent (Cole and Deuel 1937:16), and "by 1938, the [Kincaid] excavation . . . established the basic sequence: Kincaid-Lewis-Baumer, appearing in the region in that order" (from top to bottom) (Bennett 1940:126).

From this point, chronology, geography, and cultural content became nearly inseparable dimensions of terms such as Middle Mississippian. Even an attempt to distinguish a chronological scheme from a culture sequence, Ford and Willey's (1941) Burial Mound I-II and Temple Mound I-II succession, resulted in little practical difference from an Early-Middle Woodland, Late Woodland–Mississippian formulation:

> Middle Mississippi is a term first used by W. H. Holmes [1903] to characterize the typical shell-tempered pottery found in such great quantities accompanying burials in the central part of the Mississippi Valley.
>
> This division of eastern ceramics has come to be accepted as a term applying to the entire cultural complex which usually accompanies this characteristic pottery, and Deuel [1937] has attempted to define a Middle Mississippi culture unit. This paper is not using the term exactly as defined by Deuel. While essentially similar, the Middle Mississippi manifestations vary from area to area and two recognizably distinct periods can be discerned. (Ford and Willey 1941:348)

For the next couple of decades, the basic definition of Middle Mississippian changed in detail but not in essentials. In 1958, Willey and Phillips (1958:163) described Mississippian characteristics as "the rectangular 'temple' or 'town-house' mounds, the arrangement of these mounds around a central plaza, compact villages of substantial pole-and-thatch or wattle-and-daub houses with deep and extensive refuse (other than shell middens), and the frequent and abundant finds of maize . . . along with certain characteristic pottery styles and artifact types."

Griffin (1985:55) cites trends in interpretation through the 1950s and 1960s: a better understanding of the precedents to Mississippian culture in its various areas (which largely reflects more data and better chronological control); more emphasis on social, political, and religious changes; and an interest in settlement patterns and environments. The latter trend reflected increased attention to regional survey and testing, which began to portray the diverse Mississippian settlement pattern that incorporated large and small mound centers, moundless villages, hamlets, farmsteads, and specialized sites such as quarries and hunting camps, and also was related to advances in recovery and analysis of faunal and botanical data. Even so, a widely adopted textbook of North American archaeology still could, in the mid-1960s, refer to "the essential Mississippian traits—the platform mound and plaza arrangement of sites, varieties of maize and maize agriculture, and certain ceramic features" (Willey 1966:293). This definition had changed little from the classification of circa 1940.

By the end of the 1970s, the settlement pattern/environmentalist approach gelled into a new definition of Mississippian, voiced especially by Bruce D. Smith (1978a, 1978b, 1985). To Smith (1985:64), Mississippian societies included those in the greater Mississippi Valley region "who shared a number of similarities in material culture, as well as the common practice of building earthen mounds to support public buildings and the houses of their leaders . . . similarities in their tools of bone and stone, in their pottery vessels and houses, and in their villages and 'temple mounds,'" but also who shared a common habitat and adaptation. Smith's formulation emphasized that Mississippian societies were adapted to the meander belt floodplains of the Mississippi drainage, where they concentrated on six categories of resources: backwater fish, migratory waterfowl, terrestrial animals (primarily deer, raccoon, and turkey), nuts/fruits/berries, native seeds (especially polygonum and chenopod), and a maize/beans/squash agricultural complex. The Mississippian peoples were adapted to resources that were dependable and abundant and allowed an annual cycle of harvest that supported their sophisticated life-style. They also participated in ranked societies, and their hierarchical settlement systems were a significant part of their ability to adapt to natural and social environmental conditions. Smith's model allowed for regional variation, local adaptation, and adjustments through time, and it was extremely influential.

Concurrently during the 1970s and 1980s, other researchers looked in complementary directions. To cite but two examples, Peebles and Kus (1977) studied burials at Moundville in the perspective of comparative models of chiefdom societies, refining efforts to link archaeological expressions with the ranked and powerful polities described by early European explorers in the Southeast; Knight (1983) considered aspects of Mississippian religion, reflected in part in the art styles that characterize Mississippian cultures as a symbolic community, and explored ways in which religious symbols were integrated with social and political hierarchy. Griffin (1985:62) incorporates these trends in defining Mississippian in terms of continuities with previous societies in the same areas; innovations due to communication throughout the Mississippian culture area and beyond; increasing population with greater reliance on a dependable subsistence economy including agriculture; permanent towns coordinating a complex settlement system; variations on complex social, political, and religious structures; common symbolism and ceremonial items; and extensive trade, a varied complex that achieved a "cultural crest" between A.D. 1200 and 1500.

Spurred by comments on his ecological/settlement systems model, Smith (1984) probed a couple of tacit but widespread assumptions about Mississippian societies: the idea that there was a single heartland from which Mississippian society spread and the implicit correlate that Muskogean migration legends commemorated Mississippian diffusion. He found support for neither in the archaeological data, arguing instead that the process of taking on Mississippian cultural patterns occurred throughout the Mississippian culture area. Of course, as he pointed out, a few scholars had taken this position all along (citing Griffin 1946:75, 79, 1966:126–27, 1976:5–6; Holmes 1914:427–28). (Smith did not note another important point, namely, that to say that archaeological data do not support Muskogean migration legends is not the same thing as to say that they refute the legends.)

Smith's (1985) presentation of his subsistence-settlement model of Mississippian societies led him to look forward into some of the developing research questions of the 1990s. He repeated another tacit assumption of Mississippian studies when he referred to "each of these [Mississippian] societies, politically independent and economically self-sufficient" (Smith 1985:75). In fact, it has not been demonstrated that each Mississippian village was an independent polity or economic entity. Smith (1985:77) did note that, at times, local systems did shift into larger polities, and he indicated the need to refine local chronologies so that investigators could understand "the cycles of population expansion and contraction within the centers."

This question, the nature of Mississippian social and political organization, has been at the heart of a number of scholars' recent research, including Anderson's (1990) and Scarry's (1990) considerations of cycles in chiefdom organization (based on Wright's [1984] formulation stressing the internal conflicts and inherent instability of a ranked, nonstate society), Pauketat's (1994) exploration of the origins of the great Cahokia community, Muller and Stephens's (1991) consideration of Mississippian society as an adaptive organizational system, and Muller's (1997) thoughtful exploration of Mississippian political economy—to name a few. The question of the 1990s was the nature of Mississippian chiefdom, in addition to the further refinement of all previous questions about the Mississippian people and their cultural and environmental contexts.

As a pragmatic definition, the triumvirate criteria of platform mounds, maize, and shell-tempered pottery carried through from the 1930s into the present, even while the term *Mississippian* acquired overlays that reflected the advances in methods and concerns of the archaeological discipline. The richer conception of Mississippian culture that took shape in the late 1970s and early 1980s, and new questions posed or rephrased since, informed the renewed Wickliffe project in the 1980s and 1990s.

MISSISSIPPIANS IN WESTERN KENTUCKY ARCHAEOLOGY

Clay (1963) and Lewis (1990b) have surveyed the history of Mississippian site archaeology in Kentucky west of the Tennessee River, and only the highlights need be repeated here.

Mound sites were identified in the region before the turn of the twentieth century and before any concept of a Mississippian culture had begun to emerge. Rafinesque (1824) mentioned a mound in Hickman County, although exactly which site he meant is uncertain. Thomas (1894) mentioned only the McLeod Bluff site in Hickman County. The most complete survey before A.D. 1900 must be credited to Loughridge (1888), who published maps of several of the mound complexes, including Wickliffe (Figure 1.4). Soon after the century mark, Moore (1916; Morse and Morse 1998:162) visited several sites, although he evidently was unimpressed with Wickliffe. None of the disturbances documented by the WMRC excavations can be pinned on him.

The King project was part of a surge of interest in Kentucky archaeology in the 1930s, led by William S. Webb and W. D. Funkhouser of the University of Kentucky, who published a survey of Kentucky sites (Funkhouser and Webb 1932). Webb and Funkhouser (1931) reported on investigations at the Tolu site in Crittenden County at the beginning of the decade, after which Webb visited McLeod Bluff (Webb and Funkhouser 1933); but a dispute with Fain King,

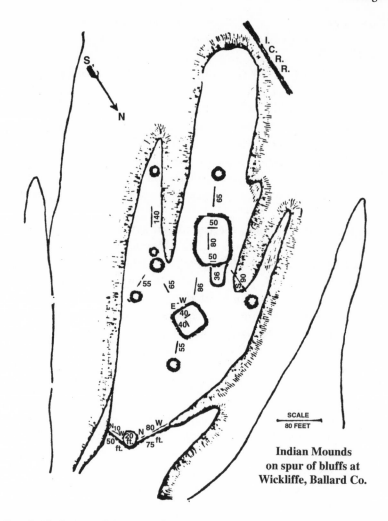

SCALE
80 FEET

**Indian Mounds
on spur of bluffs at
Wickliffe, Ballard Co.**

1.4. Loughridge's map of the Wickliffe Mounds, 1888.

who got to the latter site before him (U.K.: Webb to Guthe, 29 September 1932; King to Webb, 10 February 1933; Webb to King, 13 February 1933), so antagonized Webb that he left the west coast of Kentucky alone for some time thereafter. Also in the 1930s, the University of Chicago conducted large-scale investigations of the Kincaid site in the Black Bottom of southern Illinois, producing a material culture with clear resemblances to Wickliffe (Cole 1951).

For two decades after 1940, western Kentucky was left to collectors, of whom some collected surface artifacts and treated sites with respect and others committed extensive depredations. Webb (1952) did publish a major report of excavations at the Jonathan Creek site in Marshall County during this period.

Archaeological survey resumed in the 1960s and 1970s, with Clay's (1963) report of ceramics, Weinland and Gatus's (1979) survey of Ballard County, and inspection of an area in McCracken County by Butler, Penny, and Robinson (1981), all of which reported Mississippian sites. Southern Illinois University's project in the environs of Kincaid helped put that major site into more of a regional setting, with pertinence to the Kentucky side of the river and to the Lower Tennessee-Cumberland region (Butler 1977; Muller 1978, 1986, 1993; Riordan 1975).

In the 1980s, the pace of research quickened. Just ahead of the creation of the WMRC, University of Illinois researchers under the direction of R. Barry Lewis began survey and testing with emphasis on the Mississippian sites. The University of Illinois Western Kentucky Project has conducted studies at the Adams and Sassafras Ridge sites (Fulton County), the Turk site (Carlisle County), Wickliffe and Twin Mounds (Ballard County); revisited Tolu and Jonathan Creek; and investigated a number of other sites in the region, and has issued numerous reports and summaries (among the major works: Edging 1985, 1990, 1995; Kreisa 1988, 1990a, 1990b, 1991; Lewis 1990a, 1990b, 1991, 1996; Lewis ed. 1986; Stout 1985, 1987, 1989; Sussenbach 1993; Sussenbach and Lewis 1987; Wolforth 1987). This project, integrated with the WMRC project at Wickliffe and Pollack and Railey's (1987) excavations at the Chambers site in Marshall County, has laid the foundation for the development of a very detailed understanding of the Mississippian societies of the region.

MISSISSIPPIANS IN HISTORY

The bearers of Mississippian culture are considered to be the last of the prehistoric peoples in the Lower Mississippi Valley. In saying this, archaeologists make a distinction between people who can be studied through archaeological sources alone (the prehistoric record) and people who can be studied through two or more sets of sources, archaeological and documentary (whether written, photographic, oral, or, soon no doubt, electronic). The same distinction is made, for example, when speaking of prehistoric Europe.

In general, in the Southeast and Lower Mississippi Valley, to place the end of the Mississippi period at A.D. 1500 is entirely arbitrary and reflects coming changes in the nature of the databases in two respects: first, items of Old World manufacture begin trickling into Native American sites, providing a handy marker for a new time period in much the same way as the appearance of shell temper provides a convenient marker for the arrival of the Mississippi period; second, with descriptions by European travelers, archaeologists and historians now can begin to discuss people like the Chickasaw, Choctaw, Natchez, and many others (Figure 1.5). These peoples who are named in the historic record clearly are historic Mississippian peoples, and in some

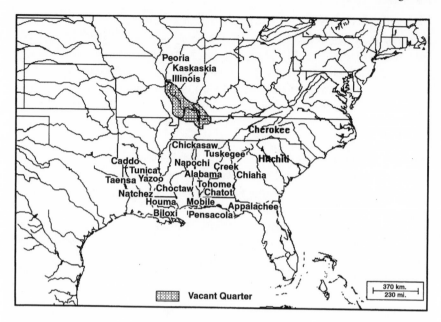

1.5. Historic Native American tribes of the Mississippian area and the hypothesized Vacant Quarter.

areas the link between groups for whom we have names and groups who created an archaeological record can be established. The written documents provide a wealth of descriptions of the later Mississippian peoples that help in interpreting their ancestral sites (Hudson 1976), although archaeologists in eastern North America have not done well at working with modern descendants to see how living traditions also can illuminate the ancestors' sites and ways of life. (For instance, Shawnee traditions place their ancestors and relatives in the Lower Ohio Valley, but they cannot yet be distinguished in the archaeological record.)

In western Kentucky, archaeologists cannot make a link between Mississippian sites and historic or modern descendants. The archaeological record is, at best, sparse for the period following about A.D. 1400. So is the historic record. When the French explorers descended the Mississippi, they recorded no villages between the Arkansas and the Illinois rivers. Eighteenth-century European and American outposts such as Fort Jefferson, a short distance south of Wickliffe, and Fort Massac, near Metropolis, Illinois, had encounters with Chickasaw and Cherokee parties, but the homelands of those groups were in northern Mississippi and along the Tennessee–North Carolina border, respectively. Western Kentucky and Tennessee are known as the Jackson Purchase because of the 1818 treaty negotiated by Isaac Shelby and Andrew

Jackson, in which the Chickasaw ceded rights to the area, but 1818 is more than four centuries after the well-documented occupations of Mississippian sites in western Kentucky. There is no historical evidence that ancestral Chickasaw lived in Kentucky, and a residential continuity in the region from which to identify Wickliffe and neighboring sites with any historic occupants is wanting.

The gap in both archaeological and documentary records has drawn some archaeologists, led by Stephen Williams (1980, 1983, 1990) to postulate a Vacant Quarter in the area of western Kentucky, southeast Missouri above the Bootheel, and southern Illinois (Figure 1.5). Williams's argument is that the lack of archaeological markers for the period circa A.D. 1400 to 1700 in this region—markers well known from sites of the time in southeast Missouri, northeast Arkansas, and southwest Indiana—indicates a lack of occupation, essentially an abandonment, by Native Americans. The scenario may take two forms: either the area was completely abandoned, or the mound centers and larger villages collapsed, leaving a much smaller, scattered, archaeologically nearly invisible population. Parenthetically, it may be noted that there is a great deal of confusion about when exactly the Vacant Quarter hypothetically begins, it being placed by various discussants at A.D. 1300, 1400, or 1450, reflecting some lack of precision in the dating of known sites in the region.

R. Barry Lewis (1984, 1988, 1990a, 1996) is probably the leading opponent of the Vacant Quarter hypothesis. He notes the lack of comprehensive archaeological survey that would demonstrate that there are no sites—and indeed the interior of Kentucky's Jackson Purchase is dismally covered by archaeological reconnaissance—and questions the adequacy of archaeological chronology in the region to distinguish sites postdating A.D. 1400 from those of the previous century. There is also a lack of any good explanation why people would abandon the area for a few years, let alone generations.

What became of the Mississippian peoples of western Kentucky, and who their living descendants may be (What tribe are they?, as so many visitors to the WMRC ask), are questions that still have no answers.

2 The King Project

The Wickliffe investigations, spread out over almost seven decades now, seem less a project than a phenomenon, and they are imbued with a somewhat swashbuckling aura of controversy, suspicion, and alienation from the mainstream of archaeology.

Since the site was donated to Murray State University in 1983, research has been directed toward reevaluating earlier excavations conducted by Fain W. King in the 1930s. The large collection of artifacts still housed on the site is a valuable resource and database, if researchers can reconstruct something of their original context. To do this, it is necessary to understand two interrelated things: the King excavation as a field project and the intent of that excavation, encompassing the academic and social milieu in which the project was conducted. In the absence of extensive field notes or an analytical report, current study must depend on provenience information on the artifacts and whatever scraps of information researchers can find in publications and archives.

The central character in this saga is Fain White King, originally of Paducah. The infamy of the Wickliffe Mounds site is due as much to King's personality as to his archaeology. King's relationships with contemporary archaeologists were often stormy and more than anything else shaped the legacy that Wickliffe Mounds Research Center researchers are trying to evaluate.

King bought the Wickliffe Mounds site in 1932 from the Wisconsin Chair Company, which had owned the land since 1895 (Ballard County Deed Book). At that time he was untrained, but was not a stranger to archaeology or archaeologists. A later newspaper story in the *St. Louis Post Dispatch* (Behymer 1946) states that King had been dealing artifacts since he was a teenager, at first with financial backing from his father. He had been in correspondence with archaeologists at the University of Kentucky since at least 1927, when he offered to show W. D. Funkhouser his collection (U.K.: King to Funkhouser, 14 November 1927), and in 1928 he discussed with William S. Webb the possibility of excavations in mounds near Barlow, in Ballard County (U.K.: King to Webb, 11 May 1928). In August 1932, King visited the University of Chicago's Lewistown project, where he was recorded as a friend of Walter B. Jones of the Alabama Museum of Natural History (Deuel 1932).

Jones sent students to help King open the Wickliffe site in September 1932 (Figure 2.1). Jones's crews had worked at the Moundville site in Alabama since

2.1. Alabama Museum of Natural History consultants, 1932.

1929 (Lyon 1996:185) and so had as much experience with this type of site as anyone. According to the *Cairo Evening Citizen and Bulletin* (Cairo, Illinois) (*CECB;* 17 October 1932, p. 3), "Even the diggers, [a] group of Alabama Negros have had long experience in the work" (Figure 2.2). It seems that King had little real idea of the task he had set himself: "Due to the vastness and tediousness of the work, Mr. King expects it to take several months to complete his job" (Ibid.).

Jones's participation apparently provoked some discussion among colleagues. Webb wrote to Carl E. Guthe, at the University of Michigan, "I am exceedingly sorry to know that the Alabama Museum of Natural History is cooperating with Mr. Fain King . . . He is not an archaeologist but is merely collecting as a fad" (U.K.: Webb to Guthe, 29 September 1932). Webb had an antipathy toward King already, because King had excavated in the McLeod Bluff site in Hickman County only weeks before Webb's arrival on the same site, leaving a swath of destruction that left Webb with little to salvage in the small area in which he had permission to work. Webb also reported that King had attempted to buy pottery from a collector by claiming to represent the University of Kentucky (Ibid.).

Jones replied, also to Guthe, that since King would excavate at Wickliffe anyway, it was better to work with him and ensure a proper methodology.

2.2. Alabama Museum of Natural History field crew, 1932.

Jones felt that he had made progress with King, who had "kept a careful record of all his purchases [of artifacts] and accessions since we met him . . . I am absolutely sure that he now realizes the scientific value of his work" (U.K.: Jones to Guthe, 17 October 1932).

Webb responded with pessimism about King's change of heart. "It is my opinion that when Dr. Jones knows him as well as I do, Dr. Jones will change his mind" (U.K.: Webb to Guthe, 29 October 1932).

Meanwhile, King was reporting to Webb (U.K.: King to Webb, 1 October 1932). King indicated that his inspiration had been the Dickson project (Harn 1980) in Illinois. In his letter of October 1, 1932, King said that they had been at work for one week and had excavated half of the main platform mound. By October 28, they had completed the two platform mound excavations, covered them with exhibit buildings, and exposed about twenty-five burials in Mound C (U.K.: King to Webb, 28 October 1932). There are some sketchy field notes, a few drawings, and a set of photographs from this initial excavation, kept at Mound State Monument, Alabama, and the University of Alabama Library Archives.

It was apparently at this point, after little more than a month of work, that the first hints of serious controversy began. Guthe wrote to Webb on November 3 that Jones had withdrawn his crew, leaving only one, Jimmy Hays, on King's payroll (U.K.: Guthe to Webb, 3 November 1932). King's work continued for a little while, though, since he wrote to S. A. Garrett of the Milwaukee Public Museum, on November 8, that they had uncovered forty burials by then (U.K.: King to Garrett, 8 November 1932). In December, T. M. N. Lewis wrote to Webb that he was expecting pottery from King, mentioning that Jones also was working on Wickliffe pottery (U.K.: Lewis to Webb, 10 December 1932). There was not yet a serious breach, and perhaps would not be with Jones, since an article in *Natural History* in 1935 cited King as a member of the Board of Regents of the Alabama Museum of Natural History (Butler 1935:400).

King filed a resume of work completed as of December 1932 with the Museum of Anthropology, University of Michigan (U.M.M.A.). He reported that the Mound C excavations had accomplished the exposure of 140 burials and that "the work here is completed; everything will be left just as it was found for the general public to see." King also wrote that "from tests outside the building" he estimated there were a thousand burials in the cemetery.

In January 1933, King encountered some serious criticism. The Science Service, in Washington, issued an announcement concerning King's exaggerated publicity about his project and, on the basis of a report by William S. Webb, gave the opinion that the project was of commercial intent and little scientific importance. Webb had reported that King had "recently broken loose in a campaign of publicity which is more than ridiculous. It is a campaign of misrepresentation intended to attract people to his show." Webb also complained that King was trying to use Webb's name to add authenticity to the publicity (U.K.: Webb to Guthe, 13 January 1933).

King wrote to Webb: "I am at a loss to understand the conflicting information I have." He claimed that, when the two had met at the recent conference of archaeologists in Birmingham, Alabama (National Research Council 1932), Webb had approved of his work. He wrote, "I will prove by all scientific investigations and reports which I am in position to do that this is a remarkable find" (U.K.: King to Webb, 4 February 1933). The National Research Council (1932) summary of the conference does not include King on the list of "members and guests," but Webb's correspondence (U.K.: Webb to King, 12 January 1933) confirms King's attendance.

King evidently asked Walter B. Jones to come to his defense and resume some active role in the Wickliffe project. Jones replied: "I believe that the program which you are about to enter upon, would act unfavorably for us, and I must therefore decline the invitation to become associated with the plan" (U.K.: Jones to King, 7 February 1933). To underscore his position, Jones copied the letter to Guthe, Webb, T. M. N. Lewis, and Warren K. Moorehead.

In a flurry of crossing letters in mid-February 1933, the story of King's preemptive strike at the McLeod Bluff site apparently was misapplied to Wickliffe. Webb set that misconception straight, but not before King made ominous statements about his friendship with Senator Alben Barkley and his plans to visit Kentucky's governor soon (U.K.: King to Webb, 10 February 1933; Webb to King, 13 February 1933).

Carl E. Guthe, consulting with the Committee on State Archaeological Surveys of the National Research Council, sent a letter to King and circulated it among most of the practicing colleagues. This letter severely criticized King's publicity and his excavations. Guthe wrote, "Frankly, you have chosen a very unsatisfactory method of [scientific investigation]. Your activities are antagonizing all professional prehistorians." He recommended that the proper way for an untrained person to approach an archaeological project would be to make "arrangements with a recognized institution" and then get out of the way (U.M.M.A.: Guthe to King, 11 February 1933).

Guthe went on to decry King's commercial publicity, reacting to such stories as that in the *New York Times* (11 January 1933, 21:6) touting Wickliffe as "the American equivalent of Tut-ankh-amen's tomb." Guthe wrote, "You are clearly catering to the romantic side of general public interest" with exaggerated and false claims (such as dating the site to an antiquity of 3,000 years). "Your news releases have made you ridiculous in the eyes of prehistorians . . . [and shown] a great ignorance of scientific methods and ethics," he wrote. In closing, Guthe expressed confidence in the scientific value of the site as well as hope that King would accept constructive suggestions in continuing the project (U.M.M.A.: Guthe to King, 11 February 1933).

Apparently, and contrary to later reputation, King took the criticism well. He wrote, "I have a letter which I am enclosing from Dr. Guthe, which without doubt the cruelest letter I have ever received. . . . I cannot but believe that the thought back of the letter is intended for my best good" (wording King's; U.K.: King to Webb, 15 February 1933). He assured Webb that he wanted to cooperate with the scientific goals of archaeologists. On the same day, Guthe wrote to Webb, "My purpose in broadcasting my letter to Mr. King was to warn professional men away from him . . . I frankly admit that I am very much annoyed with the havoc Mr. King, in his egotistical ignorance, has managed to create" (U.K.: Guthe to Webb, 15 February 1933).

Guthe wrote several suggestions to Webb about how King might best cooperate with professional archaeologists, including the possibility that King could enroll in an academic program to receive training. Webb took these suggestions to a face-to-face meeting in Lexington with King, who professed his complete willingness to become trained and to work with professionals. "However," wrote Webb, "from my knowledge of men I cannot help but feel, much as I regret to make this statement, that I did not really reach the man" (U.K.: Webb to Guthe, 23 February 1933).

King's inconsistent attitude was clear in his next letter to Guthe. He first claimed that he had grounds for a suit for "damage" on the basis of Guthe's statements about the Wickliffe project. However, King was set on having the credentials of an archaeologist. "Professor Webb has suggested a course of study, scientific contact and scientific work such suggestion I wish to follow. Might state that I intend to follow this character of work the balance of my life . . . I know now that you Archaeologists regret that such a development as I have has been made in as much that it has been made and will continue to be here. If it is at all possible to meet your viewpoint I certainly want to do it" (U.K.: King to Guthe, 24 February 1933).

Guthe sent Webb a copy of King's letter. Webb reacted with exasperation: "My present intention is to withdraw entirely from the picture." He suggested that Guthe arrange a meeting at Wickliffe with Walter B. Jones and T. M. N. Lewis, whom King still considered friends, "and thrash out with King his future conduct. I believe Jones and Lewis are in the mood to give you every support" (U.K.: Webb to Guthe, 27 February 1933).

King wrote to Guthe defending his public interpretation at Wickliffe. He assured Guthe that the Wickliffe site "has been willed" to the Commonwealth of Kentucky for use as a state park and that his lectures to visitors stressed scientific values. He said that he explained to visitors that the Wickliffe Mounds "is not a commercial enterprise, but an interest and a hobby" (U.K.: King to Guthe, 13 March 1933). Neither Guthe nor any of his critical colleagues is likely to have been mollified by the characterization of modern archaeology as a hobby.

King tried to give the appearance of serious application to studies by asking Webb and others for reading lists and books (U.K.: King to Webb, 23 March 1933). Up to this point, King was writing on letterhead entitled "Wickliffe Mounds, Museum and Burials," with promotional slogans in the margins. Soon, however, he came up with a new name. Noting that visitors often confused the Wickliffe Mounds with Mound City in Illinois (they still do!), King announced a new set of highway signs proclaiming "See Ancient Buried City, Wickliffe, Ky." (U.K.: King to Webb, 14 April 1933). Neither Webb nor Guthe reacted favorably, although Webb rather feebly allowed that the new slogan "might be the best solution" for clarity in advertising (U.K.: Guthe to King, 21 April 1933; Webb to King, 24 April 1933). King continued to write to Webb, mentioning again that he had willed the site to the state of Kentucky (U.K.: King to Webb, 2 May 1933).

King continued on both courses, cooperating with (or humoring) professional archaeologists on the one hand and enraging them with his commercial hyperbole on the other. He may genuinely have been unable to comprehend the contradiction. Guthe wrote to King in June 1933, thanking him for providing timber samples to Dr. Douglass in Arizona for dendrochronological studies. However, Guthe was "considerably disappointed" in King's new advertising brochure, providing a long critique sprinkled with such phrases as "gross exaggeration," "almost revolting," and "so much ballyhoo" (U.K.: Guthe to King, 20 June 1933). King prepared a new pamphlet in October, writing that T. M. N. Lewis had "completed it." Tellingly, he wrote on a new letterhead, still with "Wickliffe Mounds, Museum and Burials," but subtitled "Ancient Buried City" (U.K.: King to Webb, 24 October 1933).

King enrolled as a special student for the winter quarter 1934 at the University of Chicago, initiating a long acquaintance with Fay-Cooper Cole, following which at least one Chicago student became closely involved with the Wickliffe site (U.C.: Guthe memorandum, 22 October 1937; Cole to Hutchins, 16 October 1941; Cole to To Whom It May Concern, 17 November 1942).

The *Cairo Evening Citizen and Bulletin* chronicled some of the events of this period, both the tourism and King's quest for respectability. On July 21, 1933 (p. 5), the headline announced, "Wickliffe is becoming Mecca for Scientists." The paper reported that "this Buried City in Wickliffe has been donated as a gift to the State of Kentucky" (*CECB*, 7 December 1933, p. 2), which probably reflects King's view of his own public-mindedness in conducting the project "for education and posterity" (to quote the plaque in the parking lot of the Wickliffe site); although it is possible that he had indeed written a will bequeathing the site to the state, as he had told Webb and Guthe. Stories followed about King's departure to study anthropology at the University of Chicago (*CECB*, 22 January 1934, p. 1) and his return after he "did research work . . . under Dr. Cole at Chicago this winter" (*CECB*, 28 March 1934). Commercial publicity continued, however, as King boasted that "his advertising covered nine states and at least a million persons saw it every day" (*CECB*, 20 November 1934, p. 5).

In the middle 1930s, in cooperation with Cole, the whole atmosphere of the project changed. This is apparently the time when King did the major work on Mounds D, E, and F, resulting in the bulk of the artifact collections extant from the project. These artifacts are labeled with 5 × 5-foot grid coordinates, an excavation technique that King must have picked up from Cole. King (1936) refers to records including floor plans and stratigraphic drawings, which is credible since he went to the trouble of labeling all of the artifacts. Several publications during this period are preliminary but reasonably sober (Lewis 1934; B. King 1937a; F. King 1936). It seems as though King was making real efforts toward responsible archaeology. He even discussed with Cole his reservations about buying artifacts from looters (U.C.: King to Cole, 28 October 1935; Cole to King, 5 November 1935).

It is interesting that the mid-1930s also saw the attempted rise of competitors in the region, even as King had emulated Don Dickson. The Lost City at Lewisburg, Kentucky, was an imitator (NAIRCA 1936). The Reelfoot Burial Mound in Tiptonville, Tennessee, announced that "they have nothing at

Wyckliffe [*sic*] that we have not found" (*Tiptonville Times* 6[19]:1, 1935; 6[30]:1, 1935). The Tiptonville exhibit was "wantonly destroyed" by vandalism (Donaldson 1946), and recent work on the supposed site has shown no trace of Native American occupation (conversation with William Lawrence, c. 1990). It may be that the threat of even more imitators spurred Cole's effort to bring King into the fold of scientific method.

However, sometime during this period, King also acquired a wife, Blanche Busey King (Figure 2.3). Discounting oral history in Wickliffe, which is entertaining but not relevant here, there is little information available about Blanche's background. The first mentions of her in any correspondence are in December 1935 (U.K.: King to Webb, 12 December 1935) and March 1936 (U.C.: King to Cole, 14 March 1936). Blanche's arrival is interesting in that, after 1936, it was she, not King, who published about the site (B. King 1937a, 1937b, 1937c, 1939) and in that in 1937 King's relationship with a number of colleagues ruptured irreparably.

The first hints of new difficulties came in early summer of 1937. Robert McCormick Adams, working with King, submitted an article on daub to *American Antiquity*, which editor W. C. McKern accepted. King withdrew the article on the pretext that it was premature (U.K.: King to Guthe, 7 August 1937; U.C.: Guthe memorandum, 22 October 1937). At the same time, King asked Guthe for "membership blanks" to enroll in the newly formed Society for American Archaeology (U.K.: King to Guthe, 7 August 1937). At that time, prospective members had to submit an application and endorsement by two current members to be accepted.

2.3. Fain and Blanche King "and associates."

The real trouble hit the correspondence fan in September 1937. The Kings reacted with severe indignation that they should have to apply for membership: "We had expected to be solicited rather than making application. . . . Mrs. King was not interested in being a member of your society at the time that I mentioned it to her, but I thought it would be a nice compliment to your society to have her as a member . . . we are doing more to create interest in American archaeology than your entire membership . . . we are doing our work as well as any institution in America today." King closed with, "As we consider the loss to your society rather than to ourselves . . . please consider the matter closed" (U.K.: King to Guthe, 1 September 1937). Webb commented that King was "running true to form" (U.K.: Webb to Guthe, 17 September 1937).

Guthe, considering the matter closed, did not reply, which further aroused King's ire. King, in a flurry of letters, cited Guthe's record of "decided effrontery" based on the Science Service memo and Guthe's letter of February 11, 1933 (quoted above), attacked Webb for statements about the Wickliffe Mounds in the 1932 Archaeological Survey of Kentucky, demanded of Watson Davis of the Science Service that his organization handle press releases for King's project, and generally threatened legal action against all and sundry (U.C.: Guthe memorandum, 22 October 1937; King to Cole, 19 October 1937; U.K.: King to Webb, 4 October 1937; King to Webb, 12 October 1937; King to Guthe, 12 October 1937).

The reaction of Guthe, Webb, and colleagues was one of shock and dismay at King's overreaction and his sudden citing of incidents dating back to 1932 and 1933, which he had seemed to take in stride at the time (U.C.: Cole to King, 21 October 1937; Guthe to King, 21 October 1937; Guthe to Cole, 22 October 1937; King to Cole, 23 October 1937). Webb wrote, "I am unable to understand why he should have chosen this time to bring up this matter since I have had no communication with him for many years" (U.K.: Webb to Guthe, 15 October 1937). Guthe then apprised Webb of the Society for American Archaeology application escapade (U.K.: Guthe to Webb, 22 October 1937). Cole wrote to Guthe, "Apparently the man has gone wild," and could only express hope that King would cool off (U.C.: Cole to Guthe, 26 October 1937). Guthe and Webb decided to leave further efforts at diplomacy to Cole (U.K.: Guthe to Webb, 14 October 1937; Webb to Guthe, 26 October 1937).

King replied to Cole's attempt at conciliation: "Just as I was greatly surprised to find you had the strength of character to leave an institution because you felt you had been injured . . . (for as a general thing college professors are given to much talk and little action)—even so, no doubt you are surprised to know my real character. A man who never forgets, vindictive if you wish, one who had every night for years promised himself retribution" (U.C.: King to Cole, 23 October 1937).

Cole did manage to patch up his own relationship with King, since by late December, King was reporting to Cole that he had dropped plans for a widely publicized suit (U.C.: King to Cole, 26 December 1937). Cole replied with a positive tone (U.C.: Cole to King, 4 January 1938), and by July was thanking the Kings for their "generous hospitality" (U.C.: Cole to King, 12 July 1938).

Acrimony in regional archaeology, and Cole's role as hopeful peacemaker, was by no means limited to the Wickliffe project in the mid to late 1930s. The New Deal era of archaeology was in progress, linked with what Lyon (1996:145) calls "multidimensional conflict." Particularly, William S. Webb was highly critical of T. M. N. Lewis's work in Tennessee, and Cole attempted to mediate in this controversy as well (Lyon 1996:144–45, 152, 159). One wonders whether Lewis's prior association with King (Lewis 1934), limited though it may have been, was a contributing factor to Webb's opinion of him.

King and Cole's correspondence continued amicably. In November 1938, King wrote to Cole that he was about to be appointed Kentucky's State Research Director, Division of Archaeology, by Governor Chandler (U.C.: King to Cole, 10 November 1938), which must have irritated Webb. By the end of the month, King was writing on Kentucky Department of Conservation stationery (U.C.: King to Cole, 19 November 1938). This chapter of the story needs more investigation. The *Louisville Courier-Journal* referred to "Fain King, State Archaeologist" in 1939 (22 September 1939, section 1, p. 17) and later noted his reappointment as "director of the Archaeology Division in the State Conservation department" and that "King serves without compensation" (14 January 1945, section 4, p. 7).

More important, in late 1938 King and Cole began discussing joint publication of site reports on the Wickliffe and Kincaid sites (U.C.: King to Cole, 19 November 1938). Cole suggested that there were several possibilities for publication (U.C.: Cole to King, 25 November 1938). King replied, "We are inclined towards your suggestion of a comparative study of this site and Kincaid . . . Mrs. King and I will consider being co-authors and collaborating with you" (U.C.: King to Cole, 19 November 1938). Cole suggested that there were various possible forms for a collaborative report or set of reports (U.C.: Cole to King, 25 November 1938).

King's renewed cooperation did not extend to other colleagues, however. He created an exhibit called "Comedy of Errors" at Wickliffe, disparaging Webb's work, and he threatened to add material on Guthe (U.C.: King to Cole, 18 January 1939; U.M.M.A.: King to Griffin, 7 October 1938).

Cole continued to work for better relations all around. As 1939 progressed, he welcomed news that Blanche King was writing a book, planned to send students to study King's ceramics, and negotiated peace offers between King and Webb (U.C.: Cole to King, 1 April 1939). King replied in kind, accepting the students, removing the Comedy of Errors exhibit as a gesture to Webb, and noting complimentary references to Guthe, Webb, and James B. Griffin in Blanche King's manuscript (U.C.: King to Cole, 4 April 1939; King to Cole, 6 June 1939). In April 1939, Cole sent graduate students to study pottery at Wickliffe. King wrote to Cole that the "boys" had arrived and would be offered lodging and other help (U.C.: King to Cole, 4 April 1939).

But by August, things fell apart again. Cole and a colleague, Edward Spicer, visited the Kings at Wickliffe, and talked generally about comparing Wickliffe and Kincaid. The Kings apparently felt that their contribution and, perhaps, Blanche's book already in print (B. King 1939) were not properly valued. King wrote to Cole that any plan to collaborate would be called off. "*We do not want any comparison or mention of the King mounds . . .* We wish this site to be ignored in every way in publications unless it can be done right by ourselves" (emphasis in the original). He threatened legal action if Cole used any Wickliffe data. "This is a notice that you are not to use in any manner, shape or form any of the materials excavated from this site without our knowledge or permission, and which permission we are not granting . . . (What D—— fools you must have thought we were!)" (U.C.: King to Cole, 20 August 1939).

At the same time, he evicted Cole's students John Bennett and Karl Schmitt from the Wickliffe site, accusing them of stealing his data. Bennett's report to Cole suggests that it was Blanche King who was the prime mover, with King himself standing back helplessly. During this exchange, Blanche King referred to Cole and Deuel's *Rediscovering Illinois* (1937) as a theft of Dickson's rights to publish his site, vowing that Cole would not do the same to them (U.C.: King to Cole, 20 August 1939; Bennett to Cole, 21 August 1939; King to Cole, 29 August 1939; King to Cole, 14 September 1939). Bennett wrote, "She was deathly afraid we were going to publish over her head and steal all their seven years of work . . . The Colonel is all right and knows the ropes. The madam is impossible" (U.C.: Bennett to Cole, 21 August 1939). Bennett and Schmitt gave up their notes and left.

Cole wrote to King, "I scarcely know how to reply" (U.C.: Cole to King, undated but clearly in response to King to Cole, 20 August 1939). Cole assured King that he had no intention of publishing Wickliffe, only wishing to make comparisons. King replied, reiterating his refusal to permit "any *mention* of the King mounds" in any publication (King's emphasis; U.C.: King to Cole, 29 August 1939).

Immediately following this brouhaha, King wrote to W. D. Funkhouser a very cordial letter thanking Funkhouser for a copy of the McLeod Bluff report. Funkhouser's answer must have been brusque, because King's next letter, nine days later, accused him of lying repeatedly and incidentally charged Cole with wanting to steal the Wickliffe data (U.C.: King to Funkhouser, 5 September 1939; King to Funkhouser, 14 September 1939). "The stupidity and ignorance of the majority of Mississippi Valley pseudo archaeologists and anthropologists is truly amazing . . . So in conclusion I wish to say the more I see certain instructors the more I like my dogs," wrote King (U.C.: King to Funkhouser, 14 September 1939). He followed with another letter to Cole, referring to Funkhouser as deceitful, and continued, "Most of you College professors are tricky and stupid," and again denied permission to use any information from the Wickliffe site (U.C.: King to Cole, 14 September 1939).

Cole was astonished and conciliatory, saying that King's attitude is "beyond my understanding." He assured King that Don Dickson had fully cooperated in all publications mentioning the Dickson Mounds (U.C.: Cole to King, 5 October 1939). King replied, in a chilly letter, that he still considered the Coles the "best of friends," and ostensibly the two agreed to "wipe the slate clean" (U.C.: King to Cole, 3 November 1939; Cole to King, 11 November 1939); however, King implied that any misunderstanding was entirely Cole's fault. So ended 1939.

The relationship remained cool from that point. Cole asked permission to acknowledge King's help in dendrochronology studies in April 1940, and King declined (U.C.: Cole to King, 18 April 1939; King to Cole, 19 April 1939).

By late 1941, King was ill, citing pneumonia and typhoid, and apparently was tired of the whole affair. He offered the Wickliffe site to the University of Chicago, which declined it (U.C.: King to Cole, 10 October 1941; Cole to Hutchins, 16 October 1941). Cole wrote to Robert M. Hutchins, president of the university, that King "is a difficult person, with many enemies, whose actions from day to day are quite unpredictable" (U.C.: Cole to Hutchins, 16 October 1941). King's remaining correspondence to Cole refers to buying and attempting to sell artifacts, and to other matters, but never again to field or analytical work (U.C.: various letters). King even asked Cole for a recommendation to join the military as an officer in 1942; Cole's reference was tepid (U.C.: King to Cole, 12 November 1942; Cole to To Whom It May Concern, 17 November 1942).

King offered the site for sale in 1946, asking $400,000 (Behymer 1946), and finally turned it over to Western Baptist Hospital in Paducah, then called the Western Kentucky Baptist Memorial Hospital. The *Louisville Courier-Journal* repeated the $400,000 valuation and stated that the property held 35 mounds (3 October 1946, section 2, p. 15; *Courier-Journal* Sunday Magazine, 24 November 1946, pp. 8–9). King had never stopped exaggerating the site.

Pamphlets and advertising brochures in the WMRC files are the primary source for the history of the Ancient Buried City between about 1940 and 1983, when Murray State University accepted the site. None bears a date. Two items apparently belong to the King era. The first, entitled "It's Never Too Late to Discover America," is a quadrifold glossy brochure. The second is a saddle-stitched pamphlet identifying the site both as the Ancient Buried City and as

King Mounds. Neither has a person's name listed as contact, only the address, and the texts and photographs closely follow Blanche King's published articles.

In fact, the texts of the brochures never did stray much from Blanche King's works until the final revision circa 1980, which was simplified. A brochure with the heading "Come and see this amazing discovery" went through three versions. The first, listing Robert P. Stratton, Superintendent, and Lucille Champion Stratton, Assistant, with their photograph, apparently belongs to a brief period immediately following the Kings' relinquishment of the site. The second is identical except for the replacement of the Strattons' names and portrait with those of George L. Johnson, "horticulturist," and Mrs. George L. Johnson, "connoisseur." The third lists the Johnsons as Superintendent and Assistant Superintendent and is organized slightly differently but otherwise is essentially the same.

The final, circa 1980, revision of the Ancient Buried City brochure is a trifold pamphlet with fewer illustrations and noticeably less text, clearly a less expensive production. The earlier of the two versions in the Wickliffe Mounds files presents the name of Frank M. Bodkin as the person to contact, who was the superintendent for about two years around 1980. When he was replaced by Darrell Unsell, who managed the site until Murray State's acquisition, the contact name and address were replaced by a rubber stamp. The text, though synopsized, betrays little if any change in the style or content of the site's interpretation since Blanche King set the pattern in the late 1930s.

None of King's own papers have been found, whether field notes, personal correspondence, or an analytical report he told Funkhouser he was writing in 1939 (U.C.: King to Funkhouser, 5 September 1939). However, the notes and correspondence cited above, and the few publications, provide glimpses of the field work, and the artifacts and open excavations left at the site supplement the picture.

The King project, for all its infamy, is promising in reanalysis. The archival information is a critical part of the analysis, necessary to understanding how the project was conducted. This background gives a perspective that researchers might not otherwise take into account. King is remembered as a showman, an entrepreneur, and an unpleasant personality. Yet it is clear from the labels on some 80,000 artifacts, from his travel to the University of Chicago, and from his references to field notes, that at least during the middle years of his work he made a conscientious effort to approach the standards of his day. He sent artifact samples to Guthe and Griffin, to Cole, to T. M. N. Lewis, to Walter B. Jones; he sent botanical samples to Melvin R. Gilmore at the University of Michigan and to Iowa State University (Brown and Anderson 1947). In the end, in part because of his personality, in part perhaps because of his wife's, in part because of lack of academic background, these attempts at collaboration fell apart.

The correspondence makes it clear that professional archaeologists varied in their response. Webb wanted nothing to do with him. Guthe offered blunt admonition. Jones tried to help, on the grounds that King would go ahead and dig anyway, but then pulled out. Cole persevered in trying to salvage a working relationship, but ultimately failed to maintain anything but a chilly acquaintance.

Blanche King's death in 1982 was the event that allowed the Wickliffe Mounds site to be returned to the province of professional archaeology, when Western Baptist Hospital was able to divest itself of the site by donating it to Murray State University.

3   Excavations

Soon after Murray State University accepted the donation of the Wickliffe site in 1983, Wickliffe Mounds Research Center researchers realized that the artifacts left from the Fain King collection would not be very useful without some indication of their contexts within the site. As the WMRC staff sorted and cataloged the King collection, they also planned a series of excavations, whose primary goal would be to reinvestigate the areas around the 1930s locations in order to establish their boundaries, obtain comparative artifact assemblages, and assess adjacent stratigraphic and feature patterning in the hope of extrapolating from undisturbed contexts to those previously removed.

The WMRC conducted excavations annually from 1984 through 1996. Summer field schools through Murray State University expanded into cooperative arrangements with the Kentucky Junior Historical Society, the Council for International Educational Exchange, and since 1991 the Middle Mississippi Survey, a consortium arrangement with Southeast Missouri State University and guest institutions (which have included Southern Illinois University at Carbondale, Eastern Kentucky University, and the University of Tennessee at Knoxville). The Western Kentucky Project of the University of Illinois at Urbana-Champaign also contributed to the effort by excavating a test unit and taking radiocarbon samples in the summer of 1983, shortly before the site was transferred to Murray State University (Lewis 1986).

King excavated in six areas, which he labeled Mounds A through F. The WMRC investigated in and around five of those sites, Mounds A through D and Mound F, and, by process of elimination, indicated the most likely location of Mound E. Additional WMRC projects targeted areas that had not been investigated previously, for a more representative sample of the village site.

This chapter summarizes the excavation data, closely following Wesler 1997. More detailed information on each excavation unit, including photographs and drawings, and the available data from the King excavations are included on the accompanying CD-ROM (Chapter 18).

THE KING EXCAVATIONS, 1932–1939

The King excavations at Wickliffe began with a scattered set of test units in September 1932 under the direction of personnel from the Alabama Museum of Natural History. Walter B. Jones consulted with King on the initial testing, bringing a crew of students from the University of Alabama under the field direction of David L. DeJarnette. The involvement of the Alabama workers was very brief, but Jones or DeJarnette made a sketchy record of work in progress in the first months of the excavation. These notes are on file at the University of Alabama, in the Library Archives and at Mound State Monument (cited as M.S.M.).

A sketch map in the Alabama notes (M.S.M.) places two rectangular test units on Mound A, one on Mound B, one at the north end of Mound D, and three in a triangular pattern in the northwest sector of the site (Figure 3.1). The Alabama crew extended the initial tests in the platform mounds into major excavation blocks and also began excavations in Mound C, apparently without establishing a grid.

The notes do not describe field methods explicitly. The note-taker referred to levels in each test: "levels depth of one spade average 6"" (M.S.M.). To judge by extant collections (scarce) and by the contents of backfill in a disturbance in Mound D that probably is the 1932 test (see below and Chapter 18), the excavators did not screen the soils. F. King's later comments that "very few artifacts were found elsewhere" (1936:38) and "the other three mounds [i.e., A, B, C; this discussion is about Mound D] excavated to date are composed of almost sterile soil" (1936:37) tend to support the idea that no screens were used. The excavators recorded features and kept artifacts that caught their eye, without apparent system.

In the mid-1930s King's association with Fay-Cooper Cole led to the introduction of the Chicago methods, which also became influential in New Deal and subsequent archaeology throughout the southeast (Lyon 1996:150, fn. 88). Blanche King (1939:33) described the system as "the five-foot method of excavating." The excavation area was gridded in 5 × 5-foot (1.5 × 1.5 meter) squares, with base lines designated as though along cardinal compass lines. Within squares, excavators proceeded by 12-inch (30 centimeter) levels, numbered from the surface down. Blanche King's description fits the labels on some 85,000 artifacts in the Wickliffe Mounds collection. She neglected to say that Mound E was gridded on a left-right grid rather than a compass-direction grid, that "north" was a convenience and had little to do with compass direction, and that each excavation area within the site—Mounds D, E, and F—had its own grid and datum point.

She went on to say that "care must be taken to keep the vertical face as smooth and straight as possible. Each profile is carefully studied . . . to detect easily any signs of kitchen midden, post molds, fire pits, outlines of buildings, and charcoal" (B. King 1939:34–35). Those King profiles so far identified, particularly in the East Midden and Mound F, are closer to 45 degrees than vertical. Blanche King (1939:35) further mentioned a daily record of finds and

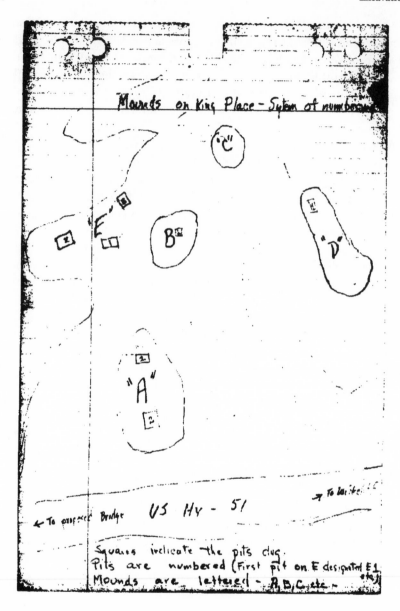

3.1. Sketch of initial test locations, 1932.

photographs or drawings "showing the position and relation of objects," and in various correspondences Fain King mentioned a detailed map of finds and features. Unfortunately, none of these records can be found. Nowhere is there a mention of screens; the ceramics and stone items in the collections at the WMRC, and most of the faunal remains, indicate that if the soils were sifted, the screen size must have been about 1 inch (2.5 centimeters).

THE WICKLIFFE MOUNDS RESEARCH
CENTER EXCAVATIONS, 1984–1996

The WMRC project began in 1984 by establishing a grid, with a prime datum (assumed elevation 100 meters) near the center of the site, consistent with the datum of the 1983 University of Illinois project (Lewis ed. 1986). All later excavations were coordinated within the same grid.

Excavation generally proceeded within units aligned with the grid. Soils were removed by shovel-shaving and troweling and sifted through ¼-inch hardware cloth. Excavators shifted to small tools for features and final trimming of profiles or level floors. All materials that failed to fall through the screen were placed in bags labeled by unit and level and boxed until laboratory processing began.

The excavators generally removed soils in arbitrary levels of 10 or 15 centimeters (4 or 6 inches), unless natural soil changes could be discerned. Where a soil change indicated a new depositional zone, the excavators terminated the level and commenced a new level. Expansion or extension units, where there was a profile to guide interpretation, usually proceeded by depositional zone, subdivided by levels if they were deep enough.

Features and postholes were defined whenever possible and the soils within them were removed, screened, and bagged separately. Features, often crossing excavation unit boundaries, were numbered within the site, in order as defined, so that adjacent features often do not have sequential numbers. Feature numbers for the WMRC excavations began with 101, to allow for numbering and recording of remnant features of the King excavations. Postholes, however, are numbered within the excavation unit. Narrative field notes, photographs, and scaled sketches recorded each level floor and feature. Unit profiles were recorded in similar fashion. Elevations were measured by transit relative to the prime datum.

The 1984 Mound A excavations obtained a stratified series of ceramic assemblages that formed the definition of three intrasite periods, Early, Middle, and Late Wickliffe. Subsequent excavations demonstrated the essentially consistent nature of the ceramic complexes, with particular significance in the changing proportions of incised and red-filmed sherds. In the following descriptions of the excavations, deposits are assigned where possible to one of the three periods (unless historically disturbed and except in other special circumstances to be detailed). Chapter 5 discusses the chronology and characterizes the periods more fully.

Mound A

Mound A is the larger platform mound, which forms the western boundary of the plaza. The mound was excavated first in 1932, with a large block excavation that revealed several buried mound summits that supported the wall trenches

3.2. Mound A, upper exposed summit, 1932.

3.3. Mound A at or near completion, 1932.

3.4. Mound A, corner of lower exposed summit, 1932.

and charred debris of structures (Figures 3.2, 3.3, and 3.4). The University of Illinois Western Kentucky Project obtained charcoal samples from the buried structures in 1983, resulting in dates of cal A.D. 1160–1280 (830 ± 70 B.P., ISGS 1143) and cal A.D. 1220–1300 (760 ± 70 B.P., ISGS 1152) (Lewis ed. 1986). (Wickliffe radiocarbon dates have been calibrated using CALIB Rev 3.0.3 [Stuiver and Reimer 1993].) Close inspection of a cleaned profile of the King excavation indicated that the charred building zones were entirely architectural, with no sign of midden (Wesler and Neusius 1987), suggesting that Mound A was primarily ceremonial in function.

The 1984 WMRC excavation placed a 2 × 8-meter test trench in the east side of Mound A, revealing at least six mound construction stages and an underlying midden. Analysis of ceramics allowed the construction of a three-period intrasite sequence (Table 3.1; Wesler 1985). The Early Wickliffe period, represented by the basal midden, was characterized by a 3:1 ratio of red-slipped to incised (including punctate) sherds. The Mound Core, comprising five of six identifiable construction zones, belonged to the Middle Wickliffe period, in which the percentage of incised sherds nearly matched that of red-slipped sherds. The final mantle of Mound A was deposited in the Late Wickliffe period, and in this zone, incised sherds occurred more frequently than red-slipped sherds at a nearly 3:1 ratio.

Table 3.1. Mound A Ceramic Frequencies and Percentages

	Outer Mound		Mound Core		Midden	
	#	%	#	%	#	%
Missippippi Plain	3732	92.5	247	88.5	595	91.0
Incised	61	1.5	5	1.8	3	0.5
Bell Plain	144	3.6	6	2.2	19	2.9
Negative Painted			1	0.4		
Red Filmed	23	0.6	8	2.9	20	3.1
Kimmswick Fabric Impressed	47	1.2	12	4.3	16	2.4
Wickliffe Thick	22	0.5			1	0.2
Cord Marked	5	0.1				
Total	4034	100.0	279	100.1	654	100.1

This sequence, and the consistency of the ceramic assemblages, was confirmed by subsequent excavations in varied settings throughout the site. The carbon 14–dated structure zones belonged stratigraphically to the Mound Core and the Middle Wickliffe period.

Mound B

Mound B, the smaller platform mound, marks the north side of the village plaza. Like Mound A, it was plumbed in 1932 by a single excavation block, this one reaching subsoil and exposing the plan of a large wall-trenched structure (Figures 3.5 through 3.8). A burial was recovered while digging an entrance into the excavation through the south side of the mound, but nothing is known of its context within the mound stratigraphy.

Excavations in 1990 on the north side of Mound B (Wesler 1990, 1991c) defined a stratigraphic sequence visually more complex than, but chronologically similar to, that of Mound A. An underlying Early Wickliffe midden was sealed by an Early Wickliffe mound and three or four Middle Wickliffe mound zones, capped by a Late Wickliffe final mantle.

The most significant difference between the Mound A and Mound B profiles is that at least two buried summits of Mound B supported middens. Analysis of the midden ceramics indicates two differences from the usual village assemblage: a paucity of decorated (red-slipped or incised) sherds and a large proportion of serving vessels (bowls and flare-rimmed bowls) as opposed to cooking vessels (jars) (Wesler 1991b, 1991c, 1992a). Faunal remains indicate that the Mound B residents utilized choice cuts of venison (Chapter 15; Kreisa and McDowell 1992, 1995). A family literally "living high" above the rest of the village, whose refuse is distinguishable by dietary and ceramic assemblages from that of the general village midden, is likely to have been an elite family.

3.5. Mound B during excavation, 1932.

3.6. Mound B with entrance excavated, 1932.

3.7. Mound B floor, 1932.

3.8. Mound B floor features, 1932.

Mound C

Mound C was excavated first in 1932. It became the centerpiece of the Wickliffe exhibits, as some 150 burials were exposed and left as an "in situ" display. The excavation was protected by a circus tent before a permanent exhibit building was constructed (Figures 3.9 and 3.10). Extended primary, bundle (secondary), and possible cremated burials were pointed out to visitors, and a number of artifacts, especially ceramic vessels, were exhibited in apparent association. Bundle burials are widespread in the eastern United States and represent individuals (often more than one individual) who were removed from a previous grave, exposed on a scaffold, or otherwise defleshed, and reburied. The Kings left burials on pedestals and removed the surrounding soil matrix, thus making the evaluation of contexts difficult. Only a sketch of the first ten to twelve burials is available in original field notes (M.S.M.).

The state of the cemetery display in the 1980s provoked several critical questions. It was clear from a cursory inspection that a number of skeletal elements had been badly repaired or restored and/or moved from their original positions. Many of the bundle burials looked suspiciously like modern arrangements. Artifact associations were dubious at best. A map and preliminary inventory

3.9. Mound C with circus tent, 1932.

3.10. Mound C and field camp, 1932.

(Haskins 1990) of the skeletal collection on display reinforced these concerns (Chapter 18).

The first controlled data on the depositional context resulted from excavations in 1989, when a test trench from the west intersected the edge of the cemetery (Chapter 18; Wesler 1991a). The general pattern of the burials fit well with the displayed materials: extended burials, several at quite shallow levels, were oriented with the heads toward the west, and bundle burials were interspersed among the extended burials. Artifact associations, however, were scarce. The burials were contained within a Late Wickliffe midden, in which no burial pits were discernible.

In the 1930s, observers had noted the lack of burial pits (Lewis 1934) and suggested that bodies were laid on the ground and dirt heaped upon them, thus forming the mound. This explanation was the typical interpretation of similar deposits at that time, an interpretation dispelled by Conrad's (1972) work at Dickson Mounds, which demonstrated the presence of intrusive burials even though the pits were not visible in the soil. At Wickliffe, however, this situation raised a problem: if the burials were intrusive into a Late Wickliffe midden, to what period did the cemetery date? The small test in 1989 was insufficient to answer the question.

The cemetery exhibit was dismantled in 1991 to make way for a new exhibit that did not display real human remains (Wesler 1992b, 1992c). The burials were removed following a numbering system established by the earlier inventory (Haskins 1990). After the loose elements were removed, the excavators reduced pedestals by arbitrary levels, exposed previously undisturbed portions of the burials for use as a control assemblage to help assess the formerly displayed specimens, and then cleaned and recorded the original profiles, supplementing stratigraphic information so obtained with several test units excavated to subsoil in the old floor.

The surprise was the complexity of the depositional context. Figure 3.11 is a composite profile, representing the north wall of the original excavation, extrapolated to subsoil according to information from nearby test units. Instead of "a cemetery," the profile shows five major stratigraphic events.

The basal cultural deposit is a Middle Wickliffe midden. A grey mound designated the "ash mound" is stratigraphically continuous with the midden. Artifacts within the ash mound are similar to the contents of a midden except for occasional burned human bone fragments, but the ashy, lensed aspect of the profile indicates burning episodes. The ash mound resembles a refuse mound, either cleaned from a burned area or burned periodically in place.

A basket-loaded mound, Mound C proper, partially overlies the ash mound. Appearing as a thin layer atop the basket-loaded mound, but achieving substantial depth as the mound slopes down, there is a midden that yielded a Late Wickliffe ceramic assemblage. The burials occur mainly in the upper midden zone.

Two minor stratigraphic units add to the complexity. Thin brown zones, apparently burning episodes, are visible near the top of the north wall profile (Figure 3.11). The lower burning zone can be traced down the slope of the ash mound, but the upper appears to correlate with the top of the basket-loaded mound.

Although most of the soil's context was removed from the formerly displayed burials, from their elevations and from excavation of the pedestals, their positions appear to correspond to the stratigraphy of the profiles: that is, the burial zone seems to be largely confined to the upper midden, and burials extend rarely, if at all, into the underlying basket-loaded mound. In three small areas, at the interface of burials and basket-loaded soils, remnant charcoal lenses were recorded. One lens consisted of wood charcoal, either a plank or a slab of bark, on which a bundle burial was placed. The bundle burial showed no sign of burning. The other two charred lenses yielded carbonized fibers. One sample resembled a ball of yarn, while the other contained three layers of a woven fabric (see Chapter 14). Elements of a burned human foot were associated with the fabric, suggesting that the latter may have been a

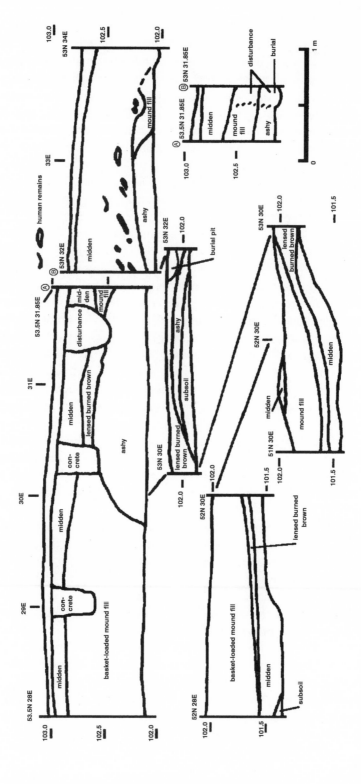

3.II. Schematic Mound C profile.

burial wrapping. This foot and other burned skeletal fragments scattered by the original excavation indicate that there was a cremation, but whether it belongs to the major cemetery event or to the top of the underlying mound is unclear. The feature that apparently contained the cremated remains was excavated in the 1930s, and without records of that excavation, it is extremely difficult to interpret.

As a final bit of depositional complexity, the northeast corner of the excavation block contained a large daub concentration, situated above the subsoil and below the upper midden/burial zone. The daub evidently belonged to a collapsed structure of some sort, but it could not be associated with either the Middle Wickliffe midden, the ash mound, or the basket-loaded mound on stratigraphic evidence. Later excavations (see below) indicated that it is a Middle Wickliffe house (Phillips 2000).

The two primary goals of the 1992 and 1993 seasons (and part of 1994) were to trace the full areal extent of the cemetery and to expose the top of the basket-loaded mound (behind the exhibit building) in search of evidence for a structure. Figure 3.12 presents the overall cemetery excavation plan.

The excavations documented only one burial south of the exhibit building. Unfortunately a cement floor covering the southeast corner of the exhibit building discourages more precise location of the cemetery perimeter in this area. The single burial on the south, Bu 258, in unit 42–45N22–23E, was oriented consistently with the cemetery norm. Only the skull and upper chest of Bu 258 were exposed. This adult female was buried with the richest assemblage of burial furniture documented at Wickliffe: a large Mississippi Plain bowl, inverted, lay on the south side of the skull, while on the north side of the skull there was a Bell Plain squash effigy bowl, which contained a poorly fired Mississippi Plain owl effigy bottle, several large mussel shells, and a smooth cobble. The burial pit was visible in the profile, confirming that the burial is intrusive to the surrounding soil matrix.

The cemetery extended substantially to the north of the cemetery building (Figure 3.12). Numerous burials, both bundle and extended, were identified, some so shallow that the plow had severely disturbed them. Burials also were recorded to the east and west sides of the building.

A block excavation also exposed a large area of the surface of the basket-loaded mound. There is no evidence of a structure on top of the basket-loaded mound. One or two dubious postholes were identified, but no posthole pattern or evidence of a burned surface. It is possible that pre-1932 plowing could have destroyed a burned surface, but postholes should not have been entirely obliterated.

Instead of a generalized burned zone or charred surface, a number of highly localized carbonized lenses, planks or bark slabs, were recorded in association with burials. In one instance, a lens of charred wood or bark had slumped into

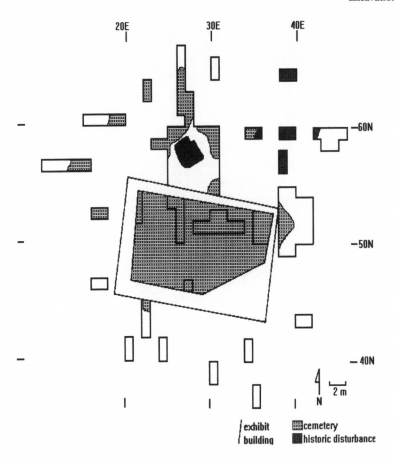

3.12. Mound C excavation plan, 1991–1994.

a burial pit, falling directly on top of the skull. In another case, a vertical slab
of charred bark or wood was found at the feet, providing convincing evidence
that at least some of the burials were placed in wooden boxes or bark envelopes
(Matternes 1993).

In the northwestern area of the excavation block, there was a concentration
of slabby conglomerate rock. In 1994, extensions were excavated to expose the
conglomerate area more fully. The slabs appear to represent a box similar to
limestone box graves of the Tennessee-Cumberland rivers area and southern
Illinois (Brown 1981), expressed in locally available materials. The box had
been disturbed, but there was no evidence that the disturbance occurred in
the historic period. Why there (apparently) should be only one such feature
in this cemetery is still a mystery.

Although the exact perimeters of the cemetery have not been located in
several areas, a tentative outline may be proposed as a large oval on an east-west

major axis. Within that area, however, burial density is not uniform. The summit of the basket-loaded mound, despite being intruded by a squarish, historic disturbance, appears to be free of burials. Moreover, there are burial-free spaces at the north-center and the east-center of the excavation block. It is possible, though data are insufficient to demonstrate, that there are delimited subareas within the cemetery, perhaps belonging to clans or lineages.

At the northeast corner of the block, there is a very revealing deposit recorded in 1992: at the edge of the mound, where the basket-loaded deposit drops off sharply and post-mound midden has accumulated deeply, ten individuals were identified within a 1 × 1-meter square. In two 1993 extensions from the mound-summit block, as the edge of the mound dropped off into midden, excavators also revealed a complex pattern of burials. Evidently, the people who created the cemetery made a point of burying around the mound but not in it.

Analysis of the skeletal material is still under way at this writing. A few preliminary statements are possible (see Matternes 1999b). On the basis of the interpolated outline and observed burial densities, the cemetery contained an estimated 800 to 900 burials. The identification of several truncated burial pits confirms the occurrence of intrusive, not heaped-over, burials. Both extended and bundle burials are attested. There is evidence for a single cremation, but its context is difficult to establish. Pathologies, whether from infection or trauma, are rare. In general, the demographic characteristics of this population compare well with those of other Mississippian groups (Matternes 1994).

Grave goods are scarce in the investigated areas of the cemetery. One Mississippi Plain (coarse, undecorated shell-tempered ware) miniature owl effigy hooded bottle was broken in half by the plow. Another small Bell Plain vessel (polished ware with finely ground shell temper) was also smashed by the plow, with only a few fragments recorded in situ. A bundle burial contained a spherical river cobble with no evidence of use alteration. These artifacts are too few to suggest any patterns, but their paucity raises serious questions about the many artifacts that had been exhibited as "burial associations."

Beyond the cemetery, the 1992–1994 excavations revealed additional complexity to the stratigraphy of the Mound C vicinity. Mound C was not an isolated mound, but a member of a complex of at least three mounds. Mound C_1, southwest of Mound C, may slightly predate the other two, but Mounds C and C_2 (to the northeast) cannot be differentiated chronologically (Wesler 1996b).

Recently, Matternes (1999a, 1999b) submitted more than a dozen samples for radiometric dating of the burial population, with two faunal bone samples from the surrounding midden as comparative samples. The specimens representing the midden produced Late Wickliffe dates, as expected, but the burial population belongs primarily to the Middle Wickliffe period. The cemetery, then, is associated with the mounds, and does not postdate the midden accumulation or the village's abandonment. The stratigraphic situation around the Mound C complex is complicated and will require further study. However, it is worth noting that the Mound C complex (basket-loaded Mound C proper, and Mounds C_1 and C_2) is layered between the Middle Wickliffe burials and the basal, Middle Wickliffe midden, thus allowing assignment of mound construction to the Middle Wickliffe period.

King Field Camp

Photographs curated at Mound State Monument, Alabama, show that the King field camp of 1932 was situated east or southeast of Mound C (Figures 3.10 and 3.13). In 1993, a set of test units was excavated in an attempt to identify the site of the field camp. Several units were excavated only slightly below the plowzone, while two units penetrated to subsoil. One of the latter units revealed the burial of a child: this burial appears to be isolated from the cemetery, yet the child was markedly older than the infants normally found buried in the village. The significance of this burial is still under study. No definite sign of the field camp was identified.

Mound D

Mound D was a pair of small rounded mounds or a long, saddled mound on the east side of the plaza (Wesler 1989). Excavations in the 1930s followed

3.13. University of Alabama field camp, 1932.

3.14. Mound D during excavation, from northeast.

a 5 × 5-foot grid, proceeding in arbitrary 1-foot levels (Figure 3.14). This excavation is best known for the large number of infant burials exposed at the subsoil level. Adult burials also were removed, apparently from within the mound, of which nothing else is known.

WMRC excavations examined soil deposits at both the north and the south ends of Mound D in 1987 (Wesler 1989, 1991d). Mound D North consists of a very small intact remnant of a Late Wickliffe mound, overlying an Early Wickliffe domestic zone. Mound D South turned out to be largely backfilled deposits, underlain by truncated features, mostly wall trenches, of Middle Wickliffe date. An infant burial in each area, both intrusive into the subsoil, matched the inferable contexts of the infants exposed in the 1930s. Thus, Mound D was constructed or completed in the Late Wickliffe period, overlying Early (north) and Middle (south) Wickliffe domestic occupations.

Distribution studies of artifacts from Mound D excavations in both the 1930s and 1987 investigations reveal unique features of this mound (Wesler 1996a). Two-thirds of the conch shell effigy ceramic fragments known from the site occur in Mound D. Mound D contained apparent caches of stone projectile points, mostly of Archaic period (8000–3000 B.P.) styles, bone tools, and discs and discoidals. Red cedar has been identified in Mound D charcoal, but not in other ethnobotanical samples from the 1930s excavations (conversation with Gail Wagner, c. 1990). Astragalus dice are lacking from

Mound D; the significance of this fact is not clear, but it contrasts Mound D with other Late Wickliffe deposits.

These special features of Mound D, together with the apparent presence of burials within the mound and the ambiguous but elongated shape of the mound, distinguish it from all other deposits—mound or midden—yet investigated on the Wickliffe site. In an attenuated or impoverished fashion, they recall the famous Mound 72 at Cahokia (Fowler 1989, 1991), an elaborate burial of a well-regarded chief. If there was an elite burial mound at Wickliffe, Mound D is the likely candidate (Wesler 1996a).

East Midden

In conjunction with the 1987 Mound D project, test excavations also studied the East Midden, at the eastern margin of the site. These deposits proved to be a dense midden, underlain by a complex pattern of intersecting wall trenches and posthole lines intruding the subsoil. The entire East Midden deposit belongs to the Late Wickliffe period (Wesler 1989).

Mound E

The 1930s' Mound E, represented by an artifact collection of more than 20,000 specimens from a gridded excavation, has not been located. Two locations of tests labeled "Mound E" are represented in the 1932 Alabama notes: three test units in the northwestern part of the site (Figure 3.1) and one near the cemetery. Northwest Village tests (below) intersected a small backfilled area that may be one of the 1932 tests, but no large block excavation. Test excavations north of Mound C in 1992 and 1993 identified a deep backfilled deposit that is probably the second 1932 Mound E site, but the disturbance is too small to be the Mound E block excavation from which the extant collections were recovered. King's final reference to Mound E (U.C.: King to Cole, 10 November 1938) placed it "across road," which probably means across the highway on the south side of the site (note the high bank across the road in the background of Figure 3.14; that bank no longer exists).

Mound F

Mound F is located on the west side of Mound A, on a slight projection of the bluff over the Mississippi River bottom. Excavated first in the 1930s (Figure 3.15), it was then identified as a "Signal Mound," because of its prominent location and numerous ashy lenses.

WMRC excavations in 1985 and 1986 cleared a large area of the floor of the old Mound F excavation block and demonstrated the presence of a small remnant of the northwest margin of the mound (Wesler and Neusius 1987). Truncated features in the old excavation floor, a shallow midden underlying the mound remnant, and the mound deposit all date to the Late Wickliffe

3.15. Mound F during excavation, from east.

period. Data are insufficient to indicate the original function or purpose of Mound F.

Northwest Village

A failed attempt to locate Mound E in 1988 and 1989 produced a series of test excavations across the north-central and northwest sector of the village (Wesler 1991a). These units identified largely undisturbed middens. Middle Wickliffe deposits occur above subsoil in the north-central areas, capped by Late Wickliffe middens, while toward the western and northern margins of the site Late Wickliffe deposits lie directly on subsoil.

House Floors

The 1994 excavations concentrated on block excavations to expose two houses previously identified. On the east side of Mound C, a daub spill had been exposed in the northeast corner of the King excavations (noted above). Two 1 × 2-meter tests in 1992, just east of the exhibit building, exposed the wall trenches of the north and south corners of the same structure. In 1994, a 4 × 4-meter unit exposed the wall trench pattern of the half to two-thirds of the house pattern that remains outside the building. It is the most complete house pattern so far documented at the Wickliffe site. The excavators noted a feature outline several levels above the floor that predicted the position of the wall trench outline, and ceramic associations in the 1992 test units suggested that the structure was a semisubterranean construction of the Late Wickliffe period. Burials rested in the soil matrix above the house floor, lending further credence to the idea that the cemetery was very late in the sequence. However, current analysis of the 4 × 4-meter excavation that exposed the house pattern (Phillips 2000) points toward a predominantly Middle Wickliffe deposit, which accords well with Matternes's (1999a, 1999b) Middle Wickliffe dates for most of the burial activity. It is possible that some burial activity continued into the earlier part of the Late Wickliffe period, introducing a smattering of ceramics to an otherwise Middle Wickliffe depositional context.

Also in 1994, a second house floor was excavated in a 4 × 4-meter block west of Mound C and north of Mound B. The southern corner of this floor had been identified in one of the Northwest Village tests in 1989. The 1994 expansion revealed sections of a fired-clay floor, part of which retained a nearly intact painting of a cross and circle, a Native American symbol that is often called a Sun Circle. The cross and circle is a widespread late prehistoric and historic Native American motif, associated in the Southeast with the sacred fire and the sun (Hudson 1976:126, 135–36). Unfortunately the intrusions of features and wall trenches made it difficult to associate the remnant floor with a clear set of walls. Preliminary ceramic analysis indicates that this floor belonged to a Middle Wickliffe construction.

Only a few sherds were associated directly with either house floor, suggesting that both were deliberately abandoned before destruction. Numerous samples from both houses are under micromorphological and microartifact analysis.

Mound G

The staff residence, constructed in the 1950s, occupied the site of a small mound that was depicted on a late nineteenth-century map (Figure 1.4; Loughridge 1888). The mound, in the southwest sector of the site, is designated Mound G by the WMRC. Excavations in 1994 and 1995 tested this area.

The first unit, a 2 × 2-meter square placed north of Mound G, penetrated a gravel layer associated with the residence, and then undisturbed midden beneath. The primary feature recorded in this unit was a corner of a house basin with a single-set-post wall pattern at its base. Analysis of the ceramics indicates that this structure belonged to the Late Wickliffe period, while the middens intruded by the basin represented Early and Middle Wickliffe zones.

The second 2 × 2-meter unit, south of Mound G, was quite interesting. There were clear signs of historic disturbance, including bricks, but also some intact prehistoric deposits. In the northwest corner, a midden of only a couple of centimeters in depth survived between subsoil and plowzone. This thin midden contained an enigmatic feature, a cluster of sherds representing at least one jar and one pan, and seven or eight deer scapulae.

Diagonally across the northeast sector, a series of three postholes penetrated the subsoil. In the hope of tracing a line that might tentatively be identified as a palisade, the excavators extended a 1 × 1-meter unit in 1994, expanded to 2 × 2 meters in 1995. There were two more postholes, but they were noticeably shallower and smaller in diameter than the previous ones and were not promising for a palisade. However, the extension revealed a section of a deep basin with a wall trench at the base. This feature is a Late Wickliffe semisubterranean house.

A final unit, 1 × 1 meters, was begun just next to the residence in an attempt to discover remaining mound deposits. Because of time limitations, this unit was abandoned before completion, after penetrating approximately 50 centimeters of dense brick rubble. The lack of surface indication of a mound under the residence and the depth of the brick rubble raise doubts about the possibility of any mound deposit surviving.

Mound H

The final set of tests in the summer of 1996 explored the southeastern sector of the Wickliffe site. The late nineteenth-century map of the Wickliffe site (Figure 1.4; Loughridge 1888) indicated a small mound toward the end of the southward-pointing ridge, designated Mound H by the WMRC. The mound is not visible at the surface today.

The 1996 tests identified middens in much of the area, and also 50 centimeters of basket-loaded mound fill overlying a shallow (ca. 15 centimeters) midden near the tip of the ridge, corresponding to Mound H. Ceramic analysis indicates that the mound and underlying midden belong to the Late Wickliffe period, although a feature intruding the subsoil is of Middle Wickliffe age. Basal middens farther north, toward Mound D, are of Middle Wickliffe deposition. The burial of a child was recorded at the top of the eastern slope, in an Early Wickliffe feature. Oxidizable Carbon Ratio (OCR) (Frink 1992, 1994, 1995) samples from several of these deposits were submitted for dating, and results fully support the Wickliffe chronology as interpreted from the radiocarbon dates (Chapter 5).

SUMMARY

From 1984 through 1996, the WMRC excavations sampled all of the major sectors of the Wickliffe site. For varying purposes in each year, the excavators first sampled an east-west transect across the center of the site, then across the northern part, and finally scattered a few tests in the southern areas. Although these tests do not create a statistically random spatial sample, there is nothing to suggest that the assemblages recovered cannot be used to conduct detailed comparisons within the site (cf. Drennan 1996:90). Future analyses will, among other things, explore the variations within the assemblages in a systematic manner.

The original goals of the testing program were to reevaluate the King excavations, in order to interpret as well as possible the original contexts of the extant artifact collections. WMRC excavators studied Mounds A, B, C, D, and F. The researchers never found direct evidence of the location of King's Mound E, in the sense of locating a sufficiently large backfilled area. Two seasons' work in the Northwest and North Central Village, and additional testing northeast of Mound C, eliminated those areas, but identified disturbances that probably are among King's 1932 tests that he originally designated Mound E. The best-guess location for the mid-1930s excavation that received the "official" Mound E designation is on the south side of the modern highway, an area now too demolished to permit any hope for archaeological traces to survive. In the search for Mound E, the WMRC crews provided a useful sample of the northern parts of the village.

As of 1994, the northern and central areas of the site were well sampled, but the southern areas were not. The south end of the site is relatively less intact: because of the highway cut, the bulldozing-out of the double driveway, the construction and destruction of historic buildings on Mound G, and the presumed loss of Mound E, a large area of the southern village is gone. The King collection from Mound E offers some potential for understanding the southern sector, but without details of context. A few tests in the southern areas in 1995 and 1996, now designated Mounds G and H, provided a small sample of middens, mound fills, and features that supplement our view of the site south of the plaza.

The eastern and western/northwestern limits of the site, confined by blufflines, are well marked. The southern limit is questionable, given the disturbances noted above. As an approximation, the Mound E grid, assuming King's grid north roughly matches his Mound D grid north (which makes sense as it aligns more or less with the highway), fits within a 40 × 40-meter square. For future site reconstructions, then, researchers may add a 1600-square-meter extension of the grid at the southwest corner, and provisionally assign the Mound E assemblage to that area.

The location of the northeastern limit of the site is not clear. However, inspection of postholes excavated in 1996 for signage to mark a small nature trail indicated no midden within the modern tree line. It is likely that the linear mound at the northeast on the Loughridge map (Figure 1.4) is in fact the formal limit of the village. Working from the grid, then, and adding the area of Mound E, the site area can be roundly estimated at 25,000 square meters, or 2.5 hectares (6.2 acres).

The excavations made clear, however, that the village covered this full area only in the Late Wickliffe period. Analysis identified Early Wickliffe deposits beneath Mounds A, B, and D, south of Mound D, and at the base of the northern Mound G test (18–20S74–76W). Three units in the Northwest and

North Central Village tests also may be listed as containing Early Wickliffe deposits, but in each case the identification rests on a single red-filmed sherd in a small ceramic sample. (For visual representations of deposits assigned to periods, see Chapter 8, Figures 8.3–8.5.) Even accepting these northern tests as Early Wickliffe deposits, the Early Wickliffe village was clustered compactly around the plaza. Among the mounds, only the basal levels of Mound B belong to the Early Wickliffe period, although quite possibly structures at the location of Mound A already had special significance.

The village expanded during the Middle Wickliffe period, and again during the Late Wickliffe period. Middle Wickliffe deposits underlie Mound C, are widely spread across the north, and extend south of Mound D and to the northern Mound G test (18–20S74–76W). It appears that the village expanded along the high ground. The cores of Mounds A and B and the Mound C complex belong to the Middle Wickliffe period. Middle Wickliffe markers in King's Mound E collection raise the possibility that the village extended south of the modern highway, as well.

At the edges of the site—Mound F, Northwest Village, East Midden, and south of Mound G (recognizing serious disturbance in this area)—the deposits belong to the Late Wickliffe period. By the end of the period, the village crowded the steep slopes of the bluff. The last mantles of Mounds A and B, the final additions to Mounds D and F (if not those entire mounds), and Mound H were constructed during the Late Wickliffe period.

There are no midden or mound deposits that can be dated to a post–A.D. 1350 period. In previous accounts of the cemetery excavation (notably Wesler 1997; Wesler and Matternes 1991), the stratigraphic position of the Mound C cemetery—within an apparent Late Wickliffe midden—and the lack of disturbances to the cemetery until the later 1800s or even 1900s were taken to argue strongly that it was the last stratigraphic Mississippian event at that location: that it postdated the Late Wickliffe village. However, recent radiocarbon data place the cemetery largely within the Middle Wickliffe period (Matternes 1999a, 1999b). There is no indication of Native American activity at the Wickliffe Mounds site after about A.D. 1350.

The WMRC project, then, accomplished its original goals and also created a dynamic picture of the founding and expansion of the Wickliffe village through about 250 years, followed by its abandonment. From this field work, questions of chronology, spatial and temporal patterning of various aspects of material culture, and the nature and organization of Mississippian life in the village may be addressed.

4 Artifacts Recovered

WICKLIFFE MOUNDS RESEARCH CENTER LABORATORY METHODS

Wickliffe Mounds laboratory procedures are designed around the principle that field and laboratory documentation must form one integrated system. Procedures in the field and in the laboratory are coordinated, so that all information—artifacts, records, photographs, reports—are cross-referenced and accessible. The reliability of project reports and future analyses, and the scholarly reputation of the laboratory, rest in large part on the thoroughness of the documentation and the maintenance of a comprehensive system. The following comments are for general information, and a more thorough explanation of Wickliffe Mounds Research Center laboratory procedures may be found in Wesler (1996c).

WMRC catalog numbers are coordinated with the master Murray State University archaeology system. Catalog numbers are tripartite, with a two-digit accession year, a sequential accession number, and a provenience lot number (e.g., *84–30.123* indicates year 1984, accession 30, provenience lot 123).

Field units are cataloged in numerical order if possible, with numerical designations preceding special designations (e.g., 29–30S4–6E, 29–30S6–8E, Mound A Test I, Mound A Test II). Within larger units, provenience lots are cataloged in order of excavation (Level 1, Level 1 troweling, Level 2, etc.). Piece-plotted (i.e., individually mapped) artifacts within a level or feature are cataloged individually, directly following the general provenience lot. Postholes are numbered within a square and cataloged following the levels or zones of the square in numerical order. Features, however, are numbered serially within the site (because they so often overlap squares) and are numbered in sequence at the end of the catalog. Each provenience unit (zone, level, mapped artifact, posthole, feature/feature section, etc.) receives a unique catalog number, in sequence following the preceding provenience unit.

Sorting for the catalog is normally done on a ½-inch screen, since pieces of pottery, fire-cracked rock, daub, and other items that fall through this screen are so small that further sorting requires more time than analytical returns justify. The small fraction is sorted by hand for chipping debris, faunal material, ethnobotanical material in undisturbed and unmixed provenience lots, and small identifiable artifacts such as beads. The remainder of the small fraction is rebagged and labeled "½" screenings" and is retained for potential future analysis.

All specimens are counted and weighed by category. That is, all sherds are weighed together, all projectile points, all daub, and so on. Most bulk materials are counted, weighed, and discarded and marked "(disc.)" on the catalog sheet. Materials routinely discarded after weighing include fire-cracked rock, unmodified gravel, brick, concrete, roofing tile, and historic coal. Individual specimens with makers marks (as on brick) or other unusual features are kept. Daub and fired clay are not discarded.

The Wickliffe Mounds collection catalog is maintained both on hand-written catalog sheets and on a computer database (dBase III+ [Ashton-Tate 1986]). The computer catalog was used to generate the summary of materials recovered in Table 4.1. The table does not include a number of special artifacts, such as beads, ear plugs, and unique items that are not easily summarized (see Table 5.15).

Most of the analysis of Wickliffe materials has concentrated on ceramics, largely to help resolve chronology, and also because of the director's own interest. Other major categories of artifacts—lithics and faunal and floral remains, in particular—form large, systematic collections that will repay detailed analysis. Chapters included on the accompanying CD-ROM, contributed by various colleagues, offer discussions of samples of these data, and indicate the potential of the Wickliffe database for further analysis.

CERAMICS

The Wickliffe ceramic assemblage in general reflects a variety of wares common to Mississippian sites of the Ohio-Mississippi confluence region. Most of the sherds can be identified according to the existing type-variety system of the Lower Mississippi Valley. The following paragraphs describe first the plain wares, then the various decorated ceramics (Table 4.2).

Most types are expected to be identified within subcategories, known as varieties. This practice aims for the identification of regional or other cultural variations within a type. Because of the fragmentary nature of the analyzed collection, the WMRC analysts have not assigned variety designations in many cases. Technically, these specimens should be listed as "var. unspecified," and this label should be understood in all cases in which a variety designation is not specified.

Plain Wares

By far the bulk of any collection of Mississippian potsherds is undecorated. The paste is distinctive for its inclusion of crushed mussel shell as a tempering agent, the hallmark of Mississippian material culture in the Lower Mississippi Valley. Generally, plain sherds are seen to fall into two categories: a coarser, more utilitarian ware known as Mississippi Plain and a more refined ware known as Bell Plain. Somewhat confusingly, there are two criteria for sorting, each of which is intended to result in the two categories. (The description of a vessel as "plain" indicates a lack of decoration on the vessel body; a sometimes substantial minority of these vessels do have decorated rims.)

One criterion suggests that sherds are either polished or not polished. The other is based on paste, with large shell particles forming a coarse paste and very small shell particles resulting in a fine paste. Of the former criterion, Phillips (1970:59) says that the distinction "has a charming simplicity and ignores the fact that sorting in specific instances is difficult if not impossible." He could have said the same of the latter.

Added to uncertainties of transitional cases of smoothing/polish and coarseness/fineness, pure shell temper is not an invariant of Mississippian ceramics in the confluence region. Of Bell Plain, Phillips (1970:60) notes that in some areas the temper is invisible or is "just not there." Williams (1954:208) admits fine clay temper within Bell Plain. The use of clay or grog temper, characteristic of the Baytown period (preceding the Mississippian), also continues in Mississippi Plain (Lewis ed. 1986:30; Williams 1974:89). Phillips says, with equal applicability to Mississippi Plain in the confluence region, "it would appear that uncertainty as to the exact nature of the paste is one of the characteristics of Bell Plain whatever the variety" (1970:60).

Wickliffe Mounds ceramics contain noticeable quantities of grog. Lewis (Lewis ed. 1986:30) found a similar situation at the Adams site (15Fu4), where grog ranged from a minor inclusion to "the dominant aplastic." The developing knowledge of the ceramic sequence in both the Mississippi River counties of Kentucky (esp. Sussenbach and Lewis 1987) and the Lower Tennessee-Cumberland area (Clay 1984) makes it clear that the grog to shell temper change was a long transition, not a sudden shift.

For the Wickliffe analyses, Mississippi Plain follows the classic definition of Phillips (1970:130ff.), based on and superseding the earlier Phillips, Ford, and Griffin (1951:105ff.) definition of Neeley's Ferry Plain. Mississippi Plain sherds contain coarse shell temper and are either rough or smooth surfaced and rarely polished. Colors range from greys to browns and occasionally to reddish. There are a total of 138,912 sherds of Mississippi Plain in the Wickliffe collections so far analyzed.

Bell Plain, in the Wickliffe analyses, essentially follows the Phillips, Ford, and Griffin (1951:122) definition, which is basically the same as that of Phillips's Bell Plain *var. New Madrid* (1970:58ff.). The only major qualification is that Phillips, Ford, and Griffin required the tempering particles to be smaller than 1 millimeter; the Wickliffe analysts sort by eyeball rather than strict

Table 4.1. Summary of Cataloged Artifacts

	1983	1984	1985	1986	1987	1988	1989	1990	1991	1992[c]	1994[c]
Sherds	827	7799	9374	6605	25,182	12,857	15,520	9885	6662	18,898	3032
Projectile points	3	9	17	9	47	15	26	16	3	32	20
Bifaces	2	5	22	15	61	28	43	25	6	26	6
Utilized flakes	15	8	17	10	96	8	18	9	23	8	
Debitage	161	5619	7013	4952	15,103	10,980	12,171	8363	3253	8638	2370
Cores	6	12	16	4	70	14	13	12	11	13	5
Ground stone		1	4	2	8	3		4	2	5	
Cobble tools	2	5	16	1	5	4	9		5	9	1
Bone tools			5		12	8	23	12	174	13	1
Faunal	283	1193	10,767	5570	30,754	15,716	34,934	14,260	14,881	14,463	3916
Shell	1	4	404	20	404	64	212	51	269	112	11
Daub[a]	b	8998.5	39,748.1	6684.8	48,857.5	12,963.7	22,470.1	13,567.9	15,513.1	26,293.6	6207
Fired clay[a]	b	15,018.2	658.7	766.7	8834.3	1515	1888.9	1729.7	2366.5	5138.5	214
Fire-cracked rock[a]	b	22,860.8	7025.8	6807.1	21,982.1	17,268.8	12,667.2	19,598.9	8119.4	17,990.9	2613
Ferrous sandstone[a]	b	13,062.1	10,042.7	4558.8	10,943.8	10,346.9	7046.2	11,170.9	13,211.6	19,196.9	2133
Gravel[a]	b	42,151.1	58,443.9	30,743.3	54,906	78,702	37,338.7	50,141.5	15,120.4	38,765.4	8179

Continued

Table 4.1. *Continued*

	1995	1996	WMRC Total	King Mound D	King Mound E[d]	King Mound F	King Collection Total	Total
Sherds	4221	5837	126,699	25,080	20,877	10,008	55,965	182,664
Projectile points	5	14	216	481	337	43	861	1077
Bifaces	10	26	275	74	235	34	343	618
Utilized flakes	2	1	215	41	35	59	135	350
Debitage	2824	3664	85,111	146	1585	276	2007	87,118
Cores			176	5	25	20	50	226
Ground stone	1		26	13	52	8	73	99
Cobble tools	6	7	74	29	70	179	278	352
Bone tools	1	5	254	1	15	1	17	271
Faunal	4455	7652	15,884		4		22,954	181,798
Shell	25	44	1621	1003	925	422	2350	3971
Daub[a]	2663.6	5041.6	209,009.5			1588.4	1588.4	210,597.9
Fired clay[a]	382	390	38,902.5	45			45	38,947.5
Fire-cracked rock[a]	4815.5	6825.7	148,575.2				0	148,575.2
Ferrous sandstone[a]	4147.3	5601.2	111,461.4	900.1	2119.8	8072.7	11,092.6	122,554
Gravel[a]	18,967.5	11,792	445,250.8	282.4	282.4		282.4	445,533.2

[a]In grams.
[b]Not weighed.
[c]Not fully cataloged.
[d]Includes unprovenienced items.

Table 4.2. Summary of Ceramics Analyzed from Wickliffe Mounds

Mississippi Plain	138,912
Bell Plain	22,318
Matthews Incised *var. Beckwith*	709
Matthews Incised *var. Manly*	378
Barton Incised	45
Mound Place Incised	27
Wallace Incised	2
Winterville Incised	19
Punctate	109
Perforated	36
O'Byam Incised *var. O'Byam*	300
O'Byam Incised *var. Stewart*	2
O'Byam Incised *var. Adams*	33
Leland Incised	30
Owens Punctate	55
Untyped incised	1326
Kimmswick Fabric Impressed	3274
Wickliffe Thick	2260
Varney or Old Town Red Filmed	1384
Carson Red-on-Buff	5
Nashville Negative Painted	79
Crosno Cord Marked	78
Baytown Plain	173
Mulberry Creek Cord Marked	41
Larto Red Filmed	4
Tolu Fabric Impressed	18
Untempered	276
Sand tempered	5
Unidentified or other	189
Total	172,087

measurement. Both criteria, fine paste and a noticeably smoothed to polished surface (at least one surface), are necessary for a sherd to be sorted as Bell Plain. Most of the specimens range from dark grey to black, but a few light grey or brown (cf. "cinnamon" in Phillips, Ford, and Griffin 1951) are included if they meet the paste and surface criteria. A few light grey sherds have thick dark-grey cores, and the surface color may have resulted from a slip. The Wickliffe collection includes 22,318 sherds of Bell Plain.

Several authors, particularly Williams (1954:225ff.) and Phillips (1970: 130ff., *vars. Coker* and *Mound Field*), have suggested that a thin variant of Mississippi Plain is characteristic of an early Mississippian period. In the Mound A sample (Wesler 1985), thin Mississippi Plain vessels do seem to be characteristic of the early occupation (Table 4.3CD). This finding should be subject to further study with a more rigorous set of sorting criteria. Only a few sherds in the Wickliffe collections are identified as thin Mississippi Plain, and they are included with Mississippi Plain in the tables.

There are also three sherds of a thin-walled, smoothed, plain-surfaced vessel with a carinated shoulder that appear to belong to a Powell Plain jar (Vogel 1975:90–93). They belong to a Middle Wickliffe context in the vicinity of Mound C and join the Ramey Incised and Cahokia Cord Marked sherds (below) in attesting contact with the American Bottom.

Effigies

The effigies generally belong to either the Mississippi Plain or Bell Plain type, more seldom are a red-filmed or negative-painted type (below), and are included in those counts in the tables. Figures 4.1CD, 4.2CD, 4.3CD, and 4.8CD are examples of effigies recovered by the WMRC excavations, the first three from Mound C and the last from Mound D North. Phillips discusses the effigies from the King collection in Chapter 9.

A brief study of the spatial distribution of the Wickliffe Mounds effigies included those recovered through 1988 but not the more recent specimens (Wesler 1991c). The only evident pattern was a concentration of conch shell effigies in Mound D, possibly a burial mound (see Chapters 5 and 18). The conch shell spiral found in 1988 shows that such effigies are found scattered around the village, too.

Decorated Sherds: Incised and Punctate

The most common sort of decoration found on Mississippian ceramics consists of breaking of the smoothed surface of the vessel, usually with incised lines, or occasionally with punctations. Typological assignments of decorated sherds are based partly on paste characteristics, following the Mississippi Plain–Bell Plain distinction, and partly on the motif and decoration placement. Sherds from the Wickliffe excavations are identified within established types where possible.

Matthews Incised, as defined by Phillips (1970:128–29), is a ware with Mississippi Plain paste as described above. Depending on the exact style of the decoration, specimens are classified within several varieties. *Variety Matthews* is identified by the presence of "running curvi- or rectilinear designs on the rim or shoulder area of jars" and may also include some punctation associated with the primary motif. *Variety Beckwith* is similar, but is distinguished by two sets of running lines that intersect at regular intervals to form guilloches (Figure 4.4CD and Figure 4.7CD, *bottom left*). *Variety Matthews* is so rare at Wickliffe that WMRC analysts have abandoned the distinction from *var. Beckwith*, tabulating a total of 709 sherds as the latter. This lumped category needs to be studied more closely for potential distinctions on the variety or subvariety level.

Matthews Incised *var. Manly*, subsuming the former Manly Punctate type of Phillips, Ford, and Griffin (1951:147; cf. Williams 1954:223), is decorated with a meandering incised line with associated punctations on the shoulder of a jar. In most instances, the sherds are fairly small, but the jar-shoulder form allows at least tentative inclusion within the named type. *Variety Manly* accounts for 378 sherds.

Another incised type, widely spread in the Lower Mississippi Valley, is Barton Incised. Phillips (1970:44ff.) attributes two varieties to the northern Lower Valley, *var. Campbell* with vertical incising on the rim and *var. Kent* with vertical incising on the body of a jar (cf. Phillips, Ford, and Griffin 1951:114–19, 126–27; Williams and Brain 1983:126ff.). The forty-five Wickliffe examples are most closely related to *var. Campbell*, but many are so crudely decorated that they should not be attributed to a variety.

The type Mound Place Incised is somewhat uncertainly defined, Phillips (1970:135) and Phillips, Ford, and Griffin (1951:147–48) having been dissatisfied with the extent of available collections. The defining characteristic seems to be the presence of at least two parallel lines below the rim of a bowl, irrespective of paste. Williams (1954:224) quite specifically described three lines on a rim effigy bowl. Wickliffe analysts accept the slightly looser definition of the type and include sherds with two or three lines below a bowl rim within the Mound Place category. There are twenty-seven sherds that fit this definition.

Williams (1954:221ff.), followed by Phillips (1970:144), defined O'Byam Incised as a Bell-paste plate form with incising on the interior of the rim. Usually this incising follows a triangular design of some sort, repeated around the rim. Williams (1954:221ff.) distinguished O'Byam Incised from O'Byam Engraved, a practice not apparently in general use. Lewis (Lewis ed. 1986:40–43) defines two varieties, distinguishing a *var. Adams* from Phillips's (1970:144) *var. O'Byam* on the basis of a thinner flange and the characteristic use of parallel line incising in the generally triangular motif. Clay (1979) defines *var. Stewart* as showing similar incising on deep plates, lending an elongation to the triangles.

Following Hilgeman (1992), Wickliffe analysts define a deep plate as one with a rim greater than 67 millimeters in width, and include the rare O'Byam Incised deep plate as *var. Stewart* (Figure 5.12CD, *top left*). Wickliffe analyses combine incised and engraved plate sherds as *var. O'Byam* (Figure 4.5CD), and incised and engraved flared bowl sherds as *var. Adams* (Figure 4.6CD). Decorative motifs vary in both varieties, and they should be studied further. Rare sherds of a plate form exhibiting sloppy incising but of Mississippi Plain paste are also listed as *var. O'Byam*. The Wickliffe collections include 300 *var. O'Byam*, 33 *var. Adams*, and 2 *var. Stewart* sherds. Both of the latter are in the King collection, one from Mound D and the other from Mound E. Two sherds of *var. Stewart* were noted in the field in 1993 and 1994; both are from plowzone contexts.

Wickliffe analysts usually list three type categories that are highly tentative designations: Winterville Incised, Wallace Incised, and Leland Incised. These categories were included in the analysis because there are sherds in the Wickliffe Mounds collection that do not seem to fit the types usually cited for the Cairo Lowland region, described above: the incising is notably wider than the published examples or available specimens of O'Byam, Matthews, or Mound Place Incised would seem to allow. Whether these specimens actually can be identified within these types is questionable. Generally, the use of the type names at Wickliffe is meant more as a shorthand description than a typological specification.

Following Phillips (1970:172), Winterville Incised includes sherds with a Mississippi Plain paste and broad-lined incising on vessel rims, shoulders, or bodies. Three mendable sherds found in 1989 show an unusually complex curvilinear design and fit the description of Winterville Incised *var. Winterville*. Another sherd has a fine Mississippi Plain paste and fairly fine incision, almost engraving. It seems to be almost a halfling between Winterville Incised and Walls Engraved: the paste is too coarse for Walls and the paste and lines quite fine for Winterville. It is listed under the latter category, for a total of nineteen Winterville Incised sherds.

Wallace Incised (Phillips 1970:168) includes those sherds that have broad-line incising on the exterior of bowls. Two sherds from the King collection fit this description and perhaps should be lumped into the Winterville Incised category, broadly defined as above.

Leland Incised, as discussed by Phillips, Ford, and Griffin (1951:137–40), Phillips (1970:104–7), and Williams and Brain (1983:171ff.), is closely related to protohistoric and historic Natchezan ceramics, which clearly does not suggest extension to the northern Lower Valley. However, there are sherds at Wickliffe Mounds that fit within the most general level of definition of Leland Incised. For this analysis, sherds of Bell Plain paste with incising (especially wide-line, curvilinear incising) that cannot be attributed to O'Byam Incised are listed as Leland. The category includes thirty sherds.

Sherds that combine punctation with incising, particularly when incised lines border punctated zones, are listed as Owens Punctate (Figure 4.7CD, *bottom right;* Phillips 1970:149–50; Phillips, Ford, and Griffin 1951:136–37; Williams and Brain 1983:193ff.). This type is represented by fifty-five specimens.

Two other categories of sherds are untyped but included in the "incised" supercategory. Specimens with incised lines, too small to identify motif or vessel form, are listed as "unknown" or "untyped incised" (1326 sherds; Figure 4.7CD, *top*). Sherds marked by punctations, but not large enough to identify as to type, are listed in the analysis simply as "punctate" (109 sherds). A few sherds (36) are actually perforated and listed separately, but may simply represent overzealous punctation.

The type Parkin Punctate (Phillips 1970:150–52) is problematic, because there is one jar with its rough finger-punched exterior in the Wickliffe collections. The WMRC staff has been chided several times for leaving it on display at Wickliffe, since it is considered to belong to a later period than the Wickliffe occupation (Mainfort 1996; Morse and Morse 1983). However, it bears a Mound D provenience label in full accord with the rest of the King collection and cannot be rejected without contesting the entire systematically labeled collection. The potential significance of this pot will be considered later.

Two incised sherds must be singled out as non–Lower Mississippi Valley types. Ramey Incised belongs to the American Bottom and is described as a jar with a globular body that makes an abrupt angle toward the mouth, a short rim, and incising on the shoulder (Griffith 1981; Vogel 1975:95). One of the Wickliffe sherds, from the Early Wickliffe midden under Mound A, is likely to have been made in the American Bottom and traded to Wickliffe (conversation with J. B. Griffin, c. 1988; conversation with John Kelly, c. 1990). The second, from Middle Wickliffe deposits in Mound B, fits the type description, but has paste differences and is probably a local copy (conversation with George Holley, c. 1990).

Painted Sherds

Mississippian potters used three kinds of painting on their vessels: direct painting of designs, large-area painting or filming (slipping), and negative or resist painting. Specimens of all three methods have been identified in the Wickliffe collections.

Red filming on Mississippian pottery is assigned to two types, Varney Red Filmed and Old Town Red Filmed. There seem to be two schools of thought on the distinction between the types. Phillips (1970:144ff., 167) restricts Varney to red-filmed pans, relegating all other red filming to sundry varieties of Old Town. Price and Price (1984:52–53), however, citing Williams (1954:209) among others, disagree. They consider the coarser or Mississippi Plain–paste specimens, including but not exclusive to the pan, to fall within Varney, while Old Town is restricted to finer paste. Ignoring Phillips's (1970:144ff.) contention that red-filmed coarse and fine paste specimens do not sort out in the same way that Bell and Mississippi Plain pastes do, Price and Price (1984:52–53) suggest that the separation of coarse-paste Varney is the "more common definition of the type."

The 1985 Mid-South Archaeological Conference seems to have pointed the way toward a consensus on this issue. Price and Williams's (1985) identification of an early or Emergent Mississippian Varney tradition in southeast Missouri seems to confirm Price's and Williams's view, at least on a general level. The Varney tradition includes red filming on a coarse or Mississippi Plain paste, characterized by jars with flaring rims, gourd-shaped hooded bottles, pans, and bowls.

Later, wares that might come under the name of Old Town developed, including more elaborate bottles, effigies, and generally thinner vessels; pans persist, but whether these will continue to be called Varney remains for the typologists to decide. On a single-sherd level, the Old Town–Varney distinction is essentially moot, since it is more on the level of assemblage patterning, particularly in vessel form, that the differences are important (conversation with S. Williams, c. 1985).

To avoid committing to a typological assignment, Wickliffe analysts list sherds simply as red-filmed, for a total of 1384 specimens.

Negative painting is a technique of applying the design in a substance that resists additional coloring, so that the design is actually the background or vessel color rather than the applied paint. Phillips (1970:139–41) defines the type Nashville Negative Painted to cover all of these vessels, with several varieties.

Plate rims with a black-on-buff design are very much like specimens from the Angel site (Kellar 1967) and sometimes are called *var. Angel.* Other black-on-buff sherds may be related to *var. Sikeston.* Sherds decorated in black-on-white, especially when the white background is a Bell Plain paste or fine slip, may be assigned to *var. Kincaid.* Most of the seventy-nine Nashville Negative Painted sherds at Wickliffe are of the black-on-white variety (Figures 4.8CD and 4.9CD exhibit a fine example from Mound D North).

Phillips (1970:62–63) applied the type name Carson Red-on-Buff to "all shell tempered red on buff pottery in the Lower Mississippi." This is a technique of direct painting, distinguished from Varney and Old Town by the application of paint in designs and not as slips over major areas of the vessel. Only five sherds of this type have been identified at Wickliffe (Figure 5.12CD, *top center*).

Surface Treated/Special Forms

Sherds with fabric-marked exteriors are assigned to the Kimmswick Fabric Impressed type, which Phillips (1970:95–96) sets up as a "supertype." These are coarsely shell-tempered sherds generally belonging to "salt" pans. Pan sherds often have extremely well-smoothed interiors, often almost polished despite the coarse temper, and probably are general-purpose griddles, frying pans, and parching vessels as well as boiling vessels. Pan sherds or rims that do not show evidence of fabric impressions are classified among the Mississippi Plain sherds. Thus the defining characteristic for the 3274 Kimmswick sherds is the exterior fabric impression, regardless of whether a pan form could be identified with certainty (Figure 4.10CD). (See Kuttruff and Drooker, Chapter 14, for further discussion of the textile impressions.)

A few sherds (18) have fabric impressions on the interior. They fit Clay's (1963:264–68) description of Tolu Fabric Impressed, with a Mississippi Plain paste and a loosely woven fabric. A fine white paste version with finely woven fabric has been noted both at Twin Mounds (Kreisa 1988) and at Wickliffe and may eventually be designated a separate variety.

The type Wickliffe Thick is an odd category, defined entirely on the basis of vessel shape (Phillips 1970:171–72). These pots are known also as Wickliffe funnels or sometimes as juice presses. They are jar-shaped to globular vessels with a wide mouth and a hole in the bottom, which, as Morse and Morse (1983:221) point out, makes this the only vessel form to have two sets of rim sherds. The vessel walls are thick, with a coarse paste. Exteriors may be plain, cord marked, incised (usually longitudinally, in a motif somehow reminiscent of a melon), or occasionally punctate (Figure 4.11CD). Williams (1954:214ff.) defined four types on the basis of surface decoration, but Phillips includes them all under the Wickliffe Thick label, on the basis of the criterion of vessel form, noting that "a term expressive of the function might be preferable, if we knew what it was" (Phillips 1970:171).

In the Wickliffe analyses, coarsely shell-tempered sherds are counted as Wickliffe Thick if they are unusually thick and seem to have an interior radius too small to belong to a pan, or if they have the characteristic melon-like incising. In practice, the incising is the most recognizable characteristic. Grog inclusions tend to be quite evident, as well, sometimes to the near exclusion of shell. Wickliffe Thick accounts for 2260 specimens.

There are a few shell-tempered sherds with cord-marked surfaces. Lewis (Lewis ed. 1986:117) lists such specimens as Crosno Cord Marked, but finds little to say about them except that they form a "consistent minority type" among his western Kentucky Mississippian samples. Williams (1954:98–100), whose work at the Crosno site would be expected to have established the type, uses the term Crosno Cord Marked but does not seem to have provided a type description. Price and Price (1984:56) mention sherds with a Mississippi Plain paste and cord marking, but state that there is no established type name for them. Clay (1963:247) applies the name McKee Island Cord Marked to similar specimens in the Lower Tennessee-Cumberland area. The Wickliffe analysts employ the term Crosno Cord Marked and have identified seventy-eight such sherds. Penelope Drooker (see Chapter 14) has cautioned that some of the apparent cord-markings may actually be faint fabric impressions.

One sherd, from the Mound E King collection, has clear cord marking and a flared jar rim that relate it much more closely to Cahokia Cord Marked than to anything in the Lower Mississippi Valley (cf. Kelly 1991:77).

Grog-Tempered Types

Broadly speaking, grog temper is characteristic of the ceramics of the Baytown period in the Cairo Lowland, which precedes the Mississippian period. Grog-tempered, plain-surfaced sherds of this earlier period are given the name Baytown Plain, cord-marked vessels are known as Mulberry Creek Cord

Marked, and red-filmed sherds as Larto Red Filmed, each with varieties (Phillips 1970:47ff., 136ff.). Phillips, Ford, and Griffin (1951:76ff.) describe a "chalky" feel for Baytown Plain, which fits the infrequent Wickliffe specimens. Sherds are identified as Baytown (173), Mulberry Creek (41), or Larto (4) only if they lack any trace of shell temper and they have a distinctly different feel from the Mississippian sherds comprising the vast bulk of the collection. No deposit at Wickliffe has yielded a pure or even predominantly grog-tempered assemblage, supporting the view, mentioned earlier, that grog temper continued as a minority ware well into the Mississippi period in western Kentucky. There is no reason to suppose a Late Woodland occupation of the Wickliffe site.

Other

A scattering of sherds are either sand-tempered or have no temper (5 and 276 specimens, respectively), these usually being small pinch-pot bowls. Among the 189 consigned to "unknown or other" there is one sherd that is coarse surfaced and limestone tempered. A number of gravel-tempered sherds with corrugated surfaces occurred in disturbed contexts in the Mound F excavations and probably belong to one or more Southwestern vessels imported for display during the King period.

There is also one other oddball worth mentioning, a jar rim with a complicated stamping in a concentric ring motif, tempered with quartzitic sand (Figure 4.12CD). This too is from the King collection, with a Mound D provenience. It appears to be a sherd of Savannah Stamped ware from northern Georgia (Wauchope 1966:77ff., fig. 219 [Wauchope captions these sherds as Etowah Stamped, but Hally (pers. com. 1997) identifies them as early Savannah Complicated Stamped]; cf. Sears 1958:193, Wilbank Complicated Stamped). The Savannah period in northern Georgia matches Middle and Late Wickliffe in date (Williams and Shapiro 1990:32, 45; Hally 1994:table 14.1), and the Mound D sherd thus links Wickliffe to the far southeast.

TOOLS (CERAMIC, BONE, SHELL, STONE)

There is a wide range of tools and implements of fired clay, chipped and ground stone, shell, and bone at Wickliffe.

Lutz (1995) provided a typological assessment of chipped stone projectile points in the King collection (summarized in Table 4.4), and Pafford (Chapter 11) discusses the points from the WMRC excavations. Briefly, most stone projectile points are related to a typical late prehistoric style (Figure 4.13CD). They are bifacially chipped, of medium to coarsely grained cherts, and are based on a small triangular pattern (cf. Justice's [1987] Late Wood-land/Mississippian small triangular cluster). Typical specimens range from 12

Table 4.4. Projectile Points in the King Collection

Type	Mound D	Mound E	Mound F	Mound ?	Total
Mississippian					
Cahokia	3		3		6
Cahokia Serrated	1				1
Triangulars	24	4	28		56
Corner Notched	4	7			11
Mississippian total	32	11	31		74
Woodland total	18	2	4	1	25
Archaic total	29	7	6	1	43
Paleoindian total	3	2			5
Unidentified	28	5	10		43
Total	110	27	51	2	190

Summarized from analysis by Lutz (1995).

to 43 millimeters in length (average 24.8 millimeters), 8 to 24 millimeters in width (average 14.1 millimeters), and 2 to 9 millimeters in thickness (average 4.4 millimeters). Rare forms are elongated triangles with excurvate sides, and a few are side- or corner-notched (cf. Justice's [1987] Cahokia and Scallorn clusters). They fit within the size range of the small triangulars and resemble notched versions of those points. Morse and Morse (1983:264) say that Scallorn points are rare in the Cairo Lowland region and more characteristic to the south. No true leaf-shaped Nodena-style points have been identified at Wickliffe, although a couple of points fit within Justice's (1987) straight-based Nodena Banks variety.

Some points stand out among the triangular types. They are large-stemmed specimens of Woodland, Archaic, and late Paleoindian (Dalton cluster, cf. Justice 1987) types. Although it is possible that there were pre-Mississippian camps on the Wickliffe site whose deposits were either ephemeral or destroyed by the Mississippian occupation—or simply not identified by the excavation program—it is equally possible that Wickliffe villagers collected points from area sites for lithic material or for other reasons (see Mound D discussion, Chapter 5).

The Mississippian people also made projectile points of antler and, rarely recovered, bone. One bone specimen looks exactly like a notched small triangular chipped stone point. Another bone item looks like a numeral 4 without the center perforation and may be a barbed projectile point. The Wickliffe collections contain a reduction sequence of antler points (Figure 4.14CD). The antler tip was grooved at an angle and snapped off. The base was drilled to fit an arrow shaft and fitted so that the diagonally cut end became a barb. At least some points were whittled to a sharper, sleeker outline.

Besides projectile points, the chipped stone assemblage contains relatively few formal tool types. Drills are found in three styles: bifacial core tools with very narrow shafts and variable base forms, bifacial cylindrical microdrills, and flakes with bifacially chipped shafts. WMRC excavators recovered only one whole hoe, although numerous flakes with characteristic "hoe" polish are a regular part of the assemblage. Another highly polished, chipped item is shaped more like an adze (Figure 4.15CD).

There are a few other chipped stone tools whose functions can be inferred. A few large flakes with steeply retouched edges probably are scrapers, as are some stemmed bifaces that probably are resharpened Archaic points. Flakes with retouched concavities on one edge are considered to be spokeshaves, and a small number have sharp projections and may be gravers. All are made of chert. Numerous fragments of unidentifiable bifacially flaked tools round out the list of chipped stone specimens.

As in most prehistoric sites, chipped stone waste flakes and chunks are numerous, with a total of more than 84,000 for the WMRC excavations, including cores. Koldehoff and Carr (Chapter 10) discuss a sample of lithics from the WMRC collection.

The WMRC excavations have recovered only a few ground stone artifacts, including fragments. There are a couple of small celts. Hammer/grinding stones, cobbles with some sign of pounding or rubbing on the surface, are scattered sparsely throughout the site.

Chunks of sandstone or burned, rough quartzite bear grooves and probably are sharpening stones. One quartzite cobble has a similar groove, exposing the rough texture of the crystalline interior. There are a number of flat fragments of sandstone and quartzite that may be fragments of grinding slabs or palettes; one or two of these have a red wash, probably the same sort of pigment found on red-filmed sherds. One sandstone artifact is a grooved ball, 67 millimeters in diameter, of unknown use or function. Unusual finds include pieces of Missouri River clinkers, resembling pumice, with sharpening grooves.

The bone tool collection is fairly varied. Pins are bone splinters that are carefully shaped and polished along their entire surface. These may be ornaments, such as hair pins, or tools for activities like basketry or weaving, while a few have eyes and are clearly needles. Other pointed bones, some with use-polish but without shaping beyond the creation of a point, are listed as awls. Bone fishhooks are often very artfully made, and unfinished specimens show that many are shaped from the long bones of deer, the shaft and inner curve carved before the hook was broken from the parent bone. Unusual bone tools in the King collection include an antler spoon or spatula and a small tool that closely resembles a crochet hook.

The King collection contains fragments of mussel shell that appear to be carved for use as spoons, but WMRC excavators have not recovered any similar pieces.

The most common ceramic tool is a pottery trowel, a mushroom-shaped object probably used to shape pots and smooth daub walls. Trowels range in size from head diameters of about 30 millimeters to 100 millimeters or more.

There are also oddball clay items, difficult to regard as tools but worth describing. One rough clay dumbbell, 34 millimeters long, 7 millimeters minimum and 15 centimeters maximum diameter, is of unknown function, but resembles a sort of clay doodle that happened to get fired. A fragment of a clay ring like a doughnut, probably slightly greater than 45 millimeters in exterior diameter, the central hole about 12 millimeters in diameter, and 10 millimeters thick, is too irregular to fit into the disc/discoidal category. One small cone, 11.5 millimeters tall and 10 millimeters in basal diameter, is of unknown function. There are two objects that were probably fired incidentally, an irregular ball 23 millimeters in diameter and an equally irregular biconical, 36 millimeters long and 44 millimeters in diameter.

ORNAMENTS AND PERSONAL ITEMS

Like the tools, ornaments, gaming pieces, and personal items are made of fired clay, stone, bone, and shell.

Mississippian shell gorgets are among the most distinctive Native American art forms of the Mid-South region and among the most promising for a study of regional style geography and interregional trade in luxury or elite goods. Even small Mississippian sites such as the Wickliffe Mounds participated in the shell gorget symbolic community.

Wickliffe excavations have produced three shell gorgets. A marine shell spider gorget was recovered in 1992. Two marine shell gorgets were found at Wickliffe in the 1930s: a Cox Mound style woodpecker gorget of unknown provenience within the site and a fragmentary human motif from Mound D. The spider gorget is the best provenienced of the three and one of the best provenienced of its type, datable to the Middle Wickliffe period (ca. A.D. 1175–1250).

One gorget (Figure 4.16a CD) is known only from a photograph in the archives of the Museum of Anthropology, University of Kentucky (UKMA Negative #574). Typical for the early data from Wickliffe Mounds, the associated notes are terse: "Shell gorget, Wickliffe Mounds, Fain King collection" (George R. Milner, pers. com. 1984). No provenience data from within the site are available. It is likely to be the gorget that King loaned to Webb at the meeting of archaeologists in Birmingham in December 1932 (U.K.: Webb to King, 12 January 1933). If so, the piece must have come from Mound A, B, or C, and of the three a Mound C (cemetery) association seems most plausible (however, the WMRC excavators found very few grave associations comparable to those described in the 1930s; see Chapters 3 and 18). In sum, there is presently no particular reason to doubt its attribution to the Wickliffe site although precise documentation is lacking. There is no suggestion as to where the specimen may be today.

From the photograph, the gorget appears to be made of shell, presumably marine shell as are most of such artifacts. There are two suspension holes penetrating the neck of one of the woodpeckers, and the triangles appear to be perforations. The surface is chipped along some edges but otherwise the specimen appears to have been recovered whole. There is no scale in the photograph.

Woodpecker and looped-square gorgets are a standard motif called the Cox Mound tentative style, defined by Muller (1966; cf. Muller 1989). Muller attributes this style to the South Central region, suggesting very broadly relationships to Moundville and its hinterland. Recently Buchner and Childress (1991) reported a slate woodpecker gorget in the Cox Mound style from Putnam County, Tennessee. They noted occurrences of similar marine shell gorgets in an area ranging from the Nashville basin to the Upper Little Tennessee Valley and to northern Alabama. There are a few marine shell woodpecker motifs from Spiro, but only one gorget, which Phillips and Brown (1978:182) suggest originated in the east.

With no provenience data, it is impossible to suggest the chronological placement of the Wickliffe gorget within the site. However, the generally interpreted A.D. 1200–1350 span of similar gorgets (Buchner and Childress 1991:1–3) matches the Middle and Late Wickliffe periods quite comfortably.

The second Wickliffe marine shell gorget (Figure 4.16b CD) does have a provenience label from the King excavations. Unfortunately the specimen is only a small fragment. It has a human figure design, with the head clearly visible and, less clearly, a raised hand holding some object. The pose is similar to the chunkey player style and also to Madeline Kneberg's (1959) Eagle Dancers of the Tennessee drainage.

Only seven chunkey player gorgets are known, or at least securely documented (Phillips and Brown 1978:110), but the diamond eye of the Wickliffe gorget is similar to the eye forms of the chunkey players of Muller's (1966, 1989) Eddyville style, characteristic of the Ohio-Mississippi confluence region. Muller (pers. com. 1993) notes, however, that the fenestration and the apparent lack of concentric rings give the Wickliffe specimen affinities to the eastern Tennessee Hightower style more than to Eddyville. He suggests, as far as can be told given the fragmentary nature of the specimen, that this gorget could have an origin in eastern Tennessee.

The human figure gorget has a provenience label in Mound D. It is possible, though difficult to establish with any confidence, that Mound D may have been an elite burial mound (Chapters 3 and 18). Apparent caches of projectile points, bone tools, and discs and discoidals, and a high frequency of conch shell effigy ceramic vessel fragments, distinguish Mound D from all other deposits yet investigated on the site. The human figure gorget was not recovered in the area of the conch effigies, but was found not far from the projectile point caches. Excavations in 1987 demonstrated that the northern margin of Mound D was a Late Wickliffe construction, but it cannot be demonstrated that Mound D was not more complex, so the gorget cannot be securely dated to the Late Wickliffe period.

Muller's Eddyville style, which Phillips and Brown (1978:III, 175) call the McAdams style and which they link to Braden A at Spiro, includes both human and spider themes. In 1992, WMRC excavators recovered the other half of the Eddyville duo: a spider gorget.

This specimen (Figure 4.16c CD) is actually only the upper half of the gorget. The edges are battered, but the pair of scallops at the top appears to be the suspension holes, and enough of the design remains to see that it matches the Eddyville style spider gorgets of the central Mississippi Valley. Esarey (1990) has done a thorough survey of spider gorgets. Almost all of the characteristics he lists are represented in the Wickliffe specimen: concentric lines defining the border, a cephalothorax cross or cross and circle, lack of additional themes, lack of fenestration or scallop, hanging with the head down, and individual segmented legs. Since the head is missing, there are no data about the fangs. The Eddyville or McAdams group is distinguishable in style from spider gorgets of the Upper Tennessee drainage and from those at Spiro, although the general theme is closely connected.

Esarey (1990) found some three dozen spider gorgets in all, nearly half of which were found within 150 kilometers of the Ohio-Mississippi confluence. In addition, the WMRC staff has seen a fragment of a coal spider gorget recovered from the Mississippian site at Cairo, Illinois. Detailed contextual data, however, are problematic. The general impression from the literature is that, when any context at all is offered, spider gorgets are attributed to mounds or burials. Esarey (1990:17) seems to assume that burial context is typical when he says that "only a few . . . have been excavated under sufficient archaeological controls to determine the age and sex of the individuals with which they were buried." Of the ten examples so controlled, the gorgets were associated with infants, children, or females; only one with a possible adult male.

For the same reasons of poorly documented contexts, close dating of spider gorgets is difficult. For the Tennessee drainage, they are generally assigned to the period A.D. 1200 to 1500. At Spiro's Great Mortuary, the range of A.D. 1200 to 1350 is offered, noting of course that this is deposition date and not necessarily manufacture date, a caveat that must be applied to all of the specimens. Muller suggests A.D. 1250 to 1350 for the Eddyville style, while noting the lack of context to lend specificity. In the Illinois Valley, spider gorgets appear in the range of A.D. 1250 to 1440. Esarey (1990) suggests a generalized dating of A.D. 1200 to 1500 for spider gorgets.

The Wickliffe spider gorget was recovered in the vicinity of Mound C, but in neither mound nor burial association (46–47N16–18E, Level 7). It was found in a midden that can be assigned to the Middle Wickliffe period, A.D. 1175 to 1200. It is likely that the Wickliffe spider is one of the best-provenienced and most securely dated of the entire group. Its context challenges "the primary objective" of Brain and Phillips's study of gorgets, in which they assert that they "find no compelling evidence . . . that any of the gorgets . . . were deposited in a context before the fifteenth century" (Brain and Phillips 1996:395, 396) and thus conclude that gorgets of the same style as the Wickliffe spider must postdate A.D. 1400.

Unfortunately, the Wickliffe specimens do not help much in dating the Cox Mound or Hightower styles. Phillips and Brown note that "Cox Mound is not a Dallas style," meaning that it does not appear in Kneberg's complexes, and that "if there is any sound information on [the Cox Mound style's] temporal position, it has escaped us" (Phillips and Brown 1978:181). The Wickliffe specimen probably dates to the period A.D. 1200 to 1350. Mound D, the source of the human gorget fragment, can be assigned to the same date range. Noting that Madeline Kneberg's (1959) early complex includes the spider and Eagle Dancer, Hightower-style gorgets in eastern Tennessee, the best that can be said is that Hightower human, Eddyville spider, and Cox Mound woodpecker gorgets are temporally compatible with the Middle to Late Wickliffe occupation.

From the perspective of style geography, the Wickliffe gorgets are an interesting mix. Certainly the spider fits comfortably within the stylistic and known geographic parameters of the Eddyville or McAdams style, belonging to the central Mississippi Valley and the upper Mid-South.

Wickliffe, however, seems out of the range for the Cox Mound gorget style, with its Tennessee–northern Alabama focus, and the lack of good provenience data does suggest some caution. But the association of the Cox Mound with the Eddyville style is not so farfetched. Gorget scholars will note the Castalian Springs gorgets, five in a single burial, including one chunkey player in the Eddyville style and two Cox Mound style woodpecker gorgets in very tight association (Phillips and Brown 1978:181). Given that a woodpecker gorget did show up as far west as Spiro, it is reasonable to suggest that the Wickliffe woodpecker extends the Mid-South range of the Cox Mound style, rather than to reject a Wickliffe provenience on the basis of previous Cox Mound style geography.

In the same vein, the Wickliffe human gorget seems outside the range for the eastern Tennessee–focused Hightower style. But the provenience label is consistent with the systematic labeling of some 85,000 other artifacts and this causes little hesitation about accepting it as a Wickliffe site recovery. Given that

Hightower-style gorgets also appear as far west as Spiro, a Wickliffe appearance for a Hightower gorget is not unreasonable.

These specimens add to the general corpus of information about Mississippian style and iconography and also establish that even a small mound center like Wickliffe participated in the extensive trade network and symbolic community that linked the Mississippian peoples. The woodpecker and human gorgets are of uncertain context, although there is some hope of making a better assessment of Mound D and the context of the human figure gorget as analysis progresses. The Wickliffe spider gorget, however, is much better provenienced and better dated and establishes the inception of the Eddyville style by the mid-thirteenth century.

It is also worth noting here that Wickliffe has yielded at least one other marine shell artifact (Figure 4.17CD). This is a section of a whelk shell, drilled, that appears to be a fragment of a ceremonial cup or trumpet. There is no sign of any engraving on it. It was recovered from Mound C in 1991, but unfortunately was found under a large chunk of concrete. So, even though the excavators recorded coordinates in three dimensions for provenience, its context in the very complicated stratigraphic setting of this mound and cemetery is uncertain.

One coal pendant or gorget was recovered in 1996, from 17–18S74–75W in the Mound G vicinity (Figure 4.16d CD). Unfortunately the crew found it while cutting profiles, so that it cannot be assigned to a Wickliffe period. It is a variation on the cross and circle motif, being a circular boss with concentric rings on a cross with scalloped edges, and is 37 millimeters wide and 8 millimeters thick at the top of the boss.

Beads, ear plugs, and other ornaments—mostly ear spool fragments—are found throughout the site. Bead materials include shell, bone, fired clay, and stone, including fluorspar. One ceramic bead or pendant is a 28-millimeter tall owl effigy with a hole piercing its neck from side to side (Figure 4.18CD). Other ceramic beads are spherical or ovoid. Most shell beads are disc shaped and centrally perforated. One, from the East Midden, was rectangular, 15.5 × 12 × 8 millimeters thick, with a central perforation.

Two irregular pebbles have holes and may be beads, and two pieces of stone are possible bead blanks, a quartz pebble with a hole drilled about two-thirds through and a fluorspar ball with a small round hole in one side. Although previous Wickliffe reports have listed perforated crinoid stem segments as possible beads, crinoid segments with natural holes are found in the local gravels, and they are currently not assumed to be beads.

An item is cataloged as an ear plug if it has a thin shaft and a bulbous end (Figure 4.19CD). Ear plugs occur in the same set of materials as beads except bone, plus there is one made of coal. They range from 15 to 32 millimeters in length. A few plugs resemble discs, except that they are small (less than 10 millimeters in diameter) and either are longer than their diameter or taper (where discs are the same diameter top and bottom).

Ear spools are ring shaped and have concave exterior surfaces. Most are ceramic and were found in fragments. The fragments may be distinguished from sherds, especially handles, by their fine finish and triangular cross section. The single whole specimen is 12 millimeters thick and 25 millimeters in exterior diameter. The thickness seems typical, but most of the fragments suggest larger diameters. One solid-centered stone specimen is listed as an ear spool because of its concave edges. A set of bone fragments may belong to an ear spool or two. The Kings described a pair of copper-covered wooden ear spools in the cemetery, but these specimens apparently were stolen and are not available for study (if indeed they were found in the Wickliffe cemetery).

One common artifact form on late prehistoric sites throughout the eastern United States is the disc or discoidal. For the WMRC analyses, the term *disc* refers to a circular object that is flat sided and thin relative to its diameter, and *discoidal* refers to concave- or convex-sided circular objects. At Wickliffe, discs and discoidals are found in baked clay, stone, and rarely bone. Most discs or fragments are ground from potsherds ("sherd discs"), and most were made from Mississippi Plain sherds, a few from Bell Plain, the occasional one from a red-filmed sherd, and at least one from a Kimmswick Fabric Impressed sherd.

Often, the smallest discs and discoidals are interpreted as lip or ear plugs, the larger ones as gaming pieces, and the largest as chunkey stones. Linn (1984) studied the discs and discoidals in the King collection, finding neither discrete size categories nor a distinction in size between materials, though the largest ones were stone. At Wickliffe, they rarely have central perforations as though used as spindle whorls. The smallest sherd disc in the 1987 collection, 15 centimeters in diameter, has a hole drilled through it and may have been a bead. It is difficult to ascribe functions to smaller disc and discoidal specimens (Figure 4.20CD).

Another recurrent artifact usually considered to be a gaming piece is a deer astragalus die, an astragalus ground flat on the wide faces and occasionally on the tops and ends as well (Figure 4.21CD). Although most astragalus dice reported previously were documented in protohistoric or contact period sites (Lewis 1988), several examples occur in Late Wickliffe deposits and one in a Middle Wickliffe deposit. One particularly fine example from the East Midden is ground flat on six sides, burned black, and polished almost to a luster (Figure 4.21CD, *left*).

Finally, the most impressive baked clay object is a large elbow pipe, 57 millimeters high, 41 millimeters wide, and 69 millimeters long. This was recovered from an early wall trench, Feature 144, under Mound D North. The WMRC excavators also recovered two other ceramic pipe fragments.

BULK MATERIALS

Bulk materials are both counted and weighed, but because of wide variation in size are most effectively reported by weight.

Daub is a low-fired clay, usually reddish to reddish brown but ranging to light tan and to charcoal grey. Many chunks have impressions of twigs and straw, and these are usually interpreted as architectural remains, fragments of wattle-and-daub walls that were accidentally fired when a house burned down. A few daub fragments have red or white paint, and some daub has extremely well-finished surfaces, nearing the consistency and smoothness of pottery. It is likely that systematic study of the daub collection will provide information about house construction and appearance. There is a total of more than 200 kilograms of daub in the collections.

"Fired clay" consists of slabby chunks of fired white clay, probably a locally available ball clay, which are scattered in small quantities throughout all of the areas excavated so far. These pieces contrast with daub by their very white color, their fine and consistent texture, and their lack of surface impressions. It is not clear what this clay was used for. Around the WMRC lab the workers sometimes refer to it as cougar litter, for lack of anything better, but the most plausible explanation offered so far is that the fired white clay was ground for use as white pigment. WMRC excavations have recovered almost 39 kilograms of fired clay.

Rock is cataloged in three groups: unmodified gravel and two kinds of fire-cracked rock. Both fire-cracked types are generally sandstones. "Ferrous sandstone" is a coarse, grainy material reddened by firing. "Fire-cracked rock" is white to yellow or buff and less granular than the ferrous sandstone. The original rationale for separating them was that very fine-grained ferrous sandstone might have been ground for pigment. The fine-grained specimens are very rare. More than 148 kilograms of fire-cracked rock, 122 kilograms of ferrous sandstone, and 445 kilograms of gravel from the WMRC excavations have been tallied, weighed, and discarded.

HISTORIC MATERIALS

A few historic artifacts, mostly nails and window glass fragments, occur in surficial and disturbed deposits on the Wickliffe site. In some cases they are instrumental in identifying disturbances. The historical archaeology of Wickliffe Mounds is a real part of the archaeological record, especially in reflecting the King excavations and their impact on the Mississippi period record (see Chapter 6). For the most part, though, the historic artifacts do not belong to a context requiring much analysis, and they will be discussed only as they become relevant.

5

Chronology and Assemblage Change

CERAMIC SEQUENCE

The first Wickliffe Mounds Research Center excavation at Wickliffe, in Mound A, defined three intrasite periods based on the changing relationship between incised and red-filmed ceramics (Table 3.1). Over the following several years, with excavations in Mound F (1985–1986), Mound D and the East Midden (1987), and the Northwest and North Central villages (1988–1989), ceramic analysis corroborated the usefulness of the construct, indicating that the incised/red-filmed relationship was consistent with stratigraphic relationships. Only in evident cases of historic disturbance, particularly the 1985 tests for the expansion of the office building, was the ceramic sequence inconcordant with depth and stratigraphy.

As the ceramic analysis employed the ceramic periods with more confidence, it became clear that other elements of the ceramic assemblages also correlated with the periods. Certain incised types and vessel forms are introduced in the Middle and Late Wickliffe periods, and thus become markers for those periods. By the time of the 1990 excavations, then, other factors than the incised/red-filmed ratio played a part in assigning deposits to periods. The initial definition of the periods, however, remained the primary criterion, since single-sherd period markers comprise a very small percentage of any assemblage.

Table 5.1CD and Figure 5.1CD (presented in the same order, top to bottom, as Table 5.1CD) present the basic ceramic chronology for all analyzed midden deposits. It is clear that Mississippi Plain dominates all assemblages. The essential complementarity of the incised and red-filmed categories also is evident. During the Middle Wickliffe period, there is a fair amount of variability in percentages, but in general the proportions of incising and red-filming usually are fairly close, with red-filming claiming the greater share more often in larger samples. Some of the variation within Middle Wickliffe is, no doubt, attributable to difficulties in separating deposits in arbitrary-level excavations.

Some patterns emerge among the other ceramic groups, most perceptibly when the figures are summarized by period (Table 5.2, Figure 5.2). Bell Plain has a slight tendency to increase in the Late period, as does Wickliffe Thick.

Table 5.2. Summary of Analyzed Ceramics

	Mississippi Plain	Incised	Bell Plain	Red Filmed	Nashville	Kimmswick	Wickliffe	Crosno	Other	Sample Size
Middens										
Late	38,205	868	5784	272	11	522	427	14	167	46,270
Middle	5134	57	571	83	3	193	27	3	27	6098
Early	2129	20	253	64		82	12	1	16	2577
Subtotal	45,468	945	6608	419	14	797	466	18	210	54,945
Features										
Late	2931	68	479	28	17	51	29	3	18	3624
Middle	600	12	55	16		17	5	2	2	709
Early	791	3	61	33		21	3	1		913
Subtotal	4322	83	595	77	17	89	37	6	20	5246
Mound deposits										
Late	10,381	190	1189	83	14	139	102	10	76	12,184
Middle	3623	35	301	50	2	156	20	3	33	4223
Early	133		12	3		9				157
Subtotal	14,137	225	1502	136	16	304	122	13	109	16,564
Disturbed	30,117	538	4590	257	6	424	242	24	218	36,416
Unassigned	466		33		1	10	1		3	514
King excavations	44,382	1279	8993	494	17	1652	1395	17	140	58,369
Total	138,892	3070	22,321	1383	71	3276	2263	78	700	172,054

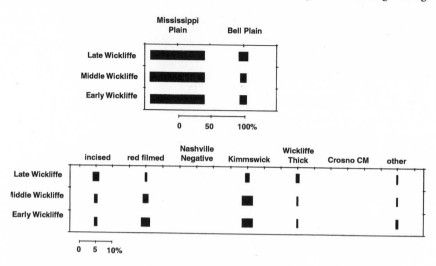

5.2. Midden ceramics, summary by period.

Kimmswick Fabric Impressed, on the other hand, decreases in the Late period. Nashville Negative Painted and Crosno Cord Marked are rare in any period, with the notable point that negative-painted sherds do not appear in the Early Wickliffe period.

The chronological pattern among features and even mound deposits confirms the midden patterns (Table 5.2, Figure 5.3CD). Since the features contain much smaller samples, the patterns are somewhat exaggerated compared with those of the middens.

Among the decorative types (Table 5.3CD, Figure 5.4CD), the period patterns are quite consistent. Matthews Incised, *vars. Beckwith* and *Manly*, Barton Incised, and Mound Place Incised are found throughout the sequence. The Early Wickliffe sherds of the latter two types tend to fit in the broadest definitions of the types. O'Byam Incised *var. Adams* appears in Middle Wickliffe. O'Byam Incised *var. O'Byam*, Owens Punctate, Winterville Incised, Leland Incised, and untyped punctate sherds mark the Late Wickliffe period. Carson Red-on-Buff is represented by a single sherd in the Late Wickliffe period. Again, the patterns are clearest when the period figures are summarized (Table 5.4, Figure 5.5) and are confirmed by the features (Table 5.4, Figure 5.6CD).

RADIOCARBON DATES

Table 5.5 lists the radiocarbon samples submitted for dating. Uncalibrated dates are cited with lower case letters (a.d.) and corrected dates with small caps (A.D.). Dates are calibrated using the decadal dataset (dataset #2) of the Stuiver

Table 5.4. Summary of Decorative Types

	Matthews/ Beckwith	Matthews/ Manly	Barton	Mound Place	Wallace	Winterville	Punctate	Perforated
Middens								
Late	149	71	16	6		7	51	28
Middle	13	5						2
Early	1	2	6	1				
Subtotal	163	78	22	7		7	51	30
Features								
Late	6	14	1				1	2
Middle		1						
Early	1							
Subtotal	7	15	1				1	2
Mound deposits								
Late	30	26		2		2	10	2
Middle	4	5						
Early								
Subtotal	34	31		2		2	10	2
Disturbed	72	40	2	1			33	1
Unassigned								
King excavations	433	214	20	17	2	10	14	1
Total	709	378	45	27	2	19	109	36

Continued

Table 5.4. Continued

	O'Byam var. O'Byam	O'Byam var. Adams	Leland Incised	Owens	Carson	Untyped Incised	Total	Assemblage Size
Middens								
Late	48	3	6	22	1	461	328	46,270
Middle		2				37	18	6098
Early						8	12	2577
Subtotal	48	5	6	22	1	506	358	54,945
Features								
Late	12		2	5		25	24	3700
Middle		1				10	1	709
Early						2	1	837
Subtotal	12	1	2	5		37	26	5246
Mound deposits								
Late	14			4		100	72	12,184
Middle		3				23	9	4223
Early								157
Subtotal	14	3		4		123	81	16,564
Disturbed	24		6	19		340	149	36,416
Unassigned								514
King excavations	204	24	16	5	4	320	711	58,369
Total	302	33	30	55	5	1326	1325	172,054

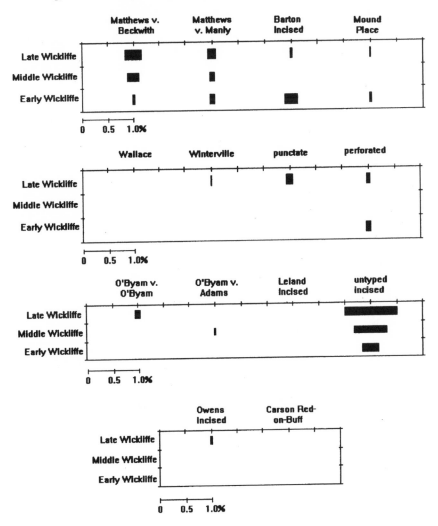

5.5. Midden decorative type summary.

and Reimer (1993) CALIB computer program, which plots intercepts of radiocarbon and dendrochronological dating curves (Stuiver and Becker 1993). CALIB calculates one- and two-sigma ranges for the intercepts, and Table 5.5 lists the one-sigma ranges. CALIB also has T-test and averaging functions for comparing a set of dates, which is a real boon to the statistically challenged.

Early Wickliffe Contexts

1. Beta 12529. Feature 106 was defined at the surface of the midden underlying Mound A. This feature was defined as a section of a circular charcoal stain,

Table 5.5. Radiocarbon Dates from Wickliffe

Provenience	Laboratory Number	Radiocarbon Age B.P.	Radiocarbon Age A.D.	Calibrated Dated A.D.
Early Wickliffe[a]				
Mound A, Feature 106	Beta-12529	520 ± 70	1430	1332 (1419) 1442
Mound A, Feature 106	Beta-25218	920 ± 60	1030	1026 (1071, 1080, 1128, 1136, 1154) 1211
Mound B, Feature 238 Zone 2	Beta-39030	1265 ± 60	685	687 (734, 736, 774) 867
Middle Wickliffe				
Mound A core	ISGS-1143	830 ± 77	1120	1157 (1218) 1280
Mound A core	ISGS-1156	765 ± 76	1185	1217 (1279) 1293
Mound A, Feature 103	Beta-25217	1030 ± 90	920	900 (1002, 1010, 1017) 1151
Middle Wickliffe average[b]		851 ± 45	1099	1158 (1212) 1259
Late Wickliffe				
Mound A, Feature 101	Beta-25216[c]	430 ± 60	1520	1431 (1445) 1610
Mound A, Feature 101	Beta-31520	620 ± 50	1330	1295 (1326, 1352, 1363, 1366, 1389) 1407
Mound A, Feature 101	Beta-31833[c]	1060 ± 70	890	898 (995) 1025
East Midden	ISGS-1171	720 ± 70	1230	1260 (1286) 1382
East Midden	Beta-25911	770 ± 60	1180	1217 (1265, 1266, 1277) 1289
Mound F, Daub Wall	Beta-25219	740 ± 70	1210	1224 (1282) 1298
Mound D North	Beta-25220	730 ± 50	1220	1262 (1284) 1295
North Village, Feature 152	Beta-27506	750 ± 60	1200	1224 (1281) 1293
North Village, Feature 152	Beta-27507	580 ± 60	1370	1305 (1334, 1338, 1402) 1422
Mound D, Feature 112, Zone 1	Beta-33584	760 ± 80	1190	1214 (1279) 1295
Mound D, Feature 112, Zone 2	Beta-33585	760 ± 90	1190	1212 (1279) 1297
Late Wickliffe average		721 ± 24	1229	1280 (1286) 1293

[a]The Early Wickliffe dates are statistically different at the 95 percent confidence level and have not been averaged (see note b).

[b]Weighted averages were obtained through CALIB (see note d). The Late Wickliffe average does not include Feature 101 dates (Beta 25216, 31520, and 31833) because of the wide spread of the three dates and the confusion caused by failing to identify large portions of the sample as corn (see note c). The Late Wickliffe average and the Middle Wickliffe average dates are not statistically the same at the 95 percent confidence level.

[c]Beta-31833, charred maize, is corrected for carbon 13/12, and Beta-25216, probably charred maize, is not corrected for carbon 13/12.

[d]Radiocarbon dates have been calibrated by Stuiver and Reimer's 1993 update of the CALIB program (Stuiver and Reimer 1993), using the decadal dataset (dataset #2). The intercept or intercepts of the radiocarbon and bristlecone pine curves are placed in parentheses between the one-sigma ranges.

truncated to the north and west by excavation walls. The feature was a basin-shaped hearth, densely packed with charcoal, ash, and faunal remains. A date in this context should define the end of the Early Wickliffe ceramic period. This first sample was submitted in 1984, but the resulting date of 520 ± 70 B.P. (a.d. 1430) is far too late to be accepted in so early a stratigraphic context. Calibration corrects this date to A.D. 1419, which does not help its acceptability.

2. Beta 25218. This is a second sample from Feature 106, submitted because the first date did not make sense. The second sample was assayed at a.d. 1030 (920 ± 60 B.P.), which calibrates to five intercepts between A.D. 1071 and 1154. Stratigraphically this date is quite acceptable. The midden produced one sherd of Ramey Incised (Griffith 1981), very likely manufactured in the American Bottom (conversation with J. B. Griffin, c. 1990), where this type is characteristic of the Stirling phase, A.D. 1100 to 1200 (Hall 1991; Pauketat 1994). The Mound A midden date compares well with the Stirling phase chronology, supporting a cross-dating by the Ramey sherd, but does not pin down the end of the early period at Wickliffe very satisfactorily.

3. Beta 39030. Feature 238, Zone 2, at the base of the midden under Mound B, was a concentration of ash and charcoal directly above the subsoil. The sample was submitted in the hope of establishing a base date for the Wickliffe occupation. The date returned, however, was a.d. 685 (1265 ± 60 B.P.), calibrating to three intercepts from A.D. 734 to 774. This date is much too early for a Mississippian deposit in the Ohio-Mississippi confluence region. Such a date should be associated with a Baytown ceramic assemblage, but the Feature 238 assemblage was entirely Mississippian. This date cannot be accepted.

The three Early Wickliffe dates are statistically different at the 95 percent confidence level. Thus, the single admissible Early Wickliffe date is Beta 25218, which has an unfortunately wide range of calibration intercepts.

Middle Wickliffe Contexts

4. ISGS 1143. This date was reported by Lewis (Lewis ed. 1986). It was taken from the lower of two dense charcoal lenses in the center of Mound A. Both lenses evidently are burned building layers from early mound summits within the mound core, representing the middle ceramic period. The date is a.d. 1120 ± 77 (830 ± 77 B.P.), calibrating to (cal.) A.D. 1218.

5. ISGS 1156. Lewis (Lewis ed. 1986) also submitted this sample, from the upper of the two Mound A burned building summits. The sample provided a date of a.d. 1185 ± 76 (765 ± 76 B.P.), cal. A.D. 1279. Both dates fit the stratigraphic sequence nicely.

6. Beta 25217. Feature 103 was defined at the base of the "wedge" in Mound A, overlaying the mound core. It appeared in the excavation as a shallow, amorphous concentration of charcoal, fire-cracked rock, and fired ball clay that extended into the south excavation wall. The date, however, was assayed

at 1030 ± 90 B.P. (a.d. 920). Calibrated to A.D. 1000–1017, this date is too early to fit the sequence.

By CALIB's T-test, however, the three Middle Wickliffe dates are statistically the same at the 95-percent confidence level. The weighted average of the three dates is 851 ± 45 B.P., cal. A.D. 1158 (1212) 1259.

Late Wickliffe Contexts

7. Beta 25216. Feature 101 was a small concentration of charcoal in the outer mantle of Mound A. It contained very little material other than charcoal. From its compact basin shape, it was originally interpreted as a hearth, though the excavators were unable to define a ground or mound surface on which a fire might have been built. The feature probably was part or most of a basket load. The sample yielded a date of 430 ± 60 B.P. (a.d. 1520), which is far later than any other date yet obtained from the site. The calibration offers an intercept at A.D. 1445—earlier but still quite late. The context is stratigraphically the latest zone of Mound A, but there is no other indication that the occupation might have lasted as late as the fifteenth century.

Two other samples from this feature were submitted to compare with the Beta 25216 result.

8. Beta 31520 yielded a date of a.d. 1330 ± 50 (620 ± 50 B.P.). Calibration provided several intercepts from A.D. 1326 to 1389, comparable to several other Late Wickliffe dates. However, after analyzing this sample, the analysis contractor (Darden Hood, pers. com. 1989) noted that the charcoal submitted included corn, which the submitter should have ascertained originally.

9. Beta 31833 was a third sample from Feature 101, for which charred maize was deliberately selected, and the date was corrected for carbon 13/12. The result, 1060 ± 70 B.P., calibrates to A.D. 995, which does not fit the Wickliffe or Mound A sequence at all.

Because of the confusion surrounding the Feature 101 maize and the variation among the three dates, all three are excluded from further discussion.

10. ISGS 1171. This sample was recovered from the East Midden by the University of Illinois team in 1983 (Lewis ed. 1986:111). The date is a.d. 1230 ± 70 (cal. A.D. 1286).

11. Beta 25911. This is the 1987 sample from the daub zone in the East Midden. It was dated to 770 ± 60 B.P. (a.d. 1180), with three intercepts from cal. A.D. 1265 to 1277. This sample was submitted because ISGS 1171 (above) and Beta 25219 and 25220 (below) were uncannily close. The two East Midden dates corroborate a mid to late thirteenth-century context in the East Midden.

12. Beta 25219. One of the odd features in the floor of King's Mound F excavation was a collapsed daub wall that King evidently left as a pedestal. This was a massive concentration of daub, with several areas of burned discoloration. The daub came up in big chunks, with numerous impressions

of grass and twigs. Charcoal from within the daub yielded a date of 740 ± 70 B.P., a.d. 1210 (cal. A.D. 1282).

13. Beta 25220. This sample is from the 1987 excavation in Mound D north. A round charcoal stain within the mound fill (5–7N28–29E, Level 5) was identified first as a posthole, but probably was simply an inclusion in the fill. The submitted sample returned a date of 730 ± 50 B.P., a.d. 1220 (cal. A.D. 1284).

14. Beta 27506. This sample, like the next one, was recovered during the 1988 excavations in the Northwest Village. Feature 152, the source of this sample, lay fairly shallowly below the plowzone, and thus is stratigraphically late for this village area. The feature produced several solid charcoal samples, probably burned beams in situ. The first of two samples submitted for dating was assessed at 750 ± 60 B.P., a.d. 1200, cal. A.D. 1281.

15. Beta 27507. The second sample submitted from Feature 152 was assessed at 580 ± 60 B.P., a.d. 1370. This is quite late and, disturbingly, 170 years variant from the previous sample from the same feature. Calibration results in the intercepts from A.D. 1334 to 1402. The earliest is quite within the range of other Late Wickliffe dates.

16. Beta 33584 was taken from Zone 1 of Feature 112, a basin-shaped intrusion into Mound D North. The sample gave a date of 760 ± 80 B.P., cal. A.D. 1279.

17. Beta 33585. This sample also came from Feature 112, but from Zone 2 of the feature. The result of 760 ± 90 B.P., cal. A.D. 1279, is consistent with the Zone 1 date.

Discounting the confusing Feature 101 dates, the Late Wickliffe dates are statistically the same at the 95 percent confidence level. Averaging them produces a weighted date of cal. A.D. 1280 (1286) 1293.

The Middle and Late Wickliffe average dates are statistically different at the 95 percent confidence level.

On the basis of these dates, recognizing that any assignment of calendrical boundaries is arbitrary and using rounded half centuries as a unit of convenience, dates for the ceramic periods may be suggested as follows:

Early Wickliffe, A.D. 1100–1200
Middle Wickliffe, A.D. 1200–1250
Late Wickliffe, A.D. 1250–1350

Recently, Matternes (1999a, 1999b) reported a number of radiocarbon dates from the Mound C cemetery, including two dates on faunal material from the Late Wickliffe midden and fourteen dates on samples of human bone. The two faunal dates average to cal. A.D. 1268 (1293) 1389, matching the previous Late Wickliffe dates very well. The burial dates average to cal. A.D. 1191 (1222) 1264, indicating a cemetery that belongs mainly to the Middle Wickliffe period. Two burial dates, however, are significantly earlier, and Matternes (1999b) suggests that they represent human remains that were curated for some time before deposition in the Mound C cemetery. This suite of dates is entirely compatible with the previously defined chronology.

OXIDIZABLE CARBON RATIO DATES

The 1996 excavations, the final Wickliffe season, provided an opportunity to compare dates from a relatively new technique, Oxidizable Carbon Ratio (OCR) (Frink 1992, 1994, 1995). OCR dating is based on the recycling of organic matter in soils, which is modeled as a linear process through time. The date is measured on a ratio of total carbon to oxidizable carbon. Because these dates are based on mean residence time (MRT) measurements, it is assumed that the results represent the mean age of all the organic carbon in the sample. Although the accuracy of these dates is generally within about ±3 percent (Frink 1994:25), because the descriptive statistics of the population are unknown for the Wickliffe samples (how much mixing of younger and older soils there is in each sample, for example), it is not possible to calculate a confidence interval with precision (Frink 1997).

The excavators took samples from 2-centimeter slices in a 20 × 20-centimeter column from a completed excavation profile. The samples were chosen to represent visible horizons or units, including plowzone and subsoil, in order to create a full chronological framework for each set of deposits. Frink (1997) suggests, especially for mound soils, that a vertical sampling interval of 5 centimeters would produce the most detailed dating sequence, but the Wickliffe samples balanced minimizing sample numbers (and analysis budget) against fully characterizing a sequence for each unit.

Table 5.6 lists the OCR dates for the 1996 excavations. The OCR dates may be compared with the Wickliffe period sequence as assigned by the ceramic assemblages, and then with the benchmark dates for the periods as interpreted from the radiocarbon dates, above.

18–20S74–76W

The stratigraphy of this unit, in the vicinity of Mound G, was difficult to characterize by period because of the contaminating effect of an intrusive house basin through each excavation level. The extension unit, 17–18S74–75W, produced ceramics that identified Zone 1 as a plow-disturbed Late Wickliffe deposit, Zone 2 as Late Wickliffe, and Zone 3 as a Middle Wickliffe zone, but failed to yield diagnostic ceramics for Zone 4. Zone 4 could therefore have belonged to either the Middle or Early Wickliffe period.

The OCR sequence fits fairly well. The Zone 1 sample gave an early Late Wickliffe date. The Zone 2 date is too early for Late Wickliffe, and even

Table 5.6. OCR Dates from Wickliffe Mounds

Provenience	Lab Number	B.P.	A.D.	Ceramic Period
18-20S74-76W				
Zone 1	ACT 2358	699	1251	L
Zone 2	ACT 2131	771	1179	L
Zone 3	ACT 2132	739	1211	M
Zone 4	ACT 2133	846	1104	M or E*
Subsoil	ACT 2359	1032	918	
77-79S28-29W				
Plowzone	ACT 2351	602	1348	L
Mound Zone 1	ACT 2352	877	1073	L
Mound Zone 2	ACT 2353	708	1242	L
Mound Zone 3	ACT 2354	764	1186	L
Midden Zone 1	ACT 2137	666	1284	L
Midden Zone 2	ACT 2138	700	1250	L
Subsoil	ACT 2355	1064	886	
76-77S14-16W				
Plowzone	ACT 2349	624	1326	L
Zone 2	ACT 2139	710	1240	L
Zone 4	ACT 2140	782	1168	E
Feature 369	ACT 2141	797	1153	E
Subsoil	ACT 2350	954	996	
57-58S16-18W				
Plowzone	ACT 2356	644	1306	L
Sample 1	ACT 2134	727	1223	L
Sample 2	ACT 2135	761	1189	M?*
Sample 3	ACT 2136	797	1153	M?*
Subsoil	ACT 2357	960	990	

L, Late Wickliffe; *M*, Middle Wickliffe; *E*, Early Wickliffe.

*Inferred from stratigraphy, no diagnostics among ceramics.

for Middle Wickliffe, but may be explained by postulating that the sample contained redeposited earlier soils—in fact, soils displaced by the house basin. The Zone 3 date is a Middle Wickliffe date. The Zone 4 date belongs in the Early Wickliffe period, answering the question evaded by the ceramics.

77–79S28–29W

Mound H, in this unit, presented a profile topped by a plowzone with a Late Wickliffe ceramic assemblage, underlain by three mound zones and two midden zones, all Late Wickliffe, and completed by a Middle Wickliffe basal feature. The purpose of taking OCR dates from this unit was to verify the Late Wickliffe assignment of the midden.

The OCR sequence matches very well. The plowzone date, representing the final occupation perhaps mixed with some later topsoil development, is a terminal Late Wickliffe date. The mound zones betray mixing of deposits from several periods, which is not surprising for a mound fill. The two midden dates are gratifyingly Late Wickliffe. The deeper midden date, A.D. 1250, suggests that the mid-century mark is a very convenient round figure marker for the transition between the two periods.

76–77S14–16W

This unit revealed a very complex stratigraphy, in which correlation of stratigraphic zones with excavation levels was somewhat problematic. Zone I yielded a Late Wickliffe ceramic assemblage, and the bottom levels and zone belonged to the Early Wickliffe period. No specifically Middle Wickliffe zone or level could be identified, but it is more than possible that traces of Middle Wickliffe activities lurked somewhere in the midlevels.

Once again, the OCR sequence fits well. Zone I yielded a date of A.D. 1326, that is, later Late Wickliffe. Zone 2, interpreted via ceramics as a Late Wickliffe zone, gave a late Middle Wickliffe date and may represent the elusive Middle Wickliffe horizon; in any case, it is difficult to quibble with a decade error in calendrics. The two deep dates, correlating with Early Wickliffe ceramics, are appropriately twelfth-century dates.

57–58S16–18W

The profile of this unit indicated a Late Wickliffe midden, the top of which was disturbed by plowing, overlying a Middle Wickliffe zone. A number of features penetrated the subsoil. Some features were visible in the profile, with points of origin at the boundary between the two midden zones. Few of the features contained diagnostic ceramics, and in the aggregate, they would most likely be assigned to the Middle Wickliffe period for lack of any more specific indicators.

The OCR sequence here is the most troubling of the four. Samples 1 and 2 represented the upper zone. Sample 1 is appropriately Late Wickliffe, but sample 2, from deeper within the Late Wickliffe midden, yielded a Middle Wickliffe date. Samples 3 and 4 were removed from within the profile of a wall trench that visually originated at the top of the Middle Wickliffe midden (actually, two mutually intruding wall trenches, only one of which may have originated at the zonal transition). Samples 3 and 4 give Early Wickliffe dates, and the two samples are dated three to four decades apart, which on their face would imply a very long filling period for the wall trench. It is of course possible that the trench fill incorporates Early Wickliffe soils from an unidentified Early horizon in this location, or even displaced subsoil. At any rate, the dates are well within the occupation of the Wickliffe site.

Summary

The date range of the OCR samples fits extremely well with the Wickliffe sequence as interpreted from the radiocarbon dates, approximately A.D.

1100 to 1350. The earliest midden OCR date is A.D. 1104, and the latest is A.D. 1348.

The sequences in each excavation unit also match fairly well, correlating with the ceramic periods, the period dates as abstracted from the radiocarbon assays, and the OCR dates. The range of OCR dates for Late Wickliffe ceramic contexts is A.D. 1223 to 1348, and the earliest OCR date belongs to a complex depositional situation that may well include some Middle Wickliffe occupation. The OCR dates from Middle Wickliffe (ceramic) contexts are A.D. 1153, 1189, and 1211, the last of which is easily Middle Wickliffe, whereas the first two seem a bit too early. The contexts are debatable, though. Dates from Early Wickliffe contexts are in the A.D. 1100s, as expected.

Only the latest Early Wickliffe and the earliest Middle Wickliffe OCR dates overlap, the overlap range being A.D. 1153 to 1168. The one-sigma range of the Middle Wickliffe averaged carbon 14 date is A.D. 1158 to 1259, which overlaps the Middle Wickliffe OCR date range extensively; the early ends of the Middle Wickliffe one-sigma range and of the OCR date range for the same ceramic period are remarkably close. It would be very easy to make an argument that the Early-to-Middle Wickliffe transition should be assigned to A.D. 1175 rather than A.D. 1200.

To do so would address another nagging problem also, that the previously interpreted Middle Wickliffe period is only half as long as either the Early or Late period. The sheer volume of deposits and assemblages of the Late Wickliffe period indeed argues for a longer, more concentrated, or both, Late compared with Middle period occupation, but the same cannot be said for the Early Wickliffe period. Setting the Early-to-Middle boundary at A.D. 1175 would incline toward a better balance among the occupation spans and intensities of the periods as evidenced by depths of deposits and quantities of material remains. To try to adjust the period markers any further by a decade here or there, however, would merely compound the essential arbitrariness of forcing a complex depositional history into a calendar created by dating techniques fraught with inherent uncertainties.

In sum, the Wickliffe sequence will be assigned dates as follows:

Late Wickliffe, A.D. 1250–1350
Middle Wickliffe, A.D. 1175–1250
Early Wickliffe A.D. 1100–1175

CHRONOLOGY OF THE KING COLLECTION

It is interesting to compare the ceramics from the King excavations (Tables 5.7CD and 5.8CD) with those from the WMRC excavations. The King excavations in aggregate, and even the deepest levels in each mound, fit the Late Wickliffe pattern. Mound F, on the west edge of the site, and Mound E, on the southern tip, could be expected to belong to the Late Wickliffe period according to the expanding village model. What of Mound D, however? WMRC excavations in Mound D North and South indicated Early and Middle Wickliffe deposits at the base of Mound D, and a ceramics analyst might expect that the deepest level of Mound D would betray these deposits. In total, they do not. It is likely that the 1-foot arbitrary levels of the King excavation simply provided too coarse a resolution to distinguish the basal midden. It is quite possible that three-dimensional mapping of chronological markers—and incised types, plus plate and handle forms (below)—will hint at some complexity in Mound D, when the site's geographic information system reaches that level of sophistication.

The collections from MF-38 and MF-39 are also disappointingly alike. If each collection represents an excavation block at the base of Mound F, given a model of an expanding village, it might be hoped that ceramic markers would indicate which assemblage belonged closer to the center of the site and which farther away, helping to place these assemblages within the Mound F excavation area. There is little help here, unfortunately.

The King collection, then, must be treated in general as a Late Wickliffe assemblage. Even though it is likely that Mound D especially incorporates earlier deposits, at this time it is not possible to winnow out Early or Middle period units. Little wonder that visiting archaeologists were unable to see the 1930s data as representative of anything but an indivisible Mississippian culture and despaired of creating any kind of internal culture sequence.

VESSEL FORMS

Although the vast majority of sherds in the assemblage are body sherds, it is the rims that offer the best indication of vessel form. The following figures are based on the rims, from midden and feature contexts, that are large enough to allow confident recognition of vessel form.

Early Wickliffe middens include seventy-seven rims of recognizable vessel form (Table 5.9, Figure 5.7CD). Jar forms predominate, followed by bowls and pans. There are two hooded bottle rims, one funnel rim, and one sherd that may be from a straight-necked bottle, although this identification is dubious. The primary Early Wickliffe assemblage, then, consists of jars, bowls, and pans.

In the Middle Wickliffe middens, represented by 152 rims, all of the same forms occur except the straight-necked bottle, and there is a new form, the flare-rimmed bowl. As noted previously, O'Byam Incised *var. Adams* occurs on this type of bowl. The form occurs only as a trace in the Late Wickliffe period. The flare-rimmed bowl, whether decorated or plain, is evidently a marker for the Middle Wickliffe period.

Table 5.9. Wickliffe Vessel Form Sequence and Serving Vessel/Jar Ratios

	Jars	Bowls	Flared Bowls	Plates	Bottles	Hooded Bottles	Pans	Funnels	Total Rims	Sample Size	Serving Ratio
Late middens											
Mound B	8	6	1	2	1		4	1	23	1212	1.12
Mound C 92	52	37	3	10	6	2	9	3	122	10,204	0.96
East Midden 83		Not analyzed								792	
East Midden 87	42	21		4	1	1	10	9	88	3823	0.6
Mound F 85		Combined with 1986									
Mound F 86	7	4		1			3	3	18	1851	0.71
NW Village	43	30		19	3	4	6	6	111	8538	1.14
NC Village 89	68	32	3	15	4	7	19	5	153	11,213	0.74
NC Village 90	4	2					1		7	1364	0.5
NC Village 94	4	4	2	4	2		1	2	19	2417	2.5
Mound G 95	38	10		7			6	4	65	2818	0.45
Mound G 96	4								4	459	0
Mound H	19	7	3	7	1		4	2	43	1579	0.89
Subtotal	289	153	12	69	18	14	63	35	653	46,270	0.81
All late deposits	327	165	12	83	20	16	73	40	736	62,154	0.8
Middle middens											
Mound B	11	2	11				9	1	34	1383	1.18
Mound C 91	21		4			1	3		29	1006	0.19
Mound C 92	7	2	1				5	1	16	639	0.42
Mound D South	4		3						7	151	0.75
NW Village	4	1					2	1	8	485	0.25

Continued

Table 5.9. *Continued*

	Jars	Bowls	Flared Bowls	Plates	Bottles	Hooded Bottles	Pans	Funnels	Total Rims	Sample Size	Serving Ratio
NC Village 89	21	5	2	2		1	6	3	40	1344	0.43
NC Village 90	4	1		1			1		7	492	0.5
NC Village 94	6	1							7	442	0.17
Mound G 96	4								4	22	0
Mound H										134	
Subtotal	82	12	21	3		2	26	6	152	6098	0.44
All middle deposits	127	21	32	4	2	4	45	7	242	11,030	0.45
Early middens											
Mound A*	12	1			1		6		20	650	0.08
Mound B										73	
Mound C 92	2	6							8	221	3
Mound D North	17	7					5		29	652	0.41
NW Village	8	1					1		10	307	0.12
NC Village 89	5	2				2		1	10	524	0.4
Mound H										150	
Subtotal	44	17			1	2	12	1	77	2577	0.39
All early deposits	47	18			1	2	13	1	82	3571	0.38
Total	501	204	44	87	23	22	131	48	1060	76,755	0.67

NW, Northwest; *NC*, North Central.
*Includes 1984 and 1985 samples.

There are 653 recognizable rims in the Late Wickliffe assemblage. True plates mark this period. (Three plate rims occur in the Middle Wickliffe middens, but two are from the North Village 1989 sample that is noted for its potential for disturbance [Chapter 18]; it is clear that the plate belongs primarily to the Late Wickliffe period. Part of the problem here is also that "flared bowl" and "plate" were defined visually and not by an objective measure.) Plate rims range in width from 25 to 67 millimeters and include both plain and incised specimens, the latter denoting O'Byam Incised *var. O'Byam.* Most plates have a fine, Bell Plain paste, but Mississippi Plain plates occur. The Late Wickliffe assemblage also includes straight-necked, short-necked, and hooded bottles and of course jars, pans, and funnels. The same patterns appear when all deposits, not just middens, are considered (Table 5.9, Figures 5.8 and 5.9).

The sequence is best marked by the bowl to flared bowl to plate develop-ment, but there are other, less conspicuous trends. This set of comparisons may be problematic. Identifiable rims comprise more than 2 percent of the Early and Middle Wickliffe sherd assemblages, but only 1.18 percent of the Late Wickliffe assemblages. Thus comparing the percentage of jar rims, for instance, among the total period assemblages may skew chronological trends. The trends must be studied in relationship both to total assemblage (Figure 5.8) and to rim totals (Figure 5.9). However, the trends are consistent by either measure.

Jars and pans diminish in the Late Wickliffe period. Bowls decrease in percentage in the Middle period, perhaps displaced by the new style of flaring

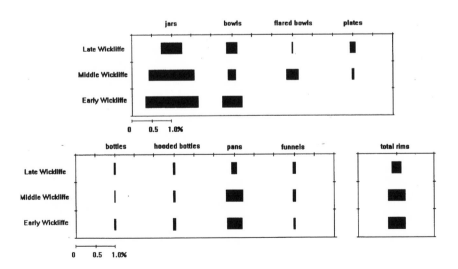

5.8. Rim forms, summary, all deposits, as percentage of assemblage.

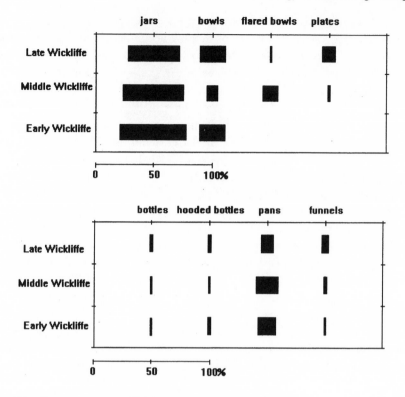

5.9. Rim forms, summary, all deposits, as percentage of rims.

the rim, then resurge in the Late period even as plates gain in popularity. Hooded bottles are present throughout the sequence. Straight-neck bottles, however, increase in proportion, and if the dubious single Early Wickliffe bottle rim is rejected, bottles appear in Middle Wickliffe and increase into the Late Wickliffe period. Funnels increase through time, by little coincidence mirroring the increase in the Wickliffe Thick type. The relationship between the pan and the Kimmswick Fabric Impressed sequences is equally intriguing but less direct, since pans include sherds that have no fabric impression and thus are identified as Mississippi Plain in the type counts.

If jars are broadly assumed to be cooking vessels, and plates and bowls taken to be serving vessels (cf. Hally 1984:59–63; Pauketat 1987), the ratio of serving to cooking vessels rises with time: from .38 in Early Wickliffe, to .45 in Middle Wickliffe, to .80 in Late Wickliffe collections (Table 5.9). Comparisons within periods emphasize one significant highlight. The Mound B Middle Wickliffe midden serving ratio is markedly high, higher even than the Late Wickliffe ratios. (The 2.5 serving ratio in the Late Wickliffe North Central Village 1994 assemblage will be disregarded for now, since the combined North Central

Village serving ratio is .82, extremely close to the overall Late period ratio.). If Mound B supported an elite residence, then evidently the elite led the trend toward increased use of serving vessels. This trend may have to do with changing foodways and, if so, may reflect styles in serving food, styles in preparing food, or choices of foods to prepare—or some combination of all three.

Pans, like jars, decrease proportionally through the sequence. Observations of similar shallow vessels in West Africa (see Wesler 1998) suggest that pans are probably general-purpose cooking vessels, boiling pans, and griddles, rather than special-purpose vessels as the common term *salt pan* would imply. Thus, the decline in pans, paralleling that in jars, reinforces the marked increase in the ratio of serving to cooking vessels.

Comparison with ceramics from the Lower Tennessee-Cumberland area and the Angel site supports the chronology by identifying horizon markers of vessel form and handle form across the Lower Ohio Valley (Clay, Hilgeman, and Wesler 1991). In particular, the Angel sequence is well documented with radiocarbon dates and seriation, and both the plate rim and handle measures presented here are adopted from Hilgeman's (1992) usage. At Angel, Hilgeman (1992:61–62) distinguishes large deep plates (rims 82–122 millimeters wide), deep plates (66–81 millimeters), large plates (56–65 millimeters), and small plates (28–55 millimeters), and by implication flared bowls with rims narrower than 28 millimeters. The most important division is between plates and deep plates, dividing at about 66 millimeters. O'Byam Incised *var. Adams,* on flared bowls, and O'Byam Incised *var. O'Byam,* on plates, are present but not abundant (Hilgeman 1992:66).

Hilgeman (1992:171) also defines handle form by a ratio of thickness to width. Wickliffe handle measurements are given below, but for now it will suffice to note that they conform closely to the Angel site sequence (Figures 5.10CD and 5.11CD).

Hilgeman's (1992:280–305) seriated and radiocarbon-dated ceramic sequence for Angel Mounds creates a strong parallel to both the Lower Tennessee-Cumberland (Clay 1979) and Wickliffe sequences. The Stephan-Steinkamp phase (potentially Angel 1) is similar to the Jonathan Creek phase (Clay 1979) and Early Wickliffe period, including characteristic loop handles and the lack of plate forms. Angel 2, A.D. 1200 to 1325, is roughly equivalent to the Angelly phase (Clay 1979; Butler 1977; cf. Pollack and Railey 1987) and Middle/Late Wickliffe, with narrow and wide intermediate handles, flared bowls, and plates. Hilgeman (1992:290) sees some indication of a division between Angel 2A, with flared bowls, and 2B, with plates, similar to the Middle-Late Wickliffe sequence. Unfortunately no Angelly phase data are available to check for this subdivision.

Hilgeman's (1992:291–92) Angel 3 phase is marked in part by wide intermediate and strap handles and deep plates. In this, it closely parallels the Tinsley

Hill phase (Clay 1979), where the decorated deep plate form is expressed as O'Byam Incised *var. Stewart.* These forms occur only as trace elements in the Wickliffe site (Figure 5.12CD), mostly in uninterpretable contexts in the King collection; two sherds of O'Byam Incised *var. Stewart* recovered in 1993 and 1994 are the only ones whose exact proveniences are known, and they were recovered from the plowzone. The small number of strap handles and deep plate rims, the plowzone context of the well-documented specimens of deep plates, and the radiocarbon dates (above) all suggest that Wickliffe was abandoned by very early in the Angel 3/Tinsley Hill phase time frame.

Late Wickliffe ceramics lack characteristics of protohistoric assemblages such as Nodena of northeastern Arkansas (Morse 1990:88–90) and Caborn-Welborn of southern Indiana and midwestern Kentucky (Green and Munson 1978), including foot rings, stirrup-neck and double bottle forms, red and white and polychrome painted pottery, and incised swastika motifs, although the seventeenth-century presence of at least some of these features in the Reelfoot Lake area of Tennessee and Kentucky is attested by recent work (Lawrence and Mainfort 1991). These elements are missing in Angel 3 and Tinsley Hill, also, indicating that these phases do not extend into the protohistoric period. Plate rims of the Caborn-Welborn phase are longer than those at Angel (Hilgeman 1992:300). Protohistoric handles in Caborn-Welborn assemblages (Green and Munson 1978; Hilgeman 1992:300) and in the Armorel phase of northeastern Arkansas (Williams 1980) become appliqué embellishments, effectively reducing the thickness-to-width ratio to 0.

The Lower Ohio Valley bowl to plate sequence parallels the Wells to Crable sequence of the American Bottom (Kelly 1984), and calibration of the American Bottom dates by the CALIB program (Hall 1991) brings the chronology reasonably in line with the Lower Ohio Valley sequence, already so calibrated.

The Angel sequence (Hilgeman 1992) was defined utilizing radiocarbon dates and seriated ceramic assemblages. The Lower Tennessee-Cumberland sequence was derived from a number of sites and associated radiocarbon dates (Clay 1979). At the Wickliffe site, radiocarbon dates, OCR dates, stratigraphy, and ceramic assemblages inform the sequence. Each of the chronological sequences was derived independently, but the concordances among them are clear. Most striking are the consistent progressions of bowl to deep plate, and loop to strap handle.

FORMULA DATING

The ceramic evidence showed that flared bowls, plate rims, and certain decorative and vessel types behaved as horizon markers for the Wickliffe periods. Parallel evidence from the Angel site (Hilgeman 1992) and the Lower

Tennessee-Cumberland region indicated that some of the markers can be extended throughout the Lower Ohio Valley (Clay, Hilgeman, and Wesler 1991), and in the flared bowl to deep plate progression perhaps into the American Bottom (Kelly 1984; Vogel 1975), as horizons that will form a framework for a coherent regional Mississippian chronological sequence.

The concepts of horizon and horizon style (Willey and Phillips 1958:32–33) are the bases of formula dating methods as utilized in historical archaeology. In creating a dating formula, the first step is to "build a chronological model" (South 1977:207). Formula dating was introduced for use on British-manufactured kaolin pipestems, in which horizons of decreasing bore-diameter size were fitted to a model characterized by a linear regression (Binford 1961; Harrington 1954). Early disapprobation of the pipestem formula (A. Noel Hume 1963) eventually subsided as repeated application demonstrated its utility (I. Noel Hume 1970:300), at least as a useful approximator.

Binford's (1961) pipestem formula was based on Binford and Maxwell's (1961) revision of Harrington's (1954) observations and trial, just as Ball's (1983) window glass regression was based in part on observation and trial by Cinadr and Brose (1978) at the Carr Mill in Warren County, Ohio. Similarly, the observed horizons in Lower Ohio Valley Mississippian ceramics will set the parameters for trial plate rim width and handle thickness dating formulas.

The date A.D. 1175 marks the introduction of the flared bowl at Wickliffe. At the Angel site, occupied until about A.D. 1450, the maximum width of plate rims is 122 millimeters (Hilgeman 1992). Thus, a formula may be constructed for date D:

$$D = \text{A.D. } 1175 + (1450 - 1175)(x/122), \text{ where } x = \text{rim width (mm)}.$$

Rim widths are vessel interior measurements taken from the outer lip to the break between the relatively flat rim and the curving bowl. Scalloped rims are measured at their widest point.

The results of the formula when applied to the small samples at Wickliffe (Table 5.10CD) are encouraging. Of seven Late Wickliffe samples, six fit within the period as defined by carbon 14 and OCR dates. The last, from the North Central Village 1994 unit, is not only a small sample, but also its rim sample is already known to be unusual (see Vessel Forms, above). The dates for all Late Wickliffe middens and for all Late Wickliffe deposits fall into the 1250s.

Of four Middle Wickliffe samples, only one (North Village 1990) yields a date later than the period limits. The late date is based on a sample size of one. The combined Middle Wickliffe middens sample yields a Middle Wickliffe date, as does the combined sample from all Middle Wickliffe deposits.

A handle formula may be similarly defined, taking Angel site data as a model. Hilgeman (1992:171) defines handle form by a ratio of thickness to width. At Angel, loop handles are those with ratios falling between .75 and 1.0; intermediate handles may be divided between narrow and wide, with ratios of .39 to .56 and .57 to .74, respectively; and strap handle ratios range from .10 to .38.

Arbitrarily setting A.D. 1000 as a base for Mississippi period handle development and A.D. 1500 for the end, and a thickness/width ratio at 1 for the first loop handles and 0 for late appliqué pseudostraps,

D = A.D. 1500 − 500r, where r = thickness/width.

Measurable handle samples from Wickliffe contexts are larger than plate samples (Table 5.11CD). Of eleven Late Wickliffe samples, five fit within the period, and two miss by five years. The Late Wickliffe midden total, and the total for all Late Wickliffe deposits, fall within the period and compare very closely to the plate formula date for all Late deposits and all Late middens.

For eight Middle Wickliffe samples, five fall within the period. Two are too late, and one too early. The dates for all Middle middens and all Middle deposits, however, fall within the period and compare tolerably well with the plate formula dates. The early date, and one of the late dates, are based on samples of one.

Finally, of five Early Wickliffe midden deposits, all with samples of one or two specimens, only one produces a handle date later than A.D. 1175, the beginning of the Middle period. The dates for all Early middens, and all Early deposits, are twelfth-century dates. Since Early Wickliffe has no serving vessels except bowls, these dates cannot be compared with plate formula dates.

In general, the larger the sample, the better its computed date fits the period parameters. In this, the parallels to the pipe stem (Binford 1961) and mean ceramic date (South 1977) formulas in historical archaeology are evident.

To date, only Gramly (1992:91) has attempted a test of one of the formulas on data from somewhere besides western Kentucky. At the Revnik site, in Stewart County, Tennessee, Gramly recovered nine plate rims ranging in width from 36 to 62 millimeters (within the Late Wickliffe/Angelly/Angel 2 range). Gramly's calculated plate rim date is A.D. 1305. He notes, however, that this date is a poor fit with the average of four (uncalibrated) radiocarbon dates, A.D. 1394 ± 41. Gramly used an earlier version of the formula (Wesler 1994), but calibrating the date and using the current version of the formula only makes the discrepancy worse.

Clearly further tests on well provenienced samples with associated radiocarbon dates are needed before the Wickliffe formulas can be accepted as having wider utility. It is possible that Gramly's data show regional differences in the chronology of the plate rim sequence, which can be explored by comparisons of both handle and plate measurements.

A comparison of dates between the chronometric (carbon 14 and OCR) and formula dating methods shows a great deal of consistency (Table 5.12). Of course, the linear regression formulas for handle and plate measurements are based on the results of radiocarbon and OCR dating, so that they are

Table 5.12. Comparison of Dating Methods (All Dates A.D.)

Carbon 14 Dates		OCR Dates		Plate Formula	Handle Formula
Late Wickliffe					
ISGS-1171	1260 (1286) 1382	ACT 2358	1251	1252	1235
Beta-25911	1217 (1265, 1266, 1277) 1289	ACT 2131	1179[a]	1256	1265
Beta-25219	1224 (1282) 1298	ACT 2351	1348	1265	1285
Beta-25220	1262 (1284) 1295	ACT 2352	1073[b]	1307	1195
Beta-27506	1224 (1281) 1293	ACT 2353	1242[b]	1213	1245
Beta-27507	1305 (1334, 1338, 1402) 1422	ACT 2354	1186[b]	1258	1220
Beta-33584	1214 (1279) 1295	ACT 2137	1284	1244	1340
Beta-33585	1212 (1279) 1297	ACT 2138	1250		1285
		ACT 2349	1326		1310
		ACT 2139	1240		1235
		ACT 2356	1306		1215
		ACT 2134	1223		
Average	1280 (1286) 1293	Range (middens)	1223-1348	Average 1258	Average 1255
Middle Wickliffe					
ISGS-1143	1157 (1218) 1280	ACT 2132	1211	1225	1205
ISGS-1156	1217 (1279) 1293	ACT 2135	1189	1205	1190
Beta-25217	900 (1002, 1010, 1017) 1151	ACT 2136	1153	1243	1340
				1315	1245
					1390
					1205
					1075
					1235
Average	1158 (1212) 1259	Range	1153-1211	Average 1225	Average 1210
Early Wickliffe					
Beta-25218	1026 (1071, 1080, 1128, 1136, 1154) 1211	ACT 2133	1104		1085
		ACT 2140	1168		1175
		ACT 2141	1153		1085
					1100
					1235
		Range	1104-1153		Average 1155
Subsoil					
		ACT 2359	918		
		ACT 2355	886		
		ACT 2350	996		
		ACT 2357	990		

[a]Redeposited by digging house basin.
[b]Mound fill.

not independent tests; but the consistency among the formula dates within periods, especially for larger samples, lends support to their potential utility.

The apparent precision of any dating method that generates a single number (read as a calendar year) is illusive. Environmental factors, measurement errors, and definitions of context in the field are flawlessly controlled only in rare cases. All dates must be evaluated with respect to all available contextual data. The current assignment of periods to units of 75 or 100 years reflects an arbitrary rounding, and the specific years chosen as period markers must be accepted as approximations. Nonetheless, the concordance between the radiocarbon and OCR dates from Wickliffe lends confidence to the general chronology of the Wickliffe periods.

ASSEMBLAGE PATTERNING

The relative standardization of the ceramic types in the scattered test areas around the Wickliffe site, especially within the intrasite periods, has been noted. Percentages of type categories vary across only a few percentage points. Decorated types, generally only about 1 percent of the entire assemblage, vary by fractions of a percentage point from sample to sample. The consistency of the assemblages is striking.

The implication of the figures is that, as regards ceramic types, the village is very homogeneous, especially in the Late Wickliffe period. A search for intravillage patterns of the subtlety required for the identification of residential or other activity sectors in a small village calls for additional measures. A modification of South's (1977) assemblage patterning method offers an alternative approach.

South, of course, developed his patterns on historic sites. Mississippian societies, though generally lumped under the label of "complex societies," are not directly comparable in geographic scale or socioeconomic complexity to the British colonial frontier. However, the reasoning behind the South method does not confine it to historical archaeology. South's "basic assumption is that each household . . . represents a system within a much larger system of complex variables, with the larger system imposing on each household a degree of uniformity in the relationships among its behavioral parts. . . . The basic postulate here is the assumption that there was a patterned casting off of behavioral by-products around an occupation site that might be viewed as a per capita, per year contribution to the archaeological record" (South 1977:86–87).

South's initial hope was to differentiate sites in settled areas and on frontiers, and eventually, with a great deal of data, to find ways of distinguishing cultural patterns such as British-American from German-American from French-American colonial settlements. The technique has been criticized.

Orser (1989), for instance, suggests that South's patterns are not useful because they are too broad and are diachronically insensitive. South (1988:25), indeed, finds that pattern recognition as usually practiced has been "particularistic, inductivistic exercises in identification and labeling."

These are problems of application rather than concept. Use of the technique on nineteenth-century sites in western Kentucky found it at least as useful for distinguishing areas within houselots (Wesler 1984, 1987) as in intersite comparisons. Either way, the pattern studies reflect South's goal of searching for "broad regularities . . . against which any deviation from such regularity can be contrasted as reflecting behavior somewhat different from expected margins" (South 1977:86).

Within a Mississippian site such as Wickliffe Mounds, the identification of an area that departs from the broader regularity would be useful to identify possible residential sectors or activity areas. These concerns are quite normal for prehistoric studies, but for the most part, the studies rely on spatial clustering of marker artifacts to distinguish such areas. Whether the markers occur in significant concentrations, thus indicating a distinct assemblage, is not always clearly measured. Artifact group patterning is a technique designed to search for assemblage variation.

The initial problem in applying South's technique to the Wickliffe site is that the categories he used do not fit directly into Mississippian data. The idea of separating functional categories, and combining artifact categories into larger groups, however, is appropriate. Several categories useful on historic sites are not transferable to Wickliffe: it is difficult to distinguish "Furniture" artifacts, for instance, and the only distinctive "Architecture" group artifact is daub, which is no more to be considered for this study than South used brick. To separate "Clothing" from "Personal" artifacts, in cases such as beads, or from "Activities," in cases such as a needle or awl, presents similar problems. South's "Tobacco" group was composed only of ball clay pipe stems, because of their usually great quantity in American colonial sites. Although tobacco pipes do of course occur in Mississippian sites, they seem to fit better into the "Activities" group, just as South included stub-stemmed pipes in historic sites.

Categories appropriate to Wickliffe, then, are Ceramics, Arms, Personal, Activities, and Debitage. In historic sites, the "Kitchen" group includes a number of artifact classes other than ceramics. In the Wickliffe database, it includes only ceramics and is so designated. South's distinction between Kitchen and Subsistence, which would include tools like hoes or fishhooks, better relegated to Activities, is also useful. Debitage is, like South's Tobacco group, a single but very numerous artifact class and thus given its own group. The Arms group includes stone, antler, and bone projectile points, in order of decreasing frequency.

The ad hoc hypothesis that inspired this experiment is that two artifact groups ought to be most significant in defining intravillage variability: a disproportionate Activities group should indicate functional areas, and a high Personal group percentage might indicate higher-status residential sectors.

The Bone group presents a particular problem, as South discussed for his historic sites. Faunal remains carry a great deal of information, but are affected differently by preservation factors than the other artifact classes. Faunal remains have not been included in this analysis.

There are clear trends in the major artifact groups (Tables 5.13CD and 5.14, Figures 5.13CD, 5.14, 5.15CD, and 5.16CD). Ceramics increase in proportion through time, and debitage decreases. Among the middens, the Personal and Activity groups are best represented in the Middle Wickliffe period. Arms (projectile points), however, are most numerous in the Late Wickliffe period. The Mound B Middle Wickliffe midden, which is the likely elite deposit, is notably lacking in distinguishing characteristics in any category, in contrast to its serving vessel ratio.

The striking note is the consistency of the patterns within periods. The Late village is represented by the most samples, the biggest samples, and the most spatially varied samples; yet the percentages of pottery types and of artifact groups are extremely consistent. The Late Wickliffe village is very homogeneous, and there is no indication at all of any differentiation in residential sectors.

Table 5.14. Wickliffe Artifact Groups, Summaries by Deposit Type and Period

	Ceramics	Arms	Personal	Activities	Debitage	Total
Middens						
Late	47,587	110	45	298	30,795	78,835
Middle	6231	7	12	71	6065	12,386
Early	2637	3	3	24	3142	5809
Subtotal	56,455	120	60	393	40,002	97,030
Features						
Late	4051	9	4	32	2222	6318
Middle	863	2	2	6	984	1857
Early	923	1	1	13	1230	2168
Subtotal	5837	12	7	51	4436	10,343
Mound deposits						
Late	12,633	16	7	68	8113	20,837
Middle	4270	1	9	30	2605	6915
Early	158		1		156	315
Subtotal	17,061	17	17	98	10,874	28,067
Total	29,353	149	84	542	55,312	135,440

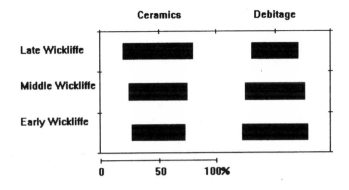

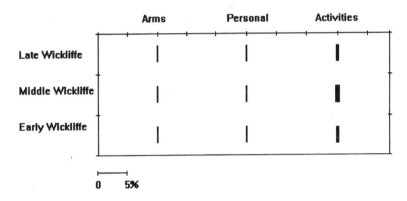

5.14. Midden artifact groups, summary by period.

Within the smaller artifact groups, Table 5.15 summarizes the distributions of various artifact classes from all midden contexts. These figures include contexts not summarized elsewhere, such as profile cuttings and balks from units in which the entire deposit was Late Wickliffe, but not similar contexts from stratified units.

The assemblage appears fairly consistent through time. Pottery trowels, astragalus dice, and most ornaments are missing in the Early Wickliffe period. However, because the Late Wickliffe sample is so much greater than that of the earlier periods, and the occurrence of these items in the Late assemblage is relatively rare, it is difficult to place much significance on the lack of any item in the Early assemblages.

On the basis of the assemblage totals in Table 5.15, the proportions of chipped stone artifacts (projectile points plus drills plus bifaces) is highest in the Middle Wickliffe period, but still much higher in Late Wickliffe than in Early Wickliffe—contrary to the generally diminishing proportion

Table 5.15. Selected Arms, Personal, and Activity Items by Period

	Late	Middle	Early	Disturbed/ Unassigned	King Mound D	King Mound E	King Mound F	Total
Clay disc/discoidal	42	12	4	13	34	12	16	133
Pottery trowel	8	3		3	30	4	13	61
Pipe		2	1		5	1	3	12
Lithic projectile point	105	8	4	77	153	26	44	417
Lithic drill	26	3	2	14	4	3	2	54
Lithic biface	123	22	4	98	89	94	36	466
Sharpener	18	2	1	9	5	3	6	44
Stone disc/discoidal	11	1	2	2	4	6	3	29
Bone awl	6	3	3	8	54	16	27	117
Bone pin	6	6	1	9	28	6	15	71
Antler projectile point	8	4	1	4	31	16	11	75
Bone fishhook	1	4	5	5	12	6	3	36
Astragalus dice	3	1				3	5	12
Bone disc					7		1	8
Bone tool	11	9	4	24	8	10	4	70
Bead*	38	14	3	141	8		1	205
Ear/lip plug*	12	4		7	1	1	2	27
Gorget*		1		1	8	1	1	12
Ornament*	7	5	2	14	9		2	37

*Any material.

of debitage. The number of drills is low throughout the occupation. The proportion of bifaces is highest in the Middle Wickliffe period, which is reflected in the minor peak of the Activities group. The proportion of chipped stone projectile points, however, rises sharply from Early to Middle and then rises again in the Late Wickliffe period. Antler projectile points in particular, and bone tools in general, fit the biface pattern, best represented in the Middle Wickliffe period.

Because of the large sample from Late Wickliffe deposits, the situation that items are present in Early or Middle deposits but not in Late deposits takes on potential significance and is relevant to two artifact classes: ceramic pipes and bone fishhooks. Pipes are rare in either earlier period. It is intuitively unlikely that smoking pipes were no longer in use in the Late period, since tobacco use is so important to Native American traditions and is well attested in the historical record. Fishhooks, however, are not so unusual an occurrence. Yet, only one was found in a Late Wickliffe deposit, and this one was from level 5 in Mound B's 40–42N6–7E, which incorporated both midden and mound fill, raising a question of whether it may have been redeposited in the mound fill.

This is a rather intriguing finding. It is unfortunate that the King collection is not analyzable well enough to assess its contexts, since it includes eighteen provenienced fishhooks. It is possible to say, however, that almost all of them occur at or near the base level of their respective excavation units (e.g., for a fishhook labeled ME 50R9 1L, Level 1 is the deepest attested level in 50R9 from Mound E). Only a single King collection fishhook does not fit this pattern (ME 80R10 1L, where there is a 3L for that square). Whether that one fishhook will disrupt the pattern is impossible to say at this time, but since Level 1 would include plowzone, it will be very difficult to place much faith in its context in any case.

SUMMARY

The occupation of the Wickliffe Mounds site can be divided into three periods: Early Wickliffe, A.D. 1100–1175; Middle Wickliffe, A.D. 1175–1250; and Late Wickliffe, A.D. 1250–1350. The periods are defined primarily on changes in ceramic sherd assemblages. The period assemblages were defined first in Mound A, raising a question about whether the mound fill deposits reflected mixing of soils from original contexts of different times, but subsequent excavations demonstrated that the period assemblages were consistent in their stratigraphic relationships throughout the site. The King collection of ceramics from Mounds D, E, and F is consistent with Late Wickliffe assemblages from the WMRC excavations, allowing for some mixture from earlier deposits, so that it may be treated provisionally as a systematic and representative assemblage. Analysis of radiocarbon and OCR samples provided calendric dates that were consistent with each other and with soils contexts as defined by the ceramic sequence.

Further study of assemblage patterns among the periods indicated that both handle thickness/width ratios and plate rim widths changed through time. Simple dating formulas based on these trends offer potential application to other regional sites.

Other patterns also distinguish assemblages from the three periods. Several trends are related to subsistence and foodways: an increase in the ratio of serving vessels to cooking vessels through time, led by the probable elite occupants of Mound B, and loss of fishhooks coupled with a sudden increase in projectile points in the Late Wickliffe period. As proportions of the entire assemblage, ceramics increase through time while debitage decreases. The Middle Wickliffe period is particularly marked by small peaks in the proportions of Personal and Activity group artifacts.

The original definition of the three Wickliffe periods, based as they were on relatively small changes in proportions among some categories of ceramics, is thus sustained by the consistency of other patterns and trends among the various samples from around the site. The Wickliffe sequence is robust and well dated and allows further analysis into temporal and spatial patterning within the village, as considered in the next chapter.

6 Subsistence and Social Patterning

The Wickliffe Mounds Research Center (WMRC) excavations at Wickliffe Mounds have produced a large body of material remains and associated data, distributed widely across the site. Not all of the data have been analyzed fully, but a number of consulting scholars have studied various samples, and their contributions have begun to create a multifaceted picture of the Mississippian people who lived at the site. Questions of subsistence practices and diets, organization of the village and activities within it, the nature of the social structure, and Wickliffe's place in a regional setting can be investigated. The archaeological record also offers some indication of human activities of the more recent past, activities alien to yet stimulated by the former Mississippian presence.

SUBSISTENCE

Faunal Remains

Both the King and the WMRC excavations recovered large assemblages of animal remains.

Reinburg (1987) analyzed the faunal remains in the King collection (Table 6.1). As with the ceramics, most of the collection represents the gridded excavations from Mounds D, E, and F. Because Reinburg undertook this rather daunting task well before WMRC researchers had made any progress toward understanding the contexts of those mounds, she treated the collection as a single assemblage in her analysis, although each specimen was coded individually and thus eventually will be studied further for distributional and perhaps temporal patterns.

Reinburg's primary goal was to test the Wickliffe data against Smith's (1975) model of animal exploitation and simultaneously to demonstrate the generally representative nature of the King collection. The King collection compares well with Smith's (1975) test sites in terms of the animals most exploited and the projected meat yields. Deer is the primary meat source, with raccoon and turkey important secondary resources. Waterfowl are diverse and slightly better represented in the King collection than in Smith's sites, perhaps because of Wickliffe's proximity to large river bottoms of the Mississippi flyway, presently celebrated for goose and duck hunting. Reinburg did not analyze the fish, reptiles, and amphibians for mean number of individuals (MNI) or projected

Table 6.1. Catalog of Faunal Remains in the King Collection (Reinburg 1987)

Species	Elements	MNI
Mammals		
Odocoileus virginianus White tailed deer	6677	185
Didelphus marsupialis Opossum	64	12
Procyon lotor Raccoon	341	29
Castor canadensis Beaver	52	6
Lutra canadensis River otter	6	2
Sylvilagus floridanus Eastern cottontail	167	23
Sylvilagus aquaticus Swamp rabbit	200	21
Sylvilagus spp. Rabbit	66	14
Sciurus carolinensis Grey squirrel	246	40
Sciurus niger Fox squirrel	826	117
Sciurus spp. Squirrel	26	3
Vulpes vulpes Red fox	3	2
Ursus americanus Black bear	20	1
Canis familiaris Dog	178	7
Spilogale putorius Spotted skunk	2	2
Mephitis mephitis Striped skunk	13	2
Mephitis/Spilogale Skunk	10	5
Marmota monax Woodchuck	10	4
Lynx rufus Bobcat	1	1
Tamias striatus Eastern chipmunk	1	1
Canis latrans Coyote	1	1
Canis/Vulpes Fox	2	1
Urocyon cinereoargenteus Grey fox	15	1
Mustela vison Mink	8	3
Ondatra zibethicus Muskrat	28	3
Felis concolor Mountain lion	1	1
Sigmodon hispidus Hispid cotton rat	2	1
Carnivore	1	
Pig	11	
Cow	16	
Rodent	10	
Oryzomys palustris Rice rat	14	
Unidentified	10,107	
Mammals total	19,125	488
Birds		
Branta canadensis Canada goose	53	19
Chen caerulescens/hyperborea Blue/snow goose	5	2
Anser albifrons White fronted goose	54	12
Anas platyrhynchos/rubripes Mallard/black duck	581	104
Anas spp. Mallard/black/pintail	146	25
Anas discors Blue winged teal	9	6
Anas strepera Gadwall	2	1
Oxyura jamaicensis Ruddy duck	21	9

Continued

Table 6.1. *Continued*

Species	Elements	MNI
Aix sponsa Wood duck	15	12
Tympanuchus cupido Greater prairie chicken	36	9
Meleagris gallopavo Wild turkey	478	45
Corvus brachyrynchos Common crow	5	1
Strix varia Barred owl	4	3
Ectopistes migratorius Passenger pigeon	67	15
Fulica americana American coot	1	1
Buteo jamaicensis Red-tailed hawk	5	1
Buteo lagopus Rough-winged hawk	1	1
Buteo lineatus Red-shouldered hawk	3	1
Circus cyaneus Marsh hawk	1	1
Falco peregrinus Peregrine falcon	1	1
Grus canadensis Sandhill crane	3	1
Podilymbus podiceps Pied-billed grebe	1	1
Cygnus columbianus (?) Whistling swan	1	1
Cygnus olor Mute swan	1	1
Phasianidae family Quail	5	2
Rallus sp. Rail	3	1
Agelaius phoenicius Redwinged blackbird	2	1
Turdus migratorius Robin	1	1
Nyctea scandiaca Snowy owl	1	1
Cathartes aura Turkey vulture	1	1
Asio flammeus Short eared owl	1	1
Bonasa umbellus Ruffed grouse	3	1
Ardea herodius Great blue heron	1	1
Campephilus principalis Ivory billed woodpecker	2	2
Megaceryle alcyon Belted kingfisher	1	1
Gallus various Chicken	19	10
Unidentified	1499	
Birds total	3033	296
Amphibians and reptiles		
Chelydra serpentina Snapping turtle	2	
Terrapene carolina Box turtle	71	
Chrysemys picta Painted turtle	8	
Pseudemys scripta/floridana Pond slider/cooter	4	
Trionyx sp. Softshell turtle	8	
Kinosternon subrubrum Mud turtle	2	
Crotalidae Poisonous snake	1	
Colubridae Nonpoisonous snake	1	
Unidentified turtle	28	
Total amphibian and reptile	125	
Fish		
Amia calva Bowfin	65	

Continued

Table 6.1. *Continued*

Species	Elements	MNI
Clupeidai sp. Shad	3	
Lepisosteus sp. Gar	105	
Catostomidae family Suckers	66	
Perciformes sp.	9	
Aplodinotus grunniens Freshwater drum	131	
Ictalurus punctatus/furcatus Channel/blue catfish	9	
Pylodictus olivarus Flathead catfish	24	
Ictalurus sp. Catfish/bullhead	39	
Ictiobus bubalus Smallmouth buffalofish	1	
Ictiobus sp. Buffalofish	5	
Unidentified	215	
Total fish	672	
TOTAL	22,955	

meat yield because of the relatively small sample—the King faunal collection clearly is biased toward large specimens, although some small and surprisingly delicate elements are included.

Kreisa and McDowell (Chapter 15) discuss provocative data from a sample of faunal remains from the WMRC excavations. They studied more than 30,000 specimens, only a sample of those available. They identified seventy-six taxa, indicating a diverse diet.

Their analysis also indicated some change through time, information that the King collection is not capable of providing at the present stage of study. Through the Wickliffe occupation, the contribution of deer to the assemblage increases, while the proportion of elements of high and medium meat utility decreases—evidently hunting of deer and utilization of their carcasses grew more intense. Among avian prey, turkeys increase in prevalence whereas waterfowl use decreases. Meat yields from fish, by contrast, decline, especially from the Early to the Middle Wickliffe period and continue to diminish into the Late Wickliffe period. The Wickliffe villagers retreated particularly from using backwater species, since the proportion of riverine species among the fish increased.

The common theme seems to be a shift in focus away from the river bottoms, toward upland mammals and fowl and riverine fish. Kreisa and McDowell (Chapter 15) suggest possible explanations: perhaps the course of the Mississippi River swung closer to the bluff at Wickliffe, destroying the adjacent floodplain, or perhaps other nearby villages became more aggressive about claiming larger shares of local bottomlands.

Kreisa and McDowell's observations are consistent with other analyses. Reinburg (1987) suggested that the small number of fish bones in the King collection probably resulted from the lack of screening in the Kings' excavations, so that small fish bones were underrepresented. However, since the ceramics from the same excavations closely resemble a Late Wickliffe assemblage, so may the faunal collection, and Reinburg's dearth of fish may well be an accurate reflection of the same trend discovered by Kreisa and McDowell.

Too, the discussion in Chapter 5 noted that fishhooks dropped out of the assemblages, and evidently out of use, in the Late Wickliffe period. It was not clear whether this situation implied a change in fishing techniques, such as an increased emphasis on nets, or a general deemphasis on fishing, so that the relative rise in chipped stone projectile points indicated increased reliance on hunting. Kreisa and McDowell's study indicates the latter.

Kreisa and McDowell's (Chapter 15) study included the Mound B middens, likely to be a Middle Wickliffe elite domestic deposit (Chapters 3 and 18). They found that, compared with a sample of the same period from elsewhere in the site, in Mound B deer made up a smaller proportion of the mammal bone but had a higher utility value. The deer in the Mound B middens thus seem to belong to choicer cuts.

Floral Remains

Edging (Chapter 16) has conducted analysis of a number of floated samples from the WMRC collections. He identified ten wood taxa, but three are dominant: hickory, oaks, and cane. These species are abundant locally and may have been utilized heavily for construction. Other tree species are mostly bottomland species. Edging suggests a regional trend toward increasing use of upland trees, perhaps encouraged by progressive clearing of the bottomlands for agricultural fields, diminishing the wood resources in the lowlands.

Edging (Chapter 16) sees variation among the western Kentucky Mississippian sites, but a general emphasis on nuts and, of course, corn. He was unable to identify either beans or tobacco seeds in his samples from Wickliffe. The lack of tobacco may be a sampling deficiency. Edging notes that beans are generally lacking in western Kentucky sites and probably became popular in the Central Mississippi Valley after Wickliffe was abandoned. Recently, Hart and Scarry (1999) reviewed radiocarbon dates and concluded that "beans do not become archaeologically visible in the Northeast until around A.D. 1300," matching Edging's observation.

Shell

Table 6.2 presents Joanna L. Casey's species analysis of the mussel shells in the King collection. Casey's (1986) thesis includes an extensive discussion of shell species, their biology, ranges, habitats, and archaeological occurrences in the lower Ohio and Tennessee-Cumberland rivers region.

Table 6.2. Catalog of Molluscan Remains in the King Collection: Frequency Data by Species and Mound

Species	MD1L	MD2L	MD3L	MD4L	MD5L	MD Misc.	MD Total	ME	MF	Other*	Grand Total
Amblema plicata	3	1	19	31	11	7	72	12	5	30	119
Fusconaia ebena	11	12	24	36	1	31	115	52	64	69	300
Quadrula cylindrica		1	2	1		1	5	1	1		7
Metanevra			2	3	1	1	7	2	3	2	14
Nodulata	1	1	3			1	6			4	10
Pustulosa		3	3	8	2	1	17	3	8	17	45
Quadrula	1		1	5	2		9	2		2	13
Megalonaias gigantea			1				1				1
Tritogonia verrucosa			4	4			8			4	12
Cyclonaias tuberculate	3		2	1	3	4	13	10	7	4	34
Elliptio crassidens	1		1	2		4	8		5		12
Dilatata	8	8	24	37	5	58	140	53	59	26	278
Plethobasus cicatricosus		1	2	2		1	6	5	1		12
Pleurobema clava			1	1			2				2
Cordatum	12	9	20	32	6	37	116	38	81	30	265
Dysnomia arcaeformis	1		1	1		1	4		2		6
Flexuosa			1				1		1	3	5
Torulosa	1	2	2	2	1	8	16	7	5		28
Plagiola lineolata	2		1	1		2	6	4	7	2	19
Lampsilis orbiculate		3		1		1	6	1	2		9
Ovata ventricosa			1	5	1		7		1		8
Radiata siliquoidea	1	1	6	16	5	4	33				33
Teres	2	3	8	10	1	4	24			1	25

Table 6.2. Continued

										Total
Lampsilis spp.						5				5
Ligumia recta		14	23		11	50	16	11	2	81
Obovaria olivaria	2	1	4	1	1	7	2	2	1	9
Retusa		5	7	2	7	24		1		29
Subrotunda		1	2			3		2		4
Proptera alata			1		1	2		3	1	5
Truncilla truncata		1	1		1	3			1	7
Cyprogenia stegaria			3			3		1		3
Dromus dromas							1			1
Ptychobranchus fasciolaris	1	2	2		5	5	2	2		9
Subtotals	52	153	245	43	184	723	210	274	203	1410
Unidentifiable	19	26	18	2	201	280	185	148	327	940
Grand totals	71	179	263	45	385	1003	395	422	530	2350

Analysis by Joanna L. Casey. Manuscript on file at Wickliffe Mounds Research Center, Wickliffe, Kentucky.

MD, Mound D; L, level; ME, Mound E; MF, Mound F.

*Proveniences absent or unreadable.

The river mussels found in archaeological contexts at Wickliffe are union-ids, one of the two groups of freshwater bivalve molluscs found in North America before European contact. (The second group, the sphaeriids, are too small to have provided much of a food resource.) There are three major unionid regions in North America, the Pacific drainage, the Atlantic region, and the Mississippian region, the latter containing an unusually numerous and diverse set of species (Simpson 1895). Researchers have identified fau-nal provinces within the Mississippian region: the Mississippian or Interior Basin, the Ozarkian, the Ohioan (the Ohio River drainage excluding the Tennessee-Cumberland), and the Cumberlandian, including the headwaters of the Tennessee and Cumberland rivers (Ortmann 1924; Johnson 1980; van der Schalie and van der Schalie 1950). Of these, the Ozarkian region is least likely to be related to the Wickliffe mussel assemblage.

From Table 6.3CD, adapted from Casey (1986:table 7), it appears that the mussels' habitat requirements are easily met in the Wickliffe vicinity. All may be found in large to small rivers, which description may be fairly applied to the Mississippi River and Mayfield Creek (5 kilometers south of Wickliffe), respectively. Otherwise it seems that all shellfish-bearing environments were harvested, from shallow (less than 1 meter) to deep (more than 1.5 meters [Casey 1986:128–30]) water, swift to weak currents, and all the mud, sand, and gravel bottom conditions of the Mississippi River.

Table 6.4CD, adapted from Casey (1986:table 5), lists the characteristic provinces of the species identified at Wickliffe. Most of the species are at home in the Mississippian province or the Ohioan, or both. Since the mouth of the Ohio River is only a few kilometers from the Wickliffe site, the presence of a few species considered Ohioan but not Mississippian should provoke little comment. Two species, however, are surprising: *Dysnomia arcaeformis* and *Dromus dromas*. Both belong to the upper reaches of the Tennessee and Cumberland drainages, and Wickliffe is well outside their modern range. Casey (1986:128), however, found both species in archaeological contexts in the Lower Tennessee-Cumberland area and suggests that "these species appear to indicate a loss of shallow-water or shoal habitats in the lower ends of these rivers between the time the sites were occupied and the present." It seems unlikely that the Mississippi period range extended to the Mississippi River at Wickliffe, but perhaps these two shells were distinctive enough to be traded as curiosities from the east side of the Jackson Purchase.

The role of freshwater shellfish in human diets is subject to discussion (Casey 1986:18–30). Shellfish provide little in the way of calories or vitamins A, B, or C, but could be significant sources of protein, calcium, phosphorus, and iron. Their availability depends on season, and particularly on periods of low water, when they are most visible and accessible. The Wickliffe villagers may have used shellfish as supplements in lean periods rather than as a dietary staple.

It is worth noting, too, that there were other reasons for gathering shellfish than their food value: quantities of burned and ground shell were added to ceramics for temper, shells were modified as tools and ornaments, and the early European observers remarked on stores of freshwater pearls among the Southeastern villages. Casey's analysis of the King collection noted a number of shell artifacts, including hoes and hoe fragments, scrapers, and spoons.

Kreisa and McDowell (Chapter 15) found that mussel shells were not well represented in their samples from Wickliffe. All of the species they identified could be found in local habitats, such as sand bars in the Mississippi River. There were too few specimens to suggest any chronological trends.

Diet at Wickliffe

Schurr and Schoeninger (Chapter 13), studying bone chemistry (and writing without the benefit of either Edging's [Chapter 16] or Kreisa and McDowell's [Chapter 15] analyses), perceive a diet heavy with corn. Their Wickliffe data show a statistically significant difference between males and females in values of nitrogen, implying that males had a higher intake of meat protein. Whether the difference is the result of men regularly enjoying the first meal from a successful hunt or of women's levels being often depleted by pregnancy and lactation is not clear.

Interestingly, Kreisa and McDowell (Chapter 15) and Edging (Chapter 16) noted similar trends toward an upland focus in the faunal and wood resources. The Wickliffe villagers relied increasingly on deer, and less on fish and waterfowl. It is difficult to discern trends in Edging's food-related plant remains when summarized per volume floated (Table 6.5). The Early Wickliffe deposits were simply more rich than the others sampled. (Edging attempted to reconcile the Wickliffe chronology with the scheme applied to his comparative sites, but Feature 106 belongs with the Early Wickliffe samples; see below for further comments on western Kentucky chronologies.) Generally in the Central Mississippi Valley, Johannessen (1988) found that Mississippian villagers emphasized corn over starchy annuals after A.D. 1250.

Table 6.5. Plant Remains per Liter Floated

	Early Wickliffe	Middle Wickliffe	Late Wickliffe	Total
Nuts	23.8	3.8	4.3	11.4
Weight (g)	0.15	0.05	0.08	0.1
Seeds	19.6		0.8	7.6
Maize	8.1	5.4	3.6	5.4
Weight (g)	0.08	0.04	0.02	0.04
Other	0.5	0.6	1.2	0.9

Summarized from Tables 16.1 and 16.2 (Edging, Chapter 16).

Although Schurr and Schoeninger find no evidence for dietary change during the period when the Mound C cemetery was in use, as they note, the cemetery probably does not represent the full period of occupation of the Wickliffe village.

Large additional samples of Wickliffe faunal and botanical remains have yet to be analyzed. Trends noted here will be reexamined when additional data can be presented.

SITE PATTERNING

Because the WMRC excavations sampled areas throughout the site, the data offer opportunities to consider the distributions of artifacts within the village, exploring both changes through time and variation within the site in each period. Brown (Chapter 8), for example, shows that there are different patterns of site use in each period in lithics, fire-cracked rock and ferrous sandstone, and daub and fired clay. Detailed analysis of the entire assemblage is necessary for these kinds of studies—as of yet, faunal and botanical remains and debitage, for instance, cannot be examined spatially at any but the most cursory level.

Ceramics

Brown (Chapter 8) notes a correlation between deposit types and sherd size: that middens and features generally contain larger sherds than mound fills. This datum is not very surprising, since the redeposition of mound soils allows additional opportunities for sherds to be broken. Brown's innovative technique for modeling clustering and separation among artifact classes will be particularly interesting when applied to typological and vessel form data. The same perspective might prove interesting if employed on fabric impressions in ceramics. Kuttruff and Drooker (Chapter 14) remark that the impressed fabrics' "most striking quality . . . is their diversity"; that diversity may have as yet unsuspected spatial and temporal patterning.

The same perspective might also be applied to effigy forms, although the sample is small. A previous attempt to detect potential clustering of effigy types (Wesler 1991b) failed to find any pattern except for a concentration of conch shell bowls in Mound D. However, the study only included those from excavations through 1988 and needs updating.

Spatial patterning in effigies should also be examined in regional perspective. Among the effigies in the King collection, Phillips (Chapter 9) observes that the most frequent types are humans and ducks and that lists from sites in the Memphis and St. Francis areas show very different frequencies (Table 9.2). Of course, the samples are not strictly comparable, the Wickliffe data

representing a single site whereas the St. Francis and Memphis area lists are
regional compilations from half a century ago (Phillips 1939). The differences,
however, are suggestive of regional variation, and a regional collation for the
Ohio-Mississippi confluence area needs to be compared with up-to-date lists
for other regions (also taking into account current developments in local
chronologies).

Lithics

Brown (Chapter 8) has created an innovative method for comparing the distributions of groups of artifacts over the area of the site, examining differences
in clustering and separation among assemblages. Consulting with Philip Carr
(cf. Koldehoff and Carr, Chapter 10), Brown divides the Wickliffe debitage
into two size categories, representing roughly manufacturing (large) and resharpening (small) flakes. The division is merely a first-order approximation
for the purposes of developing her spatial modeling technique, but the results
are interesting: each of the Wickliffe periods exhibits a different pattern.

In the Early Wickliffe period small flakes cluster, and the distributions of
small and large flakes show separation: small flakes center in the vicinity of
Mound A. In the Middle Wickliffe period, the distributions do not show
separation, but large flakes cluster in the vicinity of Mound B. The two size
grades do not show separate distributions in the Late Wickliffe period, but
small flakes tend to cluster, though not tightly.

Brown also compared three categories of chipped stone tools: utilized flakes,
projectile points, and other bifaces. The samples were too small to elicit
confidence in any patterning in the Early Wickliffe period. In the Middle
and Late Wickliffe periods, bifaces and projectile points showed very little
difference, but utilized flakes stood apart. Middle Wickliffe utilized flakes
clustered differently from projectile points and showed a separation from
bifaces. In the Late Wickliffe period, utilized flakes clustered in the Northwest
Village area.

These patterns are difficult to interpret at this stage of the analysis, but
additional analyses of lithics add perspective. Koldehoff and Carr (Chapter 10)
examine a sample of debitage from an organization-of-production perspective.
They find that local cherts, the Mounds gravels, are heavily represented by
early-stage reduction flakes, while imported cherts—Mill Creek, Kaolin, and
Burlington cherts from the north and Dover chert from the southeast—appear
more frequently as middle-stage reduction flakes (small, late-stage reduction
flakes are poorly represented as a result of the use of 1/4-inch screens in
recovery). Mounds gravel cobbles tend to be small, limiting the potential
size of both finished bifaces and flake tools, and raw materials for larger tools
had to be found outside the immediate Wickliffe area.

Mill Creek chert, imported from southern Illinois, exhibited the lowest mean weight of debitage, suggesting that this stone arrived primarily as finished items. However, Koldehoff and Carr did find some large flakes of Mill Creek chert, representing primary reduction, but they suggest that these large flakes were also brought in as blanks for flake tools rather than struck from cores on site.

Koldehoff and Carr (Chapter 10) note that the presence of Burlington chert "clearly marks some form of interaction with the Cahokia region." That interaction, judging by the relative proportion of Burlington debitage, peaked during the Middle Wickliffe period and fell to a low in the Late Wickliffe period, even as the general usage of northern stones increased through the period of Wickliffe's occupation.

Pafford (Chapter 11), concentrating on chipped stone projectile points, sees that Mounds gravels are the primary source for Mississippian arrowheads, reflecting the size limitations of local gravel cobbles also noted by Koldehoff and Carr. Pafford did not have so extensive a comparative collection as did Koldehoff and Carr and some of his material identifications (especially Kentucky Hornstone) will need to be reconciled with the latter analysts' material types. Pafford also notes a concentration of side-notched points around Mound D. His suggestion that they may be related to burials in the mound does not really seem applicable, since the East Midden is not part of the mound (see Chapters 3 and 18). Nonetheless his analysis points to differences in distributions of artifacts within the site, echoing Brown's findings, and indicates the complexity both of the Wickliffe assemblages and the human behavior they reflect.

Analysis of additional data along the lines of Koldehoff and Carr's and Pafford's work should illuminate Brown's spatial patterns and will allow her analyses to be extended in more detail. It is possible that manufacturing in exotic stones was supervised more strongly by the Mound B residents—the presumptive elite—in the Middle Wickliffe period, and one aspect that must be studied closely is whether this clustering of the manufacturing debris is disproportionately found in imported stones such as Burlington and Mill Creek, potentially implying a special elite involvement in a northern-looking exchange system. Clustering/separation studies of the different chert types must be pursued in detail. Further, the distinction between utilized flakes and bifacial tools, including projectile points, reflects the difference between an expedient tool industry (flake tools made quickly, used briefly, and discarded) and a curated tool industry (bifaces, formal tools requiring some time and skill to make, are less likely to be discarded casually), and different distributions in these categories probably reflect activity patterns within the village. Analysts will need to examine much more extensive samples of the Wickliffe debitage before making any definitive statements in this regard.

Rock and Daub

Brown (Chapter 8) applied the same spatial modeling technique to bulk materials as to lithic debitage and tools. Again, the three Wickliffe periods show different patterns.

The WMRC catalogers distinguish three categories of rough rock: gravel, fire-cracked rock, and ferrous sandstone (see Chapter 4). In the Early Wickliffe period, Brown finds that ferrous sandstone clusters significantly, but its overall distribution is not distinct from that of fire-cracked rock. Gravel, on the other hand, exhibits clustering and a separate distribution from the other two classes of rock. In the Middle Wickliffe period, ferrous sandstone and gravel both cluster, but none of the three groups displays a separate overall distribution. In the Late Wickliffe period, it is fire-cracked rock and gravel that cluster, but again there is no significant separation among the distributions.

The consistent finding is that gravel clusters. In the Late period deposits, it is possible that clustering reflects incomplete separation of Mississippian deposits from those of the historic period—the tourism era's gravel walkways and road, for example. But the Early and Middle period deposits were stratigraphically overlain by Late deposits, so that historic contamination seems less likely. It is likely that the clustering of gravel reflects natural seams and pockets in the loess subsoil.

The other two classes of stone are harder to interpret, but for now it is sufficient to note that they either cluster differently or show distributional separation from gravel and that the patterns change through time.

Brown (Chapter 8) subjected daub and fired clay to the same scrutiny. She found that fired clay clusters in the Early and Late Wickliffe periods, with distributions centering on Mound A in the former and Mound D North in the latter period. This result corresponds to feature concentrations noted during the excavation (Chapter 18). Otherwise, fired clay is distributed throughout the site at a low density. Daub, however, clusters in the Middle Wickliffe period, a fact not noted in excavation. Its distribution centers on Mound B, suggesting that Mound B supported unusually substantial structures in the Middle period. Again, the primary finding is that the two categories are distributed differently, supporting the WMRC catalogers' determination that fired clay is not a form of daub. Its purpose or function remains a mystery.

Cemetery

Both Matternes (Chapter 12) and Schurr and Schoeninger (Chapter 13) discuss possible interpretations of the orientations of burials in the Mound C cemetery. Schurr and Schoeninger note that fluorine analysis holds promise to aid in sorting out the complex depositional sequence within the cemetery.

Most of the burials were placed with their heads toward the northwest or northeast. There appears to be no lodestone either on or off the site that would focus the attention of burial parties in either direction. Solar orientation is possible, but would imply burial in specific seasons. It seems more likely that the burials are oriented to the layout of the site (see Burial 258 and adjacent, but earlier, posthole line in unit 42–44N22–23E, Chapter 18). The general village plan fits the orientation of the ridge on which the site is located, and the cemetery followed suit. No explanation predicated on astronomical alignment or other symbolism is necessary.

Matternes's analysis indicates that there are at least three general strata of burials, each with its own pattern of orientation and burial type. This inference suggests that there is some time involved in the burial activities (at least through the Middle Wickliffe period [Matternes 1999a, 1999b]). Archaeologists can only wonder what event or change in ideology would inspire such a pattern shift, analogous to a modern North American municipal cemetery's decision to inter new graves in a north-south alignment instead of an east-west position. While the psychology or symbolism of the pattern changes in the Mound C cemetery eludes analysts, it seems that several generations must have buried their dead here.

Summary

The various analyses synopsized so briefly above demonstrate that the Wickliffe site reveals a complex palimpsest of human activities and that the three Wickliffe periods may almost be regarded as three distinct villages despite the continuity of occupation. Spatial analysis of the Wickliffe data has barely begun. Distributions of ceramics may soon be studied in the perspectives of decorative type and vessel form. Varying dispersal of classes and species of food resources, or of chert materials and debitage manufacturing stages—or correlations such as vessel forms with food resources—can only be studied in detail when the entire collection is examined.

WICKLIFFE AS A CHIEFDOM

Archaeologists have generally assumed that the western Kentucky Mississippian sites represent chiefdoms. It is difficult to imagine platform mound sites in the Mississippian heartland being anything but chiefdoms ("heartland" in a geographic sense, not a developmental one [cf. Smith 1984]). We assume, surrounded as they are by the prominent centers of Cahokia (west-central Illinois), Moundville (Alabama), Kincaid (southernmost Illinois), and Angel (southern Indiana) and the well-populated Lower Mississippi Valley (see Figure 1.3), that platform mound-and-plaza villages at the Ohio-Mississippi confluence can hardly be anything but functioning members of the pan-Mississippian network, and that ideas of chiefly status were among the beliefs and practices they shared.

Mississippianists often utilize several lines of evidence to adduce chiefdom organization: hierarchical settlement pattern, which indicates centralization of authority over a region; residential differentiation within sites, which suggests social differentiation within communities; and mortuary patterns, which may demonstrate preferential treatment of certain individuals, from which we infer deferential treatment in life.

Too, the mere presence of platform mounds in the Mississippian context is often argued as a sign of a chiefdom. Hally (1996:97), for instance, contends that "the platform mound and accompanying summit structures were essential elements of the chief's role as political and religious leader, and they seemed to legitimize and sanctify the office of chief and the incumbent's claim to that position." In this perspective, the mere presence of two platform mounds at Wickliffe affirms a chief's presence. Hally (1996) and Blitz (1999) both seem to equate one mound with one chief, Blitz in particular suggesting that multiple-mound sites represent amalgamated polities; but since Wickliffe Mounds A and B seem functionally distinct (the latter a residence, the former not), they need not be assumed to reflect a rivalry.

Mississippian settlement patterns are more complex than a simple site-hierarchy model would account for. Hally (1993, 1994, 1996) has developed data that indicate "a strong tendency for contemporary mound sites in northern Georgia to be separated by distances that are either less than 18 km or more than 32 km" (Hally 1993:156). Blitz (1999) draws four different settlement patterns from the same data, of which three do not indicate site hierarchy. Both scholars seem to agree that Mississippian chiefdoms may be defined spatially as single or multiple mound centers that dominate areas of 20 kilometers or less in radius, separated by buffer zones of similar dimension.

These criteria are more easily applied in some regions than in others. In the Ohio-Mississippi confluence region, hierarchical patterns are not as apparent as in other Mississippian regions such as those centered on Cahokia or Moundville, nor are buffer zones as evident as they are in northern Georgia. Wickliffe Mounds appears to be typical of the western Kentucky sites: compact, with platform mounds on the small side, a site that could fit comfortably underneath Cahokia's Monk's Mound and never be noticed. Western Kentucky Mississippian mound sites occur every 8 or 10 kilometers along the Mississippi River (Figure 6.1), and although the site sizes vary somewhat, none of them is clearly dominant. Only Kincaid, approximately 50 kilometers up the Ohio River from Wickliffe, stands out, and it is not clear at all that the Mississippi River sites are part of a Kincaid hinterland.

Hally (1993:164) cites Muller (1986:fig. 2.1) in support of the applicability of his 20-kilometer radius/buffer zone to the Lower Ohio Valley. However,

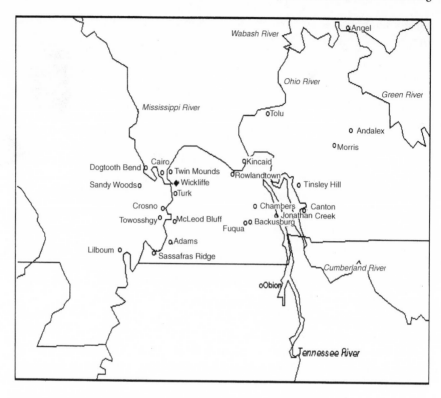

6.1. Mississippian sites in western Kentucky and the confluence area.

Muller's map is by no means a complete catalog of mound centers in the area. Figure 6.1 and Muller's more recent map (1997:fig. 5.6) are much better indicators, and even these are incomplete. A circle of 20 kilometers in radius around any of the sites is likely to include three or more mound centers, and no buffer zones are distinguishable.

However, a key element of Hally's (1993) analysis is that he considers patterns among contemporary mound centers—that is, centers with mound construction activities dated to the same phase. At present, this level of resolution is not available in the Lower Ohio Valley. Although the major Mississippian sites of Figure 6.1 are thought to have been occupied contemporaneously in broad terms, only the Wickliffe site has been excavated sufficiently to provide a chronology of mound construction. Full examination of Hally's model in the Ohio-Mississippi confluence region must await more thorough dating of mound zones in a number of sites.

Surveys and testing by the University of Illinois Western Kentucky Project have challenged the idea that sites like Wickliffe have satellite hamlets and farmsteads, as well. This work indicates that floodplain mound sites may have small outlying settlements, but blufftop sites like Wickliffe and Turk may not (Kreisa 1988; Sussenbach and Lewis 1987). On present evidence, the Wickliffe site is not part of a hierarchical settlement system, but an equal partner or competitor among a number of villages in the region.

Population figures are equally ambiguous. Estimates for western Kentucky town populations generally range around Wickliffe's 250 to 300 to Adams's (Fulton County) 600 (Stout 1989). Demographic studies have suggested that chiefdom populations typically number circa 10,000 to 12,000 (Baker and Sanders 1972:163; Trigger 1978:156–57). By this measure, twenty to forty Adams- to Wickliffe-sized villages would be expected in a chiefdom. If so many settlements were coordinated politically, surely one site would stand out as a major center.

Several studies of Mississippian mortuary patterns indicate social or political ranking. At the King site in Georgia, a very late Mississippian occupation, lower-status individuals are buried in the private or village sector, while elite burials are found in the plaza, the "public" sector (Garrett 1988). In Dallas phase sites of eastern Tennessee, comparable in scale and chronology to Wickliffe, high-status burials are isolated and are associated with public or communal features, such as mounds (Hatch 1976). In the American Bottom, Milner (1984) found that elite burials occur only in large town and mound centers; in peripheral sites, cemeteries contain graves with a common orientation and are often associated with mounds. Cahokia's Mound 72 is the quintessential elite burial mound, one of a special class of ridge-top mounds that incorporate series of smaller mounds "as well as burials and other features," the burials including a few "of especially important individuals" (Fowler 1989, 1991).

Artifact associations also characterize Mississippian burial ranking. Peebles and Kus (1977) distinguish three burial strata at Moundville, the middle stratum characterized by conch shell effigy ceramics, among other artifact types. A conch shell effigy bowl was found with an elite burial at the Dallas phase Little Egypt site (Hatch 1976). Milner's (1984) probable peripheral elite of the Cahokia system are sometimes found with marine shell cups.

Apart from those at Wickliffe, mortuary data from the western Kentucky region are scarce. At Wickliffe, there appears to be a threefold division among the burials. First, infants are buried in the village. Second, the Mound C cemetery contains children and adults. These patterns are complicated by the presence of two children in the village (field camp tests and Mound H, Chapter 18), but seem generally to hold true. They are also complicated by the likelihood that the Mound C cemetery does not contain the earliest or latest residents of the village; however, if the village residents are not represented on site, they are buried elsewhere while their infants are in the village, so that the pattern is the same. The Wickliffe cemetery resembles Milner's (1984) peripheral American Bottom cemeteries.

Third, Mound D may tentatively be identified as an elite burial mound. Mound D's conch shell effigy vessels are reminiscent of middle-stratum elite grave associations at Moundville (Peebles and Kus 1977) and the American Bottom (Milner 1984) and also of the smaller-scale chiefdom elite of the Dallas phase (Hatch 1976). Thus, the Wickliffe mortuary patterns, although problematic because of lack of detailed provenience data on grave associations recovered in the 1930s, provide some support for inferring a ranked society of smaller scale than Cahokia or Moundville, a country cousin resembling the middle levels of the Cahokia or Moundville hierarchies.

Village patterning can be expected to offer another route to the identification of a ranked society, by highlighting residential sectors characterized by elite markers. Both conceptual and ethnohistoric accounts of small chiefdoms would suggest that so identifying a chiefly sector will be difficult. Fried (1960) described a ranked society as one in which personal accumulation is not permitted, in which "strong status differentials . . . are marked by sumptuary specialization and ceremonial function . . . [by] fuss, feathers and other trappings of office. These people [chiefs] sit on stools, have big houses, and are consulted by their neighbors," but do not eat much better or own much more than others in the village (Fried 1960:719).

Hudson's (1976) survey of the Southeastern Indians supports Fried's formulation. Chiefly status is marked by "symbols of attainment," such as tattoos and special seats in council houses, and probably "icons and artifacts of the Southeastern Ceremonial Complex." Some chiefs were shown extreme deference and carried on litters. Among the Natchez, non-Suns could not eat with Suns or touch the Suns' eating vessels. "But aside from having the right to live in a special house, the only distinctive thing about the Great Sun with respect to wealth was that he wore a special feather headdress" (Hudson 1976:203, 209).

These status markers are not encouraging in terms of archaeological visibility, but they may not tell the whole story. It is unlikely that DeSoto's Spaniards, or any other European adventurer, would notice, for instance, a higher percentage of O'Byam Incised plates over Matthews Incised jars in a chief's house, or more Bell Plain than Mississippi Plain scattered across the floor. Nor might the Europeans have noticed better cuts of meat in a chief's stewpot, or a few more strings of shell beads or stone pendants, as compared to the average household in the village.

There are a few indications that these markers can be identified. At the Morgan site in coastal Louisiana, Brown (1982, 1987:162–63) and Fuller and Fuller (1987:81–83) noted a better quality of ceramics and a larger proportion of mammal remains in the mound than in the midden. At Zebree, in northeastern Arkansas, mammal bone showed a concentration suggesting differential control of meat (Morse and Morse 1990:64). Belmont and Williams (1981:35) noted the occurrence of late painted wares in mound floors and slope wash. Peebles and Kus (1977:443) cite a possible elite residential area at Moundville, admittedly a more complex site and presumably more complex society than Wickliffe Mounds.

At Wickliffe, analysis of the distributions of several artifact classes—ceramic effigy fragments, stone, antler and bone projectile points, bone tools, ornaments, discs and discoidals, and pottery trowels—revealed no patterns or concentrations other than those in Mound D (Wesler 1991b). Ceramic effigy fragments were a particular focus of the study, after Price and Griffin (1979) suggested motif patterning (as possible clan markers) at Snodgrass in southeastern Missouri. However, only the conch shell effigy fragments in Mound D occur in any concentration. A preserved fragment of fabric from Mound D is finely woven and probably an elite garment or sash (Kuttruff and Drooker, Chapter 14; Kuttruff 1990), but no other artifact type emerges as a possible elite marker.

Only Mound B reveals any indication of residential specialization. Early and Middle Wickliffe period middens on buried summits of the platform mound indicate a household separated both vertically and horizontally from the closest neighbors. The Mound B summit dwellers utilized choice cuts of venison (Kreisa and McDowell 1992, 1995; Chapter 15). A relatively large proportion of serving vessels among the rim sherds, and a low incidence of decorated sherds, mark the ceramic assemblage. No other potential "elite markers," such as fine ornaments or ceremonial vessels, were associated with the Mound B middens.

The possible elite burial mound, and the residential platform mound whose summit middens are distinguished by ceramic and faunal patterning, suggest that the Wickliffe village was occupied by a society with some internal ranking. The assemblage distinctions are subtle. The small size of the village, however, and the lack of "elite" markers such as an increased frequency of ornamental or symbolic artifacts in the mound-summit middens, indicate that the Wickliffe society was a simple and small-scale chiefdom, whose elite were few and socioeconomically little differentiated from the rest of the population. The chiefly population at Wickliffe, maybe only a single family, was distinguished primarily by "fuss, feathers and other trappings of office," in Fried's (1960) phrase, perhaps by perishable symbols such as finely woven fabrics and by the slightly better diet and more prevalent serving vessels that may be associated with a chief's diplomatic and entertainment functions. It seems likely that the major material benefit of being a chief was an elaborate funeral.

Recent models of chiefdom societies emphasize their inherent instability, which results in a "cycling" pattern of consolidation and dissolution. Anderson (1990, 1994), Scarry (1990), and Hally (1996), drawing largely on Wright's (1984) formulation, have utilized regional spatial distributions and mortuary treatments to support models of cycling in Southeastern chiefdoms. Blitz (1999) sees a more complex fission-fusion process in the northern Georgia data, but concurs with the general ascription of instability to Mississippian polities.

Data from Wickliffe Mounds take on an added dimension when viewed through a cycling model. Several patterns indicate that there was a "high point" in Wickliffe culture in the Middle Wickliffe period.

Early Wickliffe mound deposits have been identified only in the initial stage of Mound B. Five of six identifiable Mound A construction stages were built in the Middle period. Of five stages in Mound B, three belong to the Middle Wickliffe period. In each platform mound, only the final stage is a Late Wickliffe construction. If, as Hally (1996:92–93) proposes, "the construction and use of Mississippian platform mounds was largely coterminous in time with the existence of the chiefdoms in which they functioned," then the sequences of Mounds A and B argue for Middle Wickliffe as the period when a chief maintained a seat of power here.

Mound C_I is a Middle Wickliffe deposit, while Mounds C and C_2 lie stratigraphically between a Middle and a Late Wickliffe midden, indicating that they were built at the latest in the early years of the Late period. The remnants of Mounds D and F are Late Wickliffe deposits, but these mounds may have been more complex. In particular, if the Cahokia ridge-top mound model fits Mound D, it may consist of two or more mounds that were later incorporated into a longer, low mound. However, even if Mounds D and F are entirely Late Wickliffe constructions, Middle Wickliffe was the most active mound-building period.

Brown's (Chapter 8) comparison of the volume of mound soils to the volume of midden for each period supports the idea that the relative effort put into mound building was greatest in the Middle Wickliffe period, as well. She also found that the average sherd size was largest in Middle Wickliffe deposits, and that daub and large debitage clustered in the Middle period with distributions centering on Mound B, in contrast to the lack of clustering in daub and clustering in the smaller debitage in both Early and Late Wickliffe villages. Further analysis of the lithic debitage will emphasize raw material types as well as flake size categories, following Koldehoff and Carr's (Chapter 10) lead. If the clustering of Middle Wickliffe large debitage is associated with imported raw materials such as Mill Creek chert, the distribution may hint at centralization of import or manufacture by an elite power.

The proportions of ornaments, tools, and serving vessel rims are highest in the Middle period. Koldehoff and Carr state that they found fewer tools in the Middle period lithic samples, but their Middle sample is the smallest of the three period assemblages they studied. Table 6.6, summarizing their data, provides a different perspective. The most significant difference in the

Table 6.6. Summary of Lithic Debitage and Tool Data

	Debitage		Tools		Tools/ Debitage	Arrows/ Tools	Flake Tools as % of Tools
Early Wickliffe	3231	37.8%	120	30.5%	.037	16.7	45.8
Middle Wickliffe	2014	23.6%	71	18.0%	.035	18.3	56.3
Late Wickliffe	3305	30.7%	205	51.5%	.061	19.7	43.8
Total	8550	100.1%	394	100.0%			

Summarized from Tables 10.1 and 10.4 through 10.6 (Koldenhoff and Carr, Chapter 10).

tools/debitage ratio is between the combined Early and Middle periods and the Late period: the relative occurrence of tools in the Middle period is very similar to that of the Early period. The ratio of arrowheads to tools is highest in the Late period, reflecting the figures in Chapter 5, indicating an increase in projectile points. Interestingly, flake tools make up the highest proportion of tools in the Middle period, distinguishing the Middle period much as did the Activities group (Chapter 5). The Middle period is quite distinct, but not lacking in tools.

Kuttruff and Drooker (Chapter 14) note that decorated utilitarian textiles appear in the same period. Koldehoff and Carr (Chapter 10) note that Burlington chert is best represented in the Middle Wickliffe period. None of these measures appears significant in itself, but all of them distinguish the Middle Wickliffe period.

The cemetery belongs primarily to the Middle Wickliffe period (Matternes 1999a, 1999b), which indicates that earlier and later cemeteries were elsewhere and suggests more centralizing control over cemetery placement in the Middle period. It will be extremely important to try to reconstruct the construction sequence of Mound D and to place the (elite?) adult burials within the sequence. If they can be shown to belong to the Middle Wickliffe period as well, a hypothetical centripetal propensity will be powerfully affirmed. Matternes (Chapter 12) suggests a simplification of burial organization over the period in which the cemetery was used, perhaps corresponding to a simplification of social organization leading into the Late Wickliffe period.

The most distinguishing characteristics of the Late Wickliffe period are dietary changes, particularly in the diminished consumption of fish. The centralizing tendencies of the lithic manufacturing debris and intramural mortuary facility, the import of Burlington chert, the effort put into building mounds, the abundance of Activities and Personal artifact group items, all seem to fade. At the end of the Late Wickliffe period, the village is abandoned.

These data fit a scenario of village founding circa A.D. 1100, consolidation during the Middle Wickliffe period, and decline and dissolution through and after the Late Wickliffe period: a single cycle in the life of a chiefdom. The duration of the Middle Wickliffe period fits well with Hally's (1996) suggestion that a chiefdom's span of existence typically was about 75 to 100 years.

Wright's (1984) formulation distinguishes simple chiefdoms from complex chiefdoms. In a simple chiefdom, "control is exercised by figures drawn from an ascribed local elite subgroup . . . one level of control hierarchy above the level of the local community." In a complex chiefdom, "control is exercised by figures drawn from a class of people which cross-cuts many local subgroups" (Wright 1984:42). As noted previously, the Ohio-Mississippi rivers confluence region does not offer evidence of hierarchical settlement patterns, and the Wickliffe chiefdom thus resembles a simple chiefdom.

However, it is the complex chiefdoms that "characteristically cycle between one and two levels of control hierarchy above the level of the local community," with an elite " 'class' being defined as a ranked group whose members compete with each other for access to controlling positions," thus creating the instability that leads to cycling (Wright 1984:42–43). The complex chiefdom's elite support their legitimacy with "claims of geographically distant prestigious links." The cycling behavior of complex chiefdoms leads to regional abandonments of their centers.

One ceramic marker at Wickliffe may indicate extralocal chiefly linkage. Two sherds of Ramey Incised vessels have been recovered from Wickliffe in the recent excavations. Significantly, one sherd was found in each of the platform mounds, those most likely to be associated with chiefly symbolism (at least of living chiefs). In addition, sherds that closely resemble Powell Plain, an American Bottom type, were recovered in Mound C_I in 1992, further supporting some kind of direct contact with the American Bottom.

Recently, Pauketat and Emerson (1991) have discussed the symbolism of Ramey Incised as an important element in the legitimization of elite authority at Cahokia. They note that Ramey Incised may have been produced centrally, under elite control, and passed out to commoners as symbols of chiefly power. Outside the American Bottom, Ramey Incised is rare and a widely "imitated exchange item" (Pauketat and Emerson 1991; cf. Pauketat 1997:10). It is not difficult to conceive of a chief of a small town like Wickliffe using some kind of contact with the great chief of Cahokia to buttress his own power, the link symbolized by Ramey Incised jars.

Marine shell gorgets often are interpreted as prestige or display goods traded among elite, and the geographic identifications suggest elite exchange across regions. (Here, Muller's [1997:372–78] objections to associating gorgets with elite status must be recognized; indeed, the Wickliffe spider gorget was found in midden without any hint of special-status context.) As the Cox/woodpecker style may be broadly identified with the Moundville area, the Hightower/Eagle Dancer with eastern Tennessee, and the spider gorget with the Central Mississippi Valley, so too Hudson et al. (1985:732–33) relate the

Citico style to the area of early historic Coosa: "it is reasonable to conclude that the Citico gorget was symbolically associated with some institutional order or status group within the chiefdom of Coosa" (but again note Muller's [1997:75, 372–78] objections).

In this perspective, Du Pratz's (1975) early eighteenth-century comments about Natchez declarations of war, when "the hieroglyphic sign of the nation that attacks" is carved on bark, are striking. "When one nation declares war against another, they leave a picture near one of their villages . . . On the top towards the right hand is the hieroglyphic sign of the nation that declares war" (Du Pratz 1975:373, 374). It is intriguing to speculate whether the motifs found on the gorgets may be linked with the "hieroglyphic signs" of nations, and, further, whether the core areas of certain gorget motifs may have implications for Mississippian regional affiliations. This idea pushes past the bounds of speculation into the realm of a fun idea—but it would be nice to know what in the world Du Pratz was talking about.

At least, the Wickliffe gorgets may indicate both the far-flung contacts (diplomatic? kinship?—whether consanguineous, affinal, or fictive) of the people of Wickliffe and Wickliffe's association with the spider gorget region of the Central Mississippi Valley. Indeed, a number of data insinuate a connection to Cahokia, as the primary center of the central valley. There are the Ramey Incised, Powell Plain, and Cahokia Cord Marked sherds (see Chapter 4). The Ramey Incised sherd from Mound A belongs to the Early Wickliffe period, and the Mound B sherd of the same type—but more likely a local copy— belongs to Middle Wickliffe deposits. Koldehoff and Carr (Chapter 10) note that Burlington chert is most frequent in the Middle Wickliffe period, when, as argued above, the Wickliffe chiefdom was at its strongest. Kuttruff and Drooker (Chapter 14) argue that the weaving style links Wickliffe to the north rather than the south, though not specifically with Cahokia.

Nor does the chronology of Wickliffe's and Cahokia's dissolutions seem coincidental. The Sand Prairie phase of the American Bottom, A.D. 1275– 1350, is coeval with the latter three-quarters of the Late Wickliffe period, and it is the Sand Prairie phase that saw Cahokia's precipitate decline (Hall 1991:23; Pauketat 1994:47). Mehrer (1995:153) describes how populations had diminished, temple-towns had "fallen into disuse," and "regional integration was breaking down in rural areas" during and certainly by the end of the Sand Prairie phase—simultaneously with the end of the Late Wickliffe period, when Wickliffe was abandoned.

The possibility must be raised that Wickliffe indeed was part of Cahokia's rural hinterland and that Wickliffe was affiliated *at some level* with a Cahokian sphere of influence. The distance from Wickliffe to Cahokia is within histori- cally attested limits of chiefly authority in the historic period, notably Coosa in the sixteenth century (Hudson et al. 1985). It is true that the Wickliffe ceramic tradition is clearly affiliated with that of the Lower Mississippi Valley, and not the American Bottom, but of course ceramic boundaries do not constrain human community. In the Hudson et al. (1985; cf. Hudson 1997:215–17) reconstruction, Coosa incorporated several archaeological phases as defined on material, especially ceramic, criteria, much as would be the case if Wickliffe were drawn into a Cahokian orbit.

Pushing these ideas into a frankly speculative scenario, it is possible that the Ramey Incised sherd in the Early Wickliffe midden beneath Mound A marks the incorporation of Wickliffe into a Cahokian sphere. (The Early Wickliffe period corresponds temporally with the Stirling phase in the American Bottom, when that area's population was greatest [Milner 1986] and Cahokia arguably at its strongest.) This may have happened as a Cahokian representative with a large retinue appeared at the gate, calling forth the sort of diplomatic response presented by Smith and Hally (1992) whereby a chief of lesser stature established fictive kinship as an alternative to conflict; or it may have happened as an ambitious Wickliffe chief made an expedition to Cahokia to gain the anointment of a spiritually powerful leader (bringing back a Ramey Incised vessel much like bringing back a bust of Elvis to commemorate a pilgrimage to Graceland).

Relations with Cahokia may have remained close through the Middle Wickliffe period, in the sense that people from Wickliffe and Cahokia exchanged visits, Burlington chert, and ceramics (and probably foodstuffs, hides, crafts, and other perishables) on a recurrent basis. The formal or symbolic affiliation may not have been reaffirmed in any significant way—the Mound B, Middle Wickliffe Ramey Incised vessel may in fact have been a local copy, reminding Wickliffians of a relationship that did not require another personal endorsement. But then, the spider gorget belongs to a Middle Wickliffe deposit and may yet symbolize formal contact with the American Bottom.

In the Moorehead phase and Middle Wickliffe period, Cahokia's population began to decline. In Milner's (1986:235) words, "Depopulation may reflect an initiation of processes during the Moorehead phase that resulted in the Sand Prairie phase dissolution of a highly developed cultural system." Because the Late Wickliffe village covered a larger area and built up deeper middens than at any previous time, it is unlikely that Wickliffe lost population during its last century. Wickliffe's chiefs held on until the end of the period, but mound building declined and other changes presaged the dissolution of the community, as discussed above. Paraphrasing Milner, the Late Wickliffe period saw an initiation of processes that resulted in the dissolution of the village at the end of the period. The ripples of Cahokia's fall washed over Wickliffe, whose chiefs shared the greater disintegration.

It is quite unlikely that Cahokia ever held effective, day-to-day (or even season-to-season) control over Wickliffe's affairs (but then, an English king of the same period held little real control beyond the effective range of his armed henchmen [Erickson 1976:125]). Again Coosa offers a comparison, as the most distant of the Coosa towns demonstrated at most dubious subjugation (Hudson 1994:176, 1997:215–17; Hudson et al. 1985; cf. Muller 1997:chapter 2). Nonetheless, those most distant towns of the Coosa chiefdom were identified with that polity. Likewise, in the American Bottom case, Milner (1998:169) suggests that "peoples positioned towards the margins of Cahokia's influence were more likely to be situationally attached to the complex chiefdom." The possibility must be considered that Wickliffe similarly had some formal or symbolic relationship with Cahokia; the problem will be to define what that relationship actually was.

However speculative these ideas about Wickliffe's relationship to Cahokia might be, the presence of American Bottom sherds and Burlington and Mill Creek cherts and the abandonment at a cycle's end raise the question of whether Wickliffe was indeed a small-scale, simple chiefdom or whether the village could have participated in a wide political network. The answer must await detailed analysis of other Mississippian mound centers in the region, to study whether they show similar and contemporaneous boom-and-bust cycles or independent trajectories of establishment and abandonment, at different times. If a synchronous cycle, with simultaneous abandonment, can be found among the small Mississippian towns of western Kentucky, we must consider the possibility of a regional system.

None of these models explains the *rise* of a chief in a village like Wickliffe (see Pauketat 1994 for an extended discussion of the American Bottom example). In light of the finding that Mound B, the elite residence, was the first mound, insinuating that expressing the eminence of a chief was a highly significant act toward the end of the Early Wickliffe period, there are a number of alternative scenarios that may be imagined:

1. A Wickliffe family came to prominence within the village and established itself in a position of privilege.
2. A leader brought followers to Wickliffe, established the village, and then his/her grandchildren symbolized their position with a mound when the village could support a mound-building program, or when the family felt that a symbol of authority was needed. The original leader may have set out as (a) a blow for independence or (b) a sanctioned expansion of a parent group.
3. A chief may have been installed by a supervising regional elite (here in the realm of fun ideas, the third son of the fifteenth sister of the great leader at Cahokia, perhaps).
4. A village like Wickliffe could conceivably belong to a peripatetic ruler, who moved from manor to manor to eat up local surpluses and assert

his or her authority. This is a medieval European model (Dyer 1989:99), but see Smith and Hally (1992:106–7): "We propose that Southeastern paramount chiefs made periodic visits to subordinate chiefdoms for the purpose of maintaining political control over them."

In cases 1 and 2a, Wickliffe would be an independent, simple chiefdom. In cases 2b, 3, and 4, Wickliffe would be a unit of a regional, complex chiefdom. In all of the cases, a legitimizing connection to a spiritual (as opposed to effectively secular) authority at, say, Cahokia, symbolized by a souvenir Ramey Incised pot, could be involved. Each of these scenarios is more or less speculative, and more or less plausible, but none can be rejected out of hand on present evidence. To make a convincing case for any of these scenarios will tax the creativity of future researchers.

WESTERN KENTUCKY MISSISSIPPIAN SEQUENCE: A VIEW FROM WICKLIFFE

The Wickliffe project has added to the developing picture of Mississippi period subsistence and settlement systems in the Jackson Purchase region of western Kentucky. Most of the comparative data, especially for the Mississippi River counties, result from the University of Illinois Western Kentucky Project. These data have been summarized by Lewis (1990a, 1991, 1996; and see references in Chapter 1) and need not be reviewed here.

Of more immediate import is the place of Wickliffe data in the regional picture. Kreisa and McDowell (Chapter 15) and Edging (Chapter 16) already have offered comments with regard to the subsistence data. To proceed further, however, there are problems of analytical comparability.

At the beginning of the Western Kentucky Project, Lewis (1986) imposed a chronological framework based on two-century units, beginning at A.D. 900: James Bayou, A.D. 900–1100; Dorena, A.D. 1100–1300; Medley, A.D. 1300–1500; and Jackson, A.D. 1500–1700. This was a step toward establishing order where data were inadequate. The immediate problem is that the three introspective Wickliffe periods do not fit comfortably into 200-year divisions (Figure 6.2); note the difficulty Edging (Chapter 16) encountered in trying to reconcile the Wickliffe data with those from his comparative sites.

One of the key markers of the transition from Dorena into Medley is the appearance of O'Byam Incised *var. O'Byam*. This type is also a key marker from Middle to Late Wickliffe, so that the comparison of Dorena to Early-Middle Wickliffe and Medley to Late Wickliffe is not difficult even if the Wickliffe data argue for an earlier dividing date.

The Wickliffe sequence's Early to Middle and Late to post-Wickliffe transitions are, however, not easy to tease out from the Western Kentucky Project

	CAHOKIA	WICKLIFFE	LOWER TENN-CUMB. & KINCAID	ANGEL	WEST KENTUCKY PROJECT
AD 1600				Caborn-Welborn	Jackson
AD 1500	Vulcan				
	(Oneota)				Medley
AD 1400		??	Tinsley Hill	Angel 3	
AD 1300	Sand Prairie	Late Wickliffe	Angelly	Angel 2	
	Morehead	Middle Wickliffe		– – – – –	Dorena
AD 1200	Stirling	Early Wickliffe	Jonathan Creek	Angel 1	
AD 1100	Lohman	??	– – – – –	?	
	Edelhart		Douglas?	Yankeetown	James Bayou
AD 1000					

⟵ Late Woodland Cultures ⟶

Notes:
1. Cahokia sequence based on calibrated dates from Pauketat 1994 and Hall 1991.
2. Western Kentucky project sequence from Lewis 1990a.
3. Wickliffe/Lower Tenn-Cumberland/Angel from Clay, Hilgeman, and Wesler 1991.

6.2. Chronologies of the Lower Ohio Valley and American Bottom.

data. The Wickliffe sequence thus may be seen as a hypothesis for testing in the stratigraphic records of nearby Mississippian sites. Space limitations have discouraged publication of level-by-level, unit-by-unit ceramic counts for any Western Kentucky Project site except Turk (15Ce6), which is very similar to Wickliffe in size and topographic setting. Reorganizing Edging's (1995:appendix 1) ceramic data to compare with the Wickliffe analysis provides a test of the exportability of the Wickliffe sequence.

In Edging's Unit 1, Levels 1 through 3 produced incising but no red-filming and relate to the Late Wickliffe assemblages. Incised and red-filmed sherds are equally represented in Levels 4 and 5, a Middle Wickliffe pattern. The presence of a sherd of O'Byam Incised *var. Adams* in a wall trench supports the Middle Wickliffe identification.

Levels 1 and 2 of Unit 2 yielded incising but no red-filming, a Late Wickliffe assemblage. Levels 3 through 5 and the features produced a Middle Wickliffe assemblage, in which incising and red-filming are equally represented. Edging noted a sherd of O'Byam Incised *var. O'Byam* in Level 5 of this unit, but also identified an intrusive feature whose fill was included in the level excavations, to which the *var. O'Byam* sherd can be attributed.

In Level 1 of Unit 3, incising outnumbers red-filming, relating the deposit to the Late Wickliffe period. Below Level 1, however, red-filming decisively overwhelms incising, an Early Wickliffe characteristic. A sherd of O'Byam Incised *var. Adams* was recovered from a feature, indicating that Unit 3 deposits probably represent the full Wickliffe sequence, even though a Middle Wickliffe midden could not be isolated.

Finally, the top two levels of Unit 4 present a Late Wickliffe ceramic assemblage. Diagnostics are scarce in Levels 3 through 8, but as an aggregate, they fit a Middle Wickliffe pattern, confirmed by a sherd of O'Byam Incised *var. Adams* in Level 3. It seems likely, then, that the Wickliffe ceramic periods can provide useful comparability at the Turk site.

Another Mississippi period site in the Jackson Purchase, Chambers (15Ml109), provides an additional chance to test some Wickliffe dating mechanisms, in this case, the handle and plate formulas. The Chambers site was cut in two by earth borrowing for road construction. Pollack and Railey (1987) excavated two test units in the southern area, which retained a deep midden, and more extensively in the shallower northern area. Plate and handle measurements can be compared with radiocarbon dates (Table 6.7CD). By the radiocarbon dates and the ceramic totals, Chambers would seem to fit a Late Wickliffe time frame, with some indication of a component equivalent to Middle Wickliffe.

The general sequence of loop to strap handles and flared bowls to plates fits well at Chambers. The deepest level of Unit 3 yielded Late Wickliffe dates both by carbon 14 and by handle formula. In Unit 4, two identical carbon 14 dates from the deepest two levels indicate a Middle Wickliffe deposition. The plate and handle formula dates suggest that Level 6 also belongs to the Middle Wickliffe period. Combining Levels 1 through 5 as a Late Wickliffe deposit and Levels 6 through 8 as a Middle Wickliffe deposit produces formula dates consistent with the proposed sequence.

The northern area is interesting. The radiocarbon dates indicate a Late Wickliffe occupation. Plate and handle formula dates, however, imply that there is also a heavy component of Middle Wickliffe, not well represented by the radiocarbon samples. Level-by-level type counts for the ceramics are not available to check the Wickliffe assemblage analogies.

Ceramics and stratigraphy at Turk and Chambers, then, compare very closely with those from Wickliffe, and the occupation spans of the sites appear to be very similar. Radiocarbon dates at Turk, too, are broadly comparable (Table 6.8CD). The Early Turk date has a large uncertainty but overlaps considerably with Early Wickliffe. The Middle Turk dates compare well with Middle Wickliffe. The Late Turk dates overlap substantially with Late Wickliffe, but tend toward a later terminus—which brings up the problem in comparing the end of the Late Wickliffe period with the Western Kentucky Project's Medley division: compatibility of horizon markers.

The ceramic markers for the end of the Late Wickliffe ceramic period and the beginning of a postulated post-Wickliffe period are defined by analogy with the Lower Tennessee-Cumberland and Angel sequences (Clay, Hilgeman, and Wesler 1991; Hilgeman 1992): deep plates, including O'Byam Incised *var. Stewart,* and broad strap rims. The use of these traits as horizon markers in the Lower Ohio Valley is a relatively recent introduction (Clay, Hilgeman, and Wesler 1991; Wesler 1994). They were not incorporated into Western Kentucky Project analyses. Further, the Western Kentucky Project analyses do list sherds of O'Byam Incised *var. Stewart,* but the definition is not the same. Western Kentucky Project sherd analysts distinguish *Stewart* from *O'Byam* on the basis of engraving versus incising, not the length of the rim. The Wickliffe analysis lumps the Western Kentucky Project's *Stewart* together with *O'Byam.*

Thus, it is not possible to tell from extant reports whether deep plates or broad straps characterize late Turk site assemblages. The later end of the Turk radiocarbon assays admit this possibility. There are also radiocarbon dates in this range from Adams (Lewis ed. 1986:156), Twin Mounds (Kreisa 1988:49, 54), and McLeod Bluff (Lawrence 1996), and collections from the latter site at the University of Kentucky (R. B. Clay, pers. com. 1991) and in private hands include O'Byam Incised *var. Stewart.* To evaluate the late radiocarbon dates fully in the context of ceramic and assemblage periods comparable to those of the Wickliffe sequence, Mississippianists in western Kentucky will have to standardize the definitions, whatever the final agreement on a culture/chronological sequence turns out to be.

Compatibility of analyses will be crucial to a finely calibrated regional picture of assemblage change, subsistence trends, the timing of platform mound construction episodes, and abandonments of the mound centers. If Hally's (1996:112) model that the typical life span of a Mississippian chiefdom is 75 to 100 years is to be tested in western Kentucky, phases of that interval (or less) must be employed. The Wickliffe sequence meets this criterion and should be tested systematically in other sites.

THE HISTORICAL ARCHAEOLOGY OF WICKLIFFE MOUNDS

The Wickliffe Mounds site has taken its place in archaeological literature as a Mississippi period site, and the WMRC investigations on the site since 1984 have concentrated on that late prehistoric occupation. The analysis, and foregoing discussion, largely ignored the historic period artifacts recovered, except where they helped to define disturbances and to sort out where previous excavations already had explored. However, the history of the Wickliffe Mounds in the twentieth century is significant also, in its contribution to the history of Kentucky archaeology and the history of the development of tourism.

The 1930s, which saw the purchase of the Wickliffe Mounds site by Fain King as an entrepreneurial effort, were also a time of expansion of tourism.

There does not seem to be a lot of good research on tourism history, but a couple of key points are fairly clear. Tourism expanded with transportation technology, first as railhead destinations, especially spas, and then more aggressively with the advent of the family automobile, so that attractions could be developed wherever a road could be cut. With this latter expansion, the heyday of caves and archaeological sites as tourist attractions began.

A quick survey of newspapers of the period shows something of the new popularity of archaeology and, especially, of artifacts. As a single example, the *Louisville Courier-Journal,* dated March 17, 1929, had a story about a family in eastern Kentucky who had been discovered faking stone artifacts for sale "to meet the growing demand for momentos of the prehistoric race that once inhabited [Kentucky] . . . [W]hat effect the disclosure will have on the relic-hunting fad remains to be seen, for Kentucky has come to be looked on as a regular treasure trove of prehistoric relics." Unfortunately, any adverse effect on collecting was not permanent.

The fad for collecting evidently also engendered a fad for viewing, as entrepreneurs were quick to note. One area that jumped into the archaeology attraction business was that around Lewistown, Illinois. Dickson Mounds survives as a fine museum, but initially it had its rivals. The competition among the sites is reminiscent of the rivalry among commercial caves in Kentucky, including shots fired in the heat of commerce.

Western Kentucky and Tennessee saw similar competition. Besides the Wickliffe Mounds, there were would-be competitors at Tiptonville, Tennessee, and in Logan County, Kentucky. The Logan County site, known as Prehistoric Lost City, was advertised in the North American Indian Relic Collectors Association Bulletin (NAIRCA 1936), which pointed out helpfully that "Six National Continental Highways Lead to Lost City."

Although that publication did not mention the Wickliffe site, the Reelfoot Burial Mound at Tiptonville, Tennessee, was unabashedly a copy of the Wickliffe Mounds. Advertisements in the Tiptonville newspaper in 1935 announced "34 Ancient Indian skeletons unearthed and lying in their natural state, with beads, pottery, and implements of war . . . See this educational and historical sight." News reports in the same paper made the parallel explicit: "Lake County is going to have a famous buried city of its own," and, "They have nothing at Wyckliffe that we have not found at Lasater's Corner." William Lawrence (pers. com., c. 1990) tested the Tiptonville property and found no indication that there actually was a site there.

The engine for these developments was tourism, and Fain King clearly copied the Dickson Mounds as Tiptonville and Lost City copied Wickliffe. Fain King visited the University of Chicago Lewistown expedition in August 1932 (Deuel 1932). Allan Harn (pers. com., c. 1990) learned from conversations with Don Dickson that King tried to hire Dickson, then Raymond Dickson, to direct the work at Wickliffe. Both declined, perhaps because they could tell that King's motives were far less academic than their own.

King's commercial incentives were easily recognized by contemporary archaeologists, with whom he alternately feuded and attempted truces. King wrote to W. S. Webb on October 1, 1932, announcing his purchase of the Wickliffe site and his intention to set up a museum like Dickson's (see Chapter 3). King feigned (or, to be fair, perhaps sincerely believed he had) academic motives for his public program, stating that "this work is open to the public at all times and has had much to do with acquainting the great masses with Mississippi Valley archaeology" (F. King 1936).

Whether we judge this acquaintance to be a good thing or not, the statement is accurate. Questions that WMRC visitors ask give some insight into the kind of things they did learn. The questions, "Where's the guy who died in disgrace?" and "Where's the 7-foot-tall woman?" are so repetitive they drive the staff crazy. Fortunately, the visitor who insisted that he had been shown a "wooden Indian torture chamber" is, so far, unique. A large number of people did get their first glimpse of archaeology in this commercialized setting. The impact of King's project on the development of tourism in western Kentucky still cannot be clearly measured.

King's project also had an impact on Kentucky archaeology. During the years that he and Fay-Cooper Cole maintained their uneasy friendship, Cole managed to introduce Chicago-style grid excavations to the Wickliffe project. Despite King's showmanship and his private funding, his excavation was very much a part of the WPA-era establishment of archaeology in Kentucky, and it was perhaps the most publicly visible part of that history.

Thus, new methods in archaeology, and in tourism, were part of the King project in the 1930s, and part of the history of Kentucky archaeology. Archaeology and tourism are elements of human behavior. As human behaviors, should they not be reflected in the archaeological record?

The simple physical fact of the displays is a relic of King's project. They would not exist without the tourism motive, but they also freeze a moment in 1930s archaeology. More subtly, the presented moment in archaeology is a blend of what really was done and found and of what King thought would sell to an audience, a blend that results, on close analysis, in considerable ambiguity.

The WMRC researchers have been most forcefully reminded of this ambiguity in studying the cemetery. The cemetery as displayed purported to be an *in situ* exposure. The display was distorted by what King thought a cemetery ought to look like: whole skulls replaced broken ones, bones were moved to where they ought to have been, or to demonstrate situations that ought to have occurred (like families being buried together), bones were modified and outright faked. Sixty years of visitors saw King's vision of an excavated cemetery, not an intact, exposed prehistoric cemetery (Matternes 1993).

Nonetheless, the concept of exposure *in situ* is a real archaeological ideal, and a lot of visitors understood it. The exhibit in the Mound D building, however inadvertently and implicitly, also suggested controlled provenience measures: some of the pedestals are 5 × 5-foot squares, remnants of the Chicago-influenced grid. In terms of the WMRC studies, King's balks and pedestals are features belonging to an archaeologist's activity set.

Not all such features are on display. WMRC excavators have identified King test units or balks and pedestals in several excavations, in attempts to trace the limits of his work (for details, see Chapter 18). A 1932 test in the north of Mound D, plotted on the Alabama sketch map (Figure 3.1), showed up in the 1987 Mound D North excavation. Another anomalous profile, in the Northwest Village, appears to be a Mound E 1932 test, roughly mapped in the same notes. A disturbance northeast of Mound C probably represents yet another 1932 Mound E test, described but not mapped in the Alabama notes. In Mound D South, a profile puzzled excavators for some time before they realized that they had cut across a pedestal from the 1930s, where King tested deeper into subsoil on the east than on the west.

Several King profiles have considerable slope, such as the one in the remnant of Mound F, with topsoil and perhaps backfill over mound fill. Similarly, at the edge of the East Midden, the boundary of King's excavation is marked by a profile of nearly 45 degrees. Both of these were gridded excavations; is this 1930s Chicago style for perimeter profiles, or King's idiosyncratic version thereof? This question could be tested at, for example, the Kincaid site (Cole 1951).

WMRC excavators encountered a more puzzling archaeological feature in the summit of Mound C, a historic disturbance that at first looked archaeological by its squared-off corner. The excavators first thought that this was a 1932 King test that had not been recorded anywhere, since it was aligned very closely to the King tests they had already seen. However, on excavation, it turned out to be a far less regular unit than expected. The current interpretation, although analysis cannot verify the dating, is that this is a post-King test begun as a square hole to impress tourists, but abandoned in frustration when the diggers found nothing but mound fill.

Evidence of the 1932 project occurs in other contexts. In 1992, the Mound C tests penetrated a gravel road in two units. A 1932 photograph from the University of Alabama files shows this road newly cut, but not yet graveled (Figure 3.10). There are two other noteworthy aspects of this photograph: the field camp in the background and also the circus tent over the cemetery excavation. The circus tent is secured by fairly substantial stakes—one of which was identified in 1992.

The field camp was a secondary focus of the 1993 excavations. From the photographs, one tent appears to be a field laboratory and the other sleeping quarters. The excavators' question was, simply, whether there is an archaeological signature of an archaeologist's field camp. The crew excavated six test units in the general area, half of them halting at Level 2 to minimize disturbance to the intact deposits. The director was not sure quite what he was looking for: tent stakes, maybe recording artifacts, such as pen nibs, or perhaps lost labeled artifacts (WMRC staff did scoop up a pile of labeled sherds in the woods in 1984, and another unlabeled pile in 1996). Unfortunately, although there are twentieth-century artifacts from these tests, it is not clear that any of them belong to the field camp.

Past tourism facilities, more than activities, do appear in the archaeological record. WMRC tests on the west side of the office building, conducted to check for undisturbed deposits before expanding the building in 1985, produced detritus from the original office on the same location. Several features are associated with this structure. From one, excavators recovered what still stands as the single artifact from a middle Mississippian site that indisputably shows direct contact with Mexico: a cinqo centavo, dated 1953.

Another set of artifacts that betrays the tourism influence was recovered from Mound F. Mound F had an exhibit building over it, which apparently burned. WMRC excavations recovered several sherds of Southwestern corrugated ware, which must have been on display in this building. The corrugated pot is presumably a 1930s trade item, not a late prehistoric one.

Finally, Mound A was excavated first in 1932 and was left as a display of sequential mound construction, which actually was not a bad idea at all. By the time Murray State University acquired the site, the Mound A excavation was near collapse. In Test I, inside the old excavation, excavators found one rectangular posthole with shreds of uncarbonized wood in it, which does not fit the pattern of the Mississippian postholes. More than one visitor has told the WMRC staff that in previous visits they were able to go down into a deep hole in the ground, and this posthole probably is a trace of a staircase down into the mound. At least, it seems unlikely to be a Mississippian torture chamber.

Other tourist features remain to be investigated. Informants report that the Kings had a set of cabins for tourists and guests along the northern margin of the site. Probably the gravel walkway encountered in the North Central Village testing was associated with those cabins. A house just north of Mound D apparently served also as a reception area for favored visitors whom Blanche King invited for tea. Then, of course, the broad gully on the south side is also a feature, having been bulldozed out for the double driveway. This had a rather drastic impact on the topography of the site, but is purely a tourism impact. The staff residence that most likely destroyed Mound G is also a post-King but tourism-era feature. Tests in the Mound G vicinity penetrated the gravel of the residence's driveway.

There are also at least two pre-King historic features. The set of concrete piers or footings across the top of Mound C is still unexplained. Dense brick rubble in two tests in the vicinity of Mound G probably is associated with the office of the Wisconsin Chair Company, which sold the site to King, although there are no artifacts other than brick to confirm such an identification.

Some of these aspects of the archaeological record are not as well recorded or analyzed as they should have been, because it only occurred to the analyst relatively recently that the archaeology of archaeology and tourism has a contribution to make. Archaeologists know that they destroy those parts of the archaeological record that they excavate, but what more subtle traces do they leave of their own activities? Will their efforts be documented by future archaeologists, studying how methods changed through time—or how textbook ideals reflected actual practices?

Occasionally in a class in introductory anthropology, a student wants to do a paper on the impact of anthropologists on the societies they study. Very little information is available, because (perhaps in denial) very few ethnographers look for that process, and very few groups are restudied. Some important archaeological sites, however, are revisited in search of new data. Archaeologists can also document old archaeology, if we think about it.

This idea emphasizes something that archaeology professors teach, but do not always discuss explicitly in analysis: all human activities, as well as natural processes, leave traces in the archaeological record, and excavators must interpret everything that has happened to a site since the occupation in which they are most interested, to understand fully their impact on that target record. Archaeologists know this. But we tend to see a site as either prehistoric or historic. Perhaps excavators should recognize that, even in prehistoric sites, they may also have opportunities to further the studies of such arcane twentieth-century activities as tourism—and archaeology.

7 Wickliffe Mounds,

A.D. 1100–2000:

Summary and Conclusions

Wickliffe Mounds Research Center investigations have yielded a much more detailed picture of the history of the Wickliffe site than previously was achievable. WMRC crews have evaluated the deposits and chronology of the major and several minor mounds, have tested the principal sectors of the village, and have begun sorting out the extremely complex relationships of mound, village, and cemetery.

Analysis has established the characteristics of three intrasite periods based on consistent concordances of radiocarbon dates, Oxidizable Carbon Ratio dates, stratigraphic sequences, ceramic type assemblages, rim and handle forms, and assemblage groups. The investigations have indicated a pattern of village expansion from a compact, moundless settlement circa A.D. 1100, through successive construction of a number of mounds and extension of domestic areas along the crest of the ridge, to a final, intensely occupied town that crowded the edges of the bluff by about A.D. 1350. Most or all of the villagers moved away after about A.D. 1350, for reasons that are still unknown.

Although the current campaign of excavations is complete, the work of analysis, education, and preservation will continue. Many of the analyses reported here are first steps, raising questions that may be answered by more detailed, more comprehensive, or more creative further analysis. Scholars interested in portions of the database are welcome to consult the collections.

EVALUATING THE KING EXCAVATIONS

Fain King's crews excavated in six areas of the Wickliffe site and labeled Mounds A through F in order of excavation. Only a few artifacts can be traced to Mounds A, B, and C. Sketchy notes and photographs curated in Alabama provided some basic information about those first three excavations. Without additional investigation, only a few interpretations were possible: Mound A was a platform mound created in at least three stages, with large wattle-and-daub structures in the earlier two stages, exposed by excavation. Mound B was a platform mound with an internal stratigraphy, but whether there were structures at any but the deepest level was uncertain. Mound C was the location of a cemetery with extended and bundle burials. No information from these mounds allowed observers to assign any dates more specifically than to the Mississippi period.

The WMRC investigations have provided additional perspective. Mound A apparently was a ceremonial mound, without domestic middens on the mound summits, although it covered an earlier midden. Mound B did have middens on at least two summits and may be interpreted as the substructure for an elite residence. Mound C is much more complex than the cemetery, which is complicated enough by itself: the cemetery was one of several stratigraphic events, beginning with a midden and followed by a complex of three mounds, which were in turn engulfed by later midden. A lack of artifacts associated with newly identified burials raises serious doubts about the "grave goods" described in the 1930s and exhibited for many years.

Mounds D, E, and F, excavated with the benefit of University of Chicago methods and consultation, are much better represented by extant artifact collections, but do not have accompanying notes or photographs. Despite the number of artifacts, they are more difficult to interpret. Mounds D and F clearly were mounds. Mound D contained adult burials within the mound and a number of apparent artifact caches, as well as numerous infant graves. Infant burials were also attributed to Mound F, but there is no information about them, nor are there surviving specimens that can be identified as Mound F burials. The Kings identified it as a "Signal Mound" because of deposits of ash, but the structure or function of the mound is unknown.

Mound E is even more problematic. Its location is unrecorded. Two potential locations of Mound E as recorded in the Alabama notes revealed no sign of a backfilled hole large enough to have contained the reconstructed Mound E grid. Blanche King called it a village area, and not really a mound.

Again recent excavations provide perspective. It is evident that the infant burials of Mound D belonged mostly to a village level sealed beneath the mound, and not to the mound proper. The apparent artifact caches, the elongated shape of the mound, and the presence of adult burials in the mound permit the hypothesis that Mound D was an elite burial mound. A Parkin Punctate jar raises the possibility that some of the burials may be intrusive, but at present there is no indication that the jar was associated with the burials, and it can be said only to hint at some intrusion or late activity. The Mound D grid may be placed approximately on the ground with the help of known excavation limits and an existing iron pin that appears to be a datum marked on the Alabama sketch map and in King correspondence.

Mound E, by process of elimination, probably was the south end of the site, separated from the rest of the village by Highway 51/60/62. Blanche King's statement that it was a village area makes sense. Although the area of the Mound E excavation can be inferred, the orientation of the grid is unknown.

Mound F's grid may be placed on the ground with reference to the known limits of excavation. Recent excavations were able to show that a tiny remnant of the mound survives and that a few truncated features escaped excavation at the base of the mound. It is still not possible to interpret a function of this mound.

Modern excavations have allowed some insight into the chronology of the King mounds as well. Mounds A and B sealed Early Wickliffe middens. The first stage of Mound B belonged to the Early Wickliffe period. Most of the platform stages of Mounds A and B arose during the Middle Wickliffe period, and each mound received a final mantle in the Late period.

Mound C sealed a Middle Wickliffe midden and was overlain by a Middle Wickliffe cemetery. The mound itself cannot be dated by ceramics, but is bracketed by the two middens. The Mound C complex was overlain by a Late Wickliffe midden, the early deposits of which may have been intruded by late burial activity.

Mound D sealed an Early Wickliffe village midden, apparently a shallow one. The north edge of Mound D is a Late Wickliffe deposit, indicating that the mound was completed in the Late period. Analysts can discount neither the possibility that the Late Wickliffe mound incorporated earlier mound stages nor that there were late prehistoric intrusions.

There are no extant traces of Mound E deposits, and all interpretations of this area will depend on the King collection.

Both Mound F and underlying midden and feature deposits belong to the Late Wickliffe period. This conclusion must be hedged, however, since the WMRC excavations concentrated on the west end of Mound F, and the possibility of an earlier deposit on the east end, nearer the center of the site, cannot be ignored.

The typological percentages of the King collection ceramics from Mounds D, E, and F compare very well with those of the WMRC excavations. On the basis of the ceramics, even the deepest levels of each mound have Late Wickliffe ceramic assemblages. However, Mound D certainly incorporates earlier components, at least a thin basal midden masked by the 1-foot-deep excavation levels, and E and F may possibly do so. Further research on these collections will attempt to map key ceramic types and rim forms in three dimensions, exploring the possibility of internal complexity. In general, however, the artifact collections from Mounds D, E, and F can all be characterized as Late Wickliffe assemblages, with minor Early and/or Middle period inclusions.

From this perspective, Reinburg's (1987) caution that the faunal collection underrepresents fish may be reconsidered. It is quite true that smaller bone specimens probably are not as well sampled as larger ones. However, Kreisa and McDowell's (Chapter 15) samples also indicate a very small proportion of fish in the Late Wickliffe period. The King faunal sample may be as reliable as the ceramic sample appears to be, which suggests further that the large sample of shellfish also is provisionally acceptable as a Late Wickliffe assemblage.

Unfortunately, the lithic debitage was not systematically collected in the 1930s, or at least not curated subsequently, nor were other major categories of materials such as daub.

For all its faults in modern terms, given the goals of the 1930s, the King excavation project would have been considered a success if King or one of the Chicago participants had published a detailed descriptive report. It surely would have met the objectives of the University of Kentucky's visit to McLeod Bluff, which were simply to see whether that site compared more closely with Tolu, which did not have stone box graves, or with Williams, which did have them, both sites then considered to be components of a Gordon aspect (Webb and Funkhouser 1933:5). The Wickliffe assemblage and recorded features would have been an excellent comparative resource in the systematics of the Midwestern Taxonomic System and subsequent Burial Mound/Temple Mound chronological scheme. Indeed, those archaeologists who saw the Wickliffe excavations firsthand were quite aware of how it enlightened the developing picture of Middle Mississippian, and they compared it freely to other sites known at the time: Bennett's (1940:118–19) twenty-six-trait "Tentative Inventory of the Kincaid Focus" was a near-perfect fit to the Wickliffe site. Failing a Wickliffe report, the Mississippian sites of Kentucky's Mississippi River counties were exemplified only by the painfully inadequate McLeod Bluff project until the University of Illinois Western Kentucky Project and the WMRC sought to address the gap in the 1980s.

In the light of discussions of Wickliffe as a chiefdom (Chapter 6), it may be that the most unfortunate effect of the King excavations is that they destroyed the potentially elite contexts (the residences on/in Mound B, the burials in Mound D). Although the middens identified in Mound B are suggestive, they are only the peripheral scatters of the middens that must have been associated with residences on the mound and thus they provide (even with additional excavations) only small samples of this domestic assemblage. Future research in neighboring mound centers may be able to make up for this loss at Wickliffe.

EARLY WICKLIFFE, A.D. 1100–1175

Native Americans arrived at the Wickliffe site around A.D. 1100 and built a small settlement. They already were carriers of a Mississippian culture, as characterized by shell-tempered ceramics, maize agriculture, and rectangular wattle-and-daub houses surrounding a central plaza. Most of their ceramics were jars (some with loop handles) and bowls, but they also made a few bottles, hooded bottles, pans, and funnels. More pots were red-slipped than incised, and incised decorations included the patterns now identified as Matthews Incised *vars. Beckwith* and *Manly*, Barton Incised (most of these specimens are a fairly unrefined version of the pattern), and Mound Place Incised. The residents buried deceased infants within the village, and at least one older child at the edge of the village, but the location of the cemetery for older persons is unknown.

The Early Wickliffe village was a compact settlement, clustered around the plaza. There is evidence that some activities sprawled away from the town center both north and south, but either they did not cause much midden to accumulate, or the middens were disturbed by later occupation. Small flakes, more likely associated with resharpening than manufacture of stone tools, cluster, with an overall distribution that centers on Mound A.

For most of the Early Wickliffe period, the village had no mounds. Toward the end of the period, the villagers built the first stage of Mound B, which became the residence of an elite family—the only elite residence that can be identified. It is interesting that raising the elite residence apparently took precedence over raising the ceremonial mound, Mound A, which may indicate something of the consolidation of a chief's power, the priority of chiefly importance over the ceremonial sphere, the investment of both political and ceremonial power in the chief, or some combination of social, political, and spiritual power than cannot even be dissected into categories.

MIDDLE WICKLIFFE, A.D. 1175–1250

The Middle Wickliffe period saw the expansion of the village along the higher and better-drained areas of the ridge, meaning north and south more than east and west. The villagers put much more effort into raising mounds, adding several stages to both platform mounds and creating a three-mound complex around Mound C. The purpose of the Mound C complex is unknown, but it became the site for a cemetery that seems to have been established around, rather than on or in, the primary Mound C.

New ceramic characteristics mark the Middle Wickliffe period, particularly flare-rimmed bowls. The use of incising as decoration increased, although the only new incised type was O'Byam Incised *var. Adams,* which took advantage of the top of the flared bowl rims as a surface for incising. The technique of negative painting was new; specimens are rare enough that they may have been traded from elsewhere. Red-slipped pots were still common. The villagers were using more funnels for whatever they used funnels for, and in general they were using more bowls in proportion to cooking vessels, a trend in which the Mound B residents led the way.

The Mound B residents were also distinguished by relatively choosy consumption of deer—or at least by discard of better quality cuts of deer in their middens than the rest of the village. They were not, however, distinguished by other markers, such as ornaments or exotic raw materials. Only the presence of a Ramey Incised sherd, influenced by or traded from Cahokia, hints at prestige goods, but this distinction is also shared by Mound A, which apparently was not a residence. Daub clusters, with a distribution centering on Mound B, suggesting substantial architecture here. Large flakes show a similar pattern, raising the possibility of some concentration of the manufacturing of knapped lithics. These conclusions might be made with more confidence if the summits of Mound B, and their associated residences, had survived for additional study.

The Middle Wickliffe villagers continued life, in the main, with little change from previous years. They grew much the same crops. They began depending less on fish, however, and more on terrestrial birds and mammals. Wattle-and-daub was the mode of construction, and at least one building had a painted floor. The relative number of tools, flake tools among the stone tools, craft items, and personal items was greatest, though the difference is subtle, and higher quality or higher status textiles appeared in this period. A peak in the import of Burlington chert implies more interaction with the people of the American Bottom.

LATE WICKLIFFE, A.D. 1250–1350

From an archaeologist's perspective, there are a number of changes in the Late Wickliffe period.

The townspeople continued to build mounds, although their effort shifted away from the platforms. They added only the final mantle to each of the platform mounds (and plowing and 1930s excavation left no record of any structure atop the final stages of Mounds A and B, which can only be assumed to have continued their previous functions as ceremonial mound and elite residence, respectively). The people added Mounds D, F, and H to the townscape. (It is possible that Mounds D and F were begun in the Middle Wickliffe period, but no evidence has as yet demonstrated so.) The area of the village expanded yet again, to the edges of the bluff, and the depths of some of the middens imply a concentrated population. Utilized flakes cluster, with a distribution that centers on the Northwest Village, indicating a different organization of some activities from previous periods.

Plates, a wider-rimmed version of the flared bowl, appeared in the Late Wickliffe period, as did new forms of decoration, mainly more complex patterns of incising sorted into the archaeological types O'Byam Incised *var. O'Byam,* Leland and Winterville Incised, Owens Punctate, and untyped punctate. Incising in general was the dominant decorative technique. There was a trace of red-on-buff painting, called Carson Red-on-Buff by archaeologists, perhaps toward the end of the period, while red-slipped pots diminished in frequency. The trend toward an increased proportion of serving vessels to jars continued. Pans, and Kimmswick Fabric Impressed sherds, were a lesser proportion of the assemblages, while funnels and Wickliffe Thick increased. Another tendency, continuing through all three periods, was the proportional increase of potsherds in the refuse assemblages, and a complementary decrease in lithic debitage.

Trends in dietary change also continued. Fish and aquatic birds made up still less of the menu, terrestrial birds and animals more. Concurrently, fishhooks drop out of the artifact assemblage and projectile points increase in number. On the other hand, the proportion of tools, crafts, and personal items in the overall assemblage declines from Middle Wickliffe levels. Burlington chert appears least often in the Late period, perhaps reflecting the dissolution of Cahokia, although the northern focus of trade in lithics continues.

The end of the Late Wickliffe period saw a major change in the village: its abandonment.

POST-WICKLIFFE PERIOD

There is a trace of artifactual evidence of activity in the post–A.D. 1350 era. A handful of sherds—literally a handful: half a dozen deep plate rims, even fewer broad strap handles, one Parkin Punctate jar—typologically date later than the end of the Late Wickliffe period. If they were concentrated, they might have suggested a farmstead occupation, but these artifacts are widely scattered across the site. Of course, applying a date such as A.D. 1350 to a change between plates and deep plates, intermediate loops/straps to strap handles, or to the abandonment of a village, is quite arbitrary, and it is entirely possible that those late markers belong to the very last decade(s) of the Wickliffe village.

Clay (1997) suggests several regional trends: that mound construction decreased after about A.D. 1250, with few if any new mounds begun after A.D. 1300; that the late, extensive cemeteries generally show little status differentiation, arguing for a generally more egalitarian society than was found during classic Mississippian times; that the decline in mound building and creation of large cemeteries were related in expressing a shift "in the nature of veneration of a chiefly class," that is, a loss of influence or power by the chiefs (Clay 1997:29–30). In a related phenomenon, sites with fewer mounds, such as Twin Mounds (Kreisa 1988, 1990a), sometimes seen as secondary centers, instead may be recipients of populations from the disintegrating multimound centers rather than subsidiary villages. These trends must be evaluated critically with new data that fully characterize the occupational and mound-building sequences of a number of regional sites, investigating regional patterns in the light of such models as Hally's (1993, 1996) parity of chiefdom with platform mound, Blitz's (1999) fission-fusion processes, and Wright's (1984) chiefly cycling.

The Vacant Quarter hypothesis (Williams 1980, 1983, 1990) suggests that much of the Central Mississippi Valley was effectively abandoned by the early A.D. 1400s. At this time, there are no data from Wickliffe that challenge the hypothesis.

WHAT DID THE VILLAGE LOOK LIKE?

Archaeologists tend, by training and specialist preoccupation, to look at archaeological sites as collections of data: piles of potsherds and/or other artifacts, layers of soil, arrangements of features, statistical tables. They tend to set aside such apparently simple questions as, "What did the village look like?" Visitors to sites like Wickliffe ask that question all the time, however, and it is worthwhile for the professional to stop once in a while and try to visualize the site as a living place, as once it was. For one attempt to picture the vitality of the Wickliffe village, readers might consult Wesler (1991e), but they should note that it was written before the functions of Mounds A and B were interpreted as they are now.

A lifelike reconstruction of the village might begin by considering its size and population. At the end of Chapter 3, the analyst suggested that an area of 2.5 hectares (a bit more than 6 acres) would be a reasonable estimate for the Late Wickliffe village. Perhaps 10 percent of the central area was taken up by plaza and the immediately surrounding mounds.

The WMRC staff has generally estimated the peak population (again, presumably during the Late Wickliffe period) at about 250 to 300. This has always been more of a guess than an estimate, but it fits with Stout's (1989) estimate of 600 for the larger Adams site, south of Wickliffe in Fulton County, Kentucky. It also accords well with Muller's (1997:194–201) figures for historic and late prehistoric town size. The standing joke is that Wickliffe then was only a little smaller than Wickliffe now, and probably more fun on a Saturday night.

Muller (1997) settles on an average household size of five persons, as a useful figure for comparison. For a village of 250 people, then, there would be about fifty households. Historic households often had several structures in small compounds, such as a winter house, perhaps a summer house, a granary, and/or an open shed or lean-to for summer shade. The visually homogeneous nature of the Wickliffe middens, the palimpsest pattern of wall trenches at the subsoil, and the test unit peepholes of the WMRC excavations have conspired to obscure any clear view of a multistructure household at Wickliffe, but the image should be kept in mind.

If the Late Wickliffe village covered about 25,000 square meters (about 270,000 square feet), and about 10 percent was taken up with the central plaza and mounds, then about 22,500 square meters (about 240,000 square feet) would have been available to households. For fifty households, this area computes to an average of 450 square meters (about 4800 square feet) per household. This is most easily visualized within the Wickliffe grid as a 20 × 20-meter square (about 66 × 66 feet). If the average house was about 4 × 5 meters, or 20 square meters (about 13 × 16 feet, or 208 square feet), then about 5 percent of the household's area ("houselot") would be taken up by the residence.

The figures translate to about twenty households per hectare, or .05 hectare per household (8 households per acre, or one-eighth acre per household). Comparatively, this density is similar to the more populous areas of the American Bottom (Gregg [1975] as recalculated by Muller [1997:219]). Muller considers this to be quite dense for Mississippian habitation, but given the topography of Wickliffe, it makes sense: Wickliffe is well protected from flooding, but only a stone's throw from the Mississippi River and from extensive bottomlands where the main agricultural fields would have been. Why spread out in the floodplains, and sink into swamp with every flood, when a good dry ridge is so handy?

Getting past the numbers, a mental picture of the village can draw on both historic descriptions and archaeological findings. The Late Wickliffe village may have had about fifty houses scattered around a central plaza and mound complex. Some overlooked the river, others the ravines, while still others looked toward the plaza. The houses had plenty of space around them to contain household gardens with vegetables and herbs, footpaths from house to house or to the plaza, small outbuildings such as granaries and arbors, maybe racks and poles for drying food and hanging equipment, and a cooking fire near the front door. The houses were built of wattle and daub, with thatched roofs. Judging by the growth of gourds over a reconstructed house in recent years, houses were splendid vine poles, and the thatch may have been hidden by the broad leaves and heavy fruit of squashes and gourds in late summer to early autumn.

Although what survives in the ground gives us a rather dull, earth-toned mental image, in fact the village may have been quite colorful. Many houses probably had whitewash and resplendent paintings on their walls. Mats and fabrics were dyed with natural pigments. DeSoto's chroniclers wrote of colors like enamel on wood "of whatever color they like, and it gives the bow or any other wood a glaze like crockery . . . such a luster that one can see himself in them" (Clayton, Knight, and Moore 1993[2]:290, 305).

The focus of the village was the plaza, with a large thatched structure soaring above on each of the two platform mounds. These buildings, too, would have been painted with eye-catching colors. Large shedlike structures may have flanked the plaza, to offer shade for gatherings. A large pole for the ball game, precursor of lacrosse, cast a shadow across the open town center. Whether there were trees inside the village, an oft-asked question, is unknown; tree root molds are often found in the excavation, but when any particular tree grew there is impossible to say. The advantages of a few shade trees in the summer are obvious, however, and given that many historic Southeastern villages were dispersed through the woods, a mental picture of Wickliffe certainly could include a few tall, leafy trees. Blackberries and other useful weeds may have grown around the village edge, broken at intervals by footpaths into the woods.

To this picture, add people: 250 men, women, and children. Children play with each other and with dogs, rolling hoops, throwing spears at rolling stones, or hunting lizards with small bows. Some children help their mothers in gardens, weaving blankets or mats or baskets, making pottery, tanning hides stretched on poles, cooking in front of houses. A few women are walking up or down the path to the stream on the north side of the village, carrying pots or gourds for water, or following the path down the west slope toward the farm fields. Men are down at the river bank, drawing dugout canoes onto the protected banks at the mouth of a small stream; walking in from the fields with fresh game caught raiding the corn; gathered in small groups under shade arbors, fixing tools and weapons, carving shell, bone, or wooden ornaments, throwing bone dice; or standing beside their houses, patching daub walls or thatched roofs. Under the gallery next to the plaza, a chief or village elder is meeting with visitors from another village, here for a diplomatic visit or exchange of gifts. It is a kaleidoscope of motion, a medley of voices. Anything a family needs to do to make a living or maintain social harmony in a small farming village is going on.

The scene will vary by season and time of day. Most artists' renderings of these villages seem to be set in summer, with villagers stripped to the minimum of clothing because of the heat. But in spring and fall, they would be more fully, and more colorfully, clothed; in winter, mud or snow would cover the ground among bedraggled remnants of gardens, while wisps of smoke drift from small holes in the house roofs. At night, during warmer seasons, activities cluster around the glowing cook fires in front of the houses, and villagers pass like shadows back and forth as they visit friends and neighbors. Over all drifts the haunting sound of a courting flute, played with some (or little) skill by a young man hidden in the fringe of woods, hoping that his young lady will hear and recognize that his song, however inelegant, is for her.

That was Wickliffe about A.D. 1300, as nearly as we can picture it now.

CONCLUSION

The WMRC took as its logo an owl effigy hooded bottle, chosen as one of the best-known pottery vessels from the site. (The original pot, unfortunately, was stolen in 1988, by thieves whose petty selfishness or spite has deprived thousands of visitors from appreciating it and nearly twenty of its fellows.) As a symbol, perhaps it should be replaced by the painted design discovered in 1994 on the hardened clay floor of a structure in the North Central Village: the cross and circle, or Sun Circle.

The Sun Circle has many meanings, undoubtedly more varied and more profound to the Native Americans who painted it than archaeologists can guess. In one meaning, its shape symbolizes the roundness of the world: not the planet, literally, but the world's spirit; an ideal that all things are related in a great circle of life, that each person and each community is part of a greater harmony, that humans are part of the roundness and must take responsibility for their effects on the whole.

The Wickliffe Mounds are completing a turn of the circle. They began as a Native American place, a focus of culture, communication, tradition, and ceremony. As an American settler's farm, the site still in some way was dedicated to life, although not to Native American culture. As a lumberyard, and then the scene of the exploitation of the archaeological record for tourist entertainment, it drew further away from its origins.

The archaeological analysis is far from complete, yet even as we pursue these studies, today the site is changing again. The excavations are concluded. Native Americans are returning to the site to teach, to communicate, to celebrate traditions, to take care of their ancestors. They are joining archaeologists and museum professionals, students and volunteers, and museum visitors to see the Wickliffe Mounds as common ground that embodies our human heritage, to see the past in the living, to appreciate tradition, to reconcile science and spirit.

References

ARCHIVES

Ballard County Deed Book 10:302, Ballard County Courthouse, Wickliffe, Kentucky.
M.S.M. Mound State Monument, Moundville, Alabama.
U.A. University of Alabama Library Archives, University, Alabama.
U.C. University of Chicago, Joseph Regenstein Library, Department of Anthropology records.
U.K. University of Kentucky Library Archives, W. S. Webb Collection, Lexington, Kentucky.
U.M.M.A. University of Michigan, Museum of Anthropology, Ceramics Repository records and Museum archives.

NEWSPAPERS

Cairo Evening Citizen and Bulletin, Cairo, Illinois.
Louisville Courier-Journal, Louisville, Kentucky.
New York Times, New York, New York.
Tiptonville Times, Tiptonville, Tennessee.

PUBLISHED SOURCES

Anderson, David G.
1990   Stability and Change in Chiefdom-Level Societies: An Examination of Mississippian Political Evolution on the South Atlantic Slope. In *Lamar Archaeology: Mississippian Chiefdoms in the Deep South,* edited by M. Williams and G. Shapiro, pp. 187–213. University of Alabama Press, Tuscaloosa.
1994   *The Savannah River Chiefdoms: Political Change in the Late Prehistoric Southeast.* University of Alabama Press, Tuscaloosa.
Ashton-Tate
1986   *dBASE III+.* Ashton-Tate, Torrance, California.
Baker, P. T., and W. T. Sanders
1972   Demographic Studies in Anthropology. *Annual Review of Anthropology* 1:151–78. Annual Reviews, Palo Alto.
Ball, Donald B.
1983   Approaches Toward the Dating of 19th Century Ohio Valley Flat Glass.

   Proceedings of the Symposium on Ohio Valley Urban and Historic Archaeology
   1:129–37. Archaeological Survey, University of Louisville, Louisville, Kentucky.

Behymer, F. A.
   1946   For Sale—One Ancient City. *Everyday Magazine* (St. Louis Post Dispatch),
          March 3.

Belmont, John S., and Stephen Williams
   1981   Painted Pottery Horizons in the Southern Mississippi Valley. *Geoscience and
          Man* 22:19–42.

Bennett, John W.
   1940   A Preliminary Survey of the Kincaid Component and Its Affiliations. M.A.
          thesis, University of Chicago.

Binford, Lewis R.
   1961   A New Method of Calculating Dates from Kaolin Pipe Stem Samples.
          Southeastern Archaeological Conference Newsletter 9(1): 19–21.

Binford, Lewis R., and Moreau S. Maxwell
   1961   *Excavation of Fort Michilimackinac, Mackinaw City, Michigan, 1959 Season.*
          Stone Publishing, Lansing.

Blitz, John H.
   1999   Mississippian Chiefdoms and the Fission-Fusion Process. *American Antiquity*
          64(4): 577–92.

Brain, Jeffrey P., and Philip Phillips
   1996   *Shell Gorgets, Styles of the Late Prehistoric and Protohistoric Southeast.* Peabody
          Museum Press, Cambridge, Massachusetts.

Brown, Ian W.
   1981   A Study of Stone Box Graves in Eastern North America. *Tennessee Anthro-
          pologist* 6:1–26.

   1982   The Southeastern Check Stamped Tradition. *Midcontinental Journal of Ar-
          chaeology* Special Paper 4. Kent State University Press, Kent, Ohio.

   1987   Afterword—The Morgan Site in Regional Perspective. In *Excavations at
          Morgan, a Coles Creek Mound Complex in Coastal Louisiana,* by R. S. Fuller
          and D. S. Fuller, pp. 155–64. LMS Bulletin No. II. Peabody Museum,
          Harvard University, Cambridge, Massachusetts.

Brown, William L., and Edgar Anderson
   1947   The Northern Flint Corns. *Annals, Missouri Botanical Garden* 34(1): 1–20.

Buchner, C. Andrew, and Mitchell R. Childress
   1991   A Southeastern Ceremonial Complex Gorget from Putnam County, Ten-
          nessee. *Tennessee Anthropological Association Newsletter* 16(6): 1–4.

Butler, Brian M.
   1977   Mississippian Settlement in the Black Bottom, Pope and Massac Counties,
          Illinois. Ph.D. dissertation, Southern Illinois University, Carbondale. Uni-
          versity Microfilms, Ann Arbor, Michigan.

Butler, Brian M., JoAnne M. Penny, and Cathy A. Robinson

1981   *Archaeological Survey and Evaluation for the Shawnee 200 M.W. A.F.B.C. Plant, McCracken County, Kentucky.* Research Paper No. 21. Center for Archaeological Investigations, Southern Illinois University, Carbondale.

Butler, Lorine Letcher

1935   The Ancient Buried City of Kentucky. *Natural History* 36:398–404.

Casey, Joanna

1986   The Prehistoric Exploitation of Unionacean Bivalve Molluscs in the Lower Tennessee-Cumberland-Ohio River Valleys in Western Kentucky. M.A. thesis, Department of Archaeology, Simon Fraser University, Burnaby, British Columbia.

Cinadr, Thomas J., and David S. Brose

1978   The Archaeological Excavation of the Carr Mill (33WA7S), a Custom Grist Mill in Warren County, Ohio. *Archaeological Research Reports of the Cleveland Museum of Natural History* 18(2): 1–148.

Clay, R. Berle

1963   Ceramic Complexes of the Tennessee-Cumberland Region in Western Kentucky. M.A. thesis, University of Kentucky, Lexington.

1979   A Mississippian Ceramic Sequence from Western Kentucky. *Tennessee Anthropologist* 4(2): 111–28.

1984   Morris Plain: And Other West Kentucky Smoking Guns. *Tennessee Anthropologist* 9(2): 104–13.

1997   The Mississippian Succession on the Lower Ohio. *Southeastern Archaeology* 16(1): 16–32.

Clay, R. Berle, Sherri Hilgeman, and Kit W. Wesler

1991   Lower Ohio Valley Mississippian Ceramic Sequence. Presentation at the Ceramic Workshop, Kentucky Heritage Council Archaeological Conference, Bowling Green, Kentucky, March 2–3.

Clayton, Lawrence A., Vernon James Knight, Jr., and Edward C. Moore, eds.

1993   *The DeSoto Chronicles,* 2 vols. University of Alabama Press, Tuscaloosa.

Cole, Fay-Cooper

1951   *Kincaid, a Prehistoric Illinois Metropolis.* University of Chicago Press, Chicago.

Cole, Fay-Cooper, and Thorne Deuel

1937   *Rediscovering Illinois.* University of Chicago Press, Chicago.

Conrad, Lawrence A.

1972   1966 Excavation at the Dickson Mounds: A Sepo-Spoon River Burial Mound in the Central Illinois River Valley. M.A. thesis, Department of Anthropology, University of Wisconsin, Madison.

Davis, R. P. Stephen, Jr., Patrick C. Livingood, H. Trawick Ward, and Vincas P. Steponaitis

1998   *Excavating Occaneechi Town: Archaeology of an Eighteenth-Century Indian*

Village in North Carolina. CD-ROM. University of North Carolina Press, Chapel Hill.

Deuel, Thorne

1932   Report of the Week Ending August 13, 1932. Papers of the University of Chicago Lewistown Expedition, 18 August 1932. On file in the Dickson Mounds Museum Archives, Lewistown, Illinois.

1935   Basic Cultures of the Mississippi Valley. *American Anthropologist* 37:429–45.

1937   Appendix I: The Application of a Classificatory Method to Mississippi Valley Archaeology. In *Rediscovering Illinois,* by F. Cole and T. Deuel, pp. 207–19. University of Chicago Press, Chicago.

DiBlasi, Philip J., and Joseph E. Granger

1982   *A Preliminary Cultural Resource Assessment of the Ancient Buried City 15Ba4 in Wickliffe, Kentucky.* University of Louisville Archaeological Survey, Louisville.

Donaldson, R. C.

1946   The Mound Builders of the Reelfoot Lake Region. *Tennessee Archaeologist* 2(4): 77–79.

Drennan, Robert B.

1996   *Statistics for Archaeologists: A Commonsense Approach.* Plenum Publishing Corporation, New York.

Du Pratz, Antoine Simon Le Page

1975   *The History of Louisiana* (1763). J. G. Tregle, ed. Louisiana State University Press, Baton Rouge.

Dyer, Christopher

1989   *Standards of Living in the Later Middle Ages: Social Change in England c. 1200–1520.* Cambridge University Press, New York.

Edging, Richard

1985   *The Turk Site: A Mississippian Town of the Western Kentucky Border.* Department of Anthropology, University of Illinois, Western Kentucky Project, Report No. 3. Urbana.

1990   *The Turk Site: A Mississippi Period Town in Western Kentucky.* Kentucky Heritage Council, Frankfort.

1995   Living in a Cornfield: The Variation and Ecology of Late Prehistoric Agriculture in the Western Kentucky Confluence Region. Ph.D. dissertation, Department of Anthropology, University of Illinois, Urbana-Champaign. University Microfilms, Ann Arbor, Michigan.

Erickson, Carolly

1976   *The Medieval Vision: Essays in History and Perception.* Oxford University Press, New York.

Esarey, Duane

1990   Style, Geography and Symbolism of Mississippian Spiders. Paper presented at the Southeastern Archaeological Conference, Mobile, Alabama, November 7–10.

Fisher, Alton K.

1997   Origins of the Midwestern Taxonomic System. *Midcontinental Journal of Archaeology* 22(1): 117–22.

Ford, James A., and Gordon R. Willey

1941   An Interpretation of the Prehistory of the Eastern United States. *American Anthropologist* 43:325–63.

Fowler, Melvin

1989   *The Cahokia Atlas: A Historical Atlas of Cahokia Archaeology.* Illinois Historic Preservation Agency, Studies in Illinois Archaeology No. 6. Springfield.

1991   Mound 72 and Early Mississippian at Cahokia. In *New Perspectives on Cahokia: Views from the Periphery,* edited by J. B. Stoltman, pp. 1–28. Monographs in World Archaeology 2. Prehistory Press, Madison, Wisconsin.

Franklin, William A.

1974   *Regional Atlas of the Jackson Purchase, Kentucky.* Murray State University, Murray, Kentucky.

Fried, Morton H.

1960   On the Evolution of Social Stratification and the State. In *Culture and History,* edited by S. Diamond, pp. 713–31. Columbia University Press, New York, New York.

Frink, Douglas S.

1992   The Chemical Variability of Carbonized Organic Matter through Time. *Archaeology of Eastern North America* 20:67–79.

1994   The Oxidizable Carbon Ratio (OCR): A Proposed Solution to Some of the Problems Encountered with Radiocarbon Data. *North American Archaeologist* 15(1): 17–29.

1995   Application of the Oxidizable Carbon Ratio Dating Procedure and Its Implications for Pedogenic Research. In *Pedological Perspectives in Archaeological Research,* edited by M. Collins, pp. 95–106. Soil Science Society of America Special Publication 44. Madison, Wisconsin.

1997   Letter to Kit W. Wesler, 4 January 1997, on file at Wickliffe Mounds Research Center, Wickliffe, Kentucky.

Fuller, Richard S., and Diane Sylvia Fuller

1987   *Excavations at Morgan, a Coles Creek Mound Complex in Coastal Louisiana.* LMS Bulletin No. 11. Peabody Museum, Harvard University, Cambridge, Massachusetts.

Funkhouser, W. D., and William S. Webb

1932   *Archaeological Survey of Kentucky.* University of Kentucky Reports in Anthropology and Archaeology 2. Lexington.

Garrett, J.

1988   Status, the Warrior Class, and Artificial Cranial Deformation. In *The King Site: Continuity and Contact in Sixteenth-Century Georgia,* edited by R. L. Blakely, pp. 35–46. University of Georgia Press, Athens.

Gildersleeve, Benjamin, and Joseph K. Roberts

1945   *Geology and Mineral Resources of the Jackson Purchase Region.* Commonwealth of Kentucky, Department of Mines and Minerals, Lexington.

Gramly, R. Michael

1992   *Prehistoric Lithic Industry at Dover, Tennessee.* Persimmon Press, Buffalo.

Green, Thomas J., and Cheryl Ann Munson

1978   Mississippian Settlement Patterns in Southwestern Indiana. In *Mississippian Settlement Patterns,* edited by B. D. Smith, pp. 293–330. Academic Press, New York.

Gregg, Michael

1975   A Population Estimate for Cahokia. In *Perspectives in Cahokia Archaeology,* pp. 126–36. Illinois Archaeological Survey Bulletin No. 10. Urbana.

Griffin, James B.

1946   Cultural Change and Continuity in Eastern United States Archaeology. In *Man in Northeastern North America,* edited by F. Johnson, pp. 37–95. Papers of the Robert S. Peabody Foundation for Archaeology 3. Andover, Massachusetts.

1966   Mesoamerica and the Eastern United States. In *Handbook of Middle American Indians,* vol. 4, R. Wauchope, general editor, pp. 111–31. University of Texas Press, Austin.

1976   Notes on Mississippi Myths. Paper presented to the Society for American Archaeology, St. Louis, Missouri.

1985   Changing Concepts of the Prehistoric Mississippian Cultures of the Eastern United States. In *Alabama and the Borderlands, from Prehistory to Statehood,* edited by R. R. Badger and L. A. Clayton, pp. 40–63. University of Alabama Press, Tuscaloosa.

Griffith, Roberta Jean

1981   *Ramey Incised Pottery.* Illinois Archaeological Survey, Circular No. 5. Urbana.

Hall, Robert L.

1991   Cahokia Identity and Interaction Models of Cahokia Mississippian. In *Cahokia and the Hinterlands,* edited by T. E. Emerson and R. B. Lewis, pp. 3–34. University of Illinois Press, Urbana.

Hally, David J.

1984   Vessel Assemblages and Food Habits: A Comparison of Two Aboriginal Southeastern Vessel Assemblages. *Southeastern Archaeology* 3(1): 46–64.

1993   The Territorial Size of Mississippian Chiefdoms. In *Archaeology of Eastern North America, Papers in Honor of Stephen Williams,* edited by J. B. Stoltman, pp. 143–68. Archaeological Report No. 25, Mississippi Department of Archives and History. Jackson.

1994   An Overview of Lamar Culture. In *Ocmulgee Archaeology 1936–1986,* edited by D. J. Hally, pp. 144–74. University of Georgia Press, Athens.

1996   Platform-Mound Construction and the Instability of Mississippian Chiefdoms. In *Political Structure and Change in the Prehistoric Southeastern United States,* edited by J. F. Scarry, pp. 92–127. University Press of Florida, Gainesville.

Harn, Alan D.

1980   *The Prehistory of Dickson Mounds: The Dickson Excavation.* Illinois State Museum Report of Investigation No. 36. Springfield.

Harrington, J. C.

1954   Dating Stem Fragments of Seventeenth and Eighteenth Century Clay Tobacco Pipes. *Archaeological Society of Virginia Quarterly Bulletin* 9(1): 9–13.

Hart, John P., and C. Margaret Scarry

1999   The Age of Common Beans (*Phaseolus vulgaris*) in the Northeastern United States. *American Antiquity* 64(4): 653–58.

Haskins, Valerie A.

1990   Wickliffe Mounds Cemetery Project, Assessment of Human Remains from Mound C, Wickliffe Mounds KY (15Ba4): Feasibility Study. Report on file at the Kentucky Heritage Council, Frankfort, and the Wickliffe Mounds Research Center, Wickliffe.

Hatch, James W.

1976   Status in Death: Principles of Ranking in Dallas Culture Mortuary Remains. Ph.D. dissertation, Pennsylvania State University. University Microfilms, Ann Arbor, Michigan.

Hilgeman, Sherri L.

1992   Pottery and Chronology of the Angel Site, a Middle Mississippian Center in the Lower Ohio Valley. Ph.D. dissertation, Indiana University, Bloomington. University Microfilms, Ann Arbor, Michigan.

Holmes, William H.

1886   *Ancient Pottery of the Mississippi Valley.* Bureau of American Ethnology, 4th Annual Report, 1882–83. Washington, D.C.

1903   *Aboriginal Pottery of the Eastern United States.* Bureau of American Ethnology, 20th Annual Report, 1888–99. Washington, D.C.

1914   Areas of American Culture Characterization Tentatively Outlined as an Aid in the Study of Antiquities. *American Anthropologist* 16:413–46.

Hudson, Charles

1976   *The Southeastern Indians.* University of Tennessee Press, Knoxville.

1994   The Social Context of the Chiefdom of Ichisi. In *Ocmulgee Archaeology 1936–1986,* edited by D. J. Hally, pp. 175–80. University of Georgia Press, Athens.

1997   *Knights of Spain, Warriors of the Sun.* University of Georgia Press, Athens.

Hudson, Charles, Marvin Smith, David Hally, Richard Polhemus, and Chester DePratter

1985   Coosa: A Chiefdom in the Sixteenth-Century Southeastern United States. *American Antiquity* 50(4): 723–37.

Humphrey, Maurice E.
   1976   *Soil Survey of Ballard and McCracken Counties, Kentucky.* U.S.D.A. Soil
           Conservation Service, Washington, D.C.
Johannessen, Sissel
   1988   Plant Remains and Culture Change: Are Paleoethnobotanical Data Better
           than We Think? In *Current Paleoethnobotany,* edited by C. A. Hastorf and
           V. S. Popper, pp. 145–66. University of Chicago Press, Chicago.
Johnson, Richard I.
   1980   Zoogeography of North American Unionacea (Mollusca: Bivalvia) North of
           the Maximum Glaciation. *Museum of Comparative Zoology Bulletin* 419(2):
           77–189.
Justice, Noel D.
   1987   *Stone Age Spear and Arrow Points of the Midcontinental and Eastern United
           States.* Indiana University Press, Bloomington.
Kellar, James
   1967   Material Remains. In *Angel Site: An Archaeological, Historical, and Eth-
           nological Study,* by G. A. Black, pp. 431–87. Indiana Historical Society,
           Indianapolis.
Kelly, John E.
   1984   Wells Incised Plates: Their Context and Affinities with O'Byam Incised.
           Paper presented at the Paducah Ceramics Conference, Paducah, Kentucky.
   1991   Review of *Winterville: Late Prehistoric Culture Contact in the Lower Mississippi
           Valley,* by Jeffrey P. Brain. *Southeastern Archaeology* 10(1): 76–78.
King, Blanche Busey
   1937a   Ancient Buried City. *National Archaeological News* 1(3): 13–15.
   1937b   Recent Excavations at the King Mounds, Wickliffe, Kentucky. *Illinois State
           Academy of Science Transactions* 30:83–90.
   1937c   Recent Excavations at the King Mounds, Wickliffe, Kentucky. *Hobbies* 44.
   1939   *Under Your Feet.* Dodd, Mead and Company, New York.
King, Fain W.
   1936   The Archaeology of Western Kentucky. *Transactions, Illinois Academy of
           Science* 29:35–38.
Kneberg, Madeline
   1959   Engraved Shell Gorgets and Their Associations. *Tennessee Archaeologist* 15(1):
           1–39.
Knight, Vernon J.
   1983   The Institutional Organization of Mississippian Religion. Paper presented
           at the Southeastern Archaeological Conference, Columbia, South Carolina.
Kreisa, Paul P.
   1988   *Second Order Communities in Western Kentucky: Site Survey and Excavations
           at Late Woodland and Mississippi Period Sites.* Department of Anthropology,
           University of Illinois, Western Kentucky Project, Report No. 7. Urbana.

1990a   Organizational Aspects of Mississippian Settlement Systems in Western
        Kentucky. Ph.D. dissertation, Department of Anthropology, University of
        Illinois, Urbana-Champaign. University Microfilms, Ann Arbor, Michigan.

1990b   *Prehistoric Settlement Patterns in the Big Bottoms of Fulton County, Kentucky.*
        Department of Anthropology, University of Illinois, Western Kentucky
        Project, Report No. 8. Urbana.

1991   *Mississippian Sites of the Lower Ohio River Valley in Kentucky.* Department
        of Anthropology, University of Illinois, Western Kentucky Project, Report
        No. 9. Urbana.

Kreisa, Paul P., and Jacqueline M. McDowell

1992   An Analysis of Mississippian Faunal Exploitation Patterns at Wickliffe.
        Paper presented at the Kentucky Heritage Council Archaeology Conference,
        Murray, Kentucky.

1995   An Analysis of Mississippian Faunal Exploitation Patterns at Wickliffe
        Mounds. In *Current Archaeological Research in Kentucky: Volume Three,*
        edited by J. F. Doerschuk, C. A. Bergman, and D. Pollack, pp. 161–78.
        Kentucky Heritage Council, Frankfort.

Kuttruff, Jenna T.

1990   Charred Mississippian Textile Remains from Wickliffe Mounds, Kentucky
        (15BA4). Paper presented at the 1990 Southeastern Archaeological Confer-
        ence, Mobile, Alabama.

Lawrence, William L.

1996   A New Radiocarbon Date from the McLeod Bluff site (15HiI), Hickman
        County, Kentucky. *KYOPA Newsletter* 3(2): 2–3.

Lawrence, William L., and Mainfort, Robert C.

1991   40LK4: A Protohistoric Site in the Reelfoot Basin, Lake County, Tennessee.
        Paper presented at the Southeastern Archaeological Conference, Jackson,
        Mississippi, November 6–9.

Lewis, R. Barry

1984   An Examination of the Vacant Quarter Hypothesis in the Northern Lower
        Mississippi Valley. Paper presented to the Society for American Archaeology,
        Portland, Oregon.

1986   Introduction. In *Mississippian Towns of the Western Kentucky Border: The
        Adams, Wickliffe, and Sassafras Ridge Sites,* edited by R. B. Lewis, pp. 1–8.
        Kentucky Heritage Council, Frankfort.

1988   An Old World Dice Game in the Protohistoric Southern United States.
        Current Anthropology 29:759–68.

1990a   The Late Prehistory of the Ohio-Mississippi Rivers Confluence Region,
        Kentucky and Missouri. In *Towns and Temples along the Mississippi,* edited
        by D. H. Dye and C. A. Cox, pp. 38–58. University of Alabama Press,
        Tuscaloosa.

1990b   Mississippi Period. In *The Archaeology of Kentucky: Past Accomplishments and Future Directions,* vol. 2, edited by D. Pollack, pp. 375–466. Kentucky Heritage Council, Frankfort.

1991   The Early Mississippi Period in the Confluence Region and its Northern Relationships. In *Cahokia and the Hinterlands,* edited by T. E. Emerson and R. B. Lewis, pp. 274–94. University of Illinois Press, Urbana.

1996   The Western Kentucky Border and the Cairo Lowland. In *Prehistory of the Central Mississippi Valley,* edited by C. H. McNutt, pp. 47–75. University of Alabama Press, Tuscaloosa.

Lewis, R. Barry, ed.

1986   *Mississippian Towns of the Western Kentucky Border: The Adams, Wickliffe, and Sassafras Ridge sites.* Kentucky Heritage Council.

Lewis, Thomas M. N.

1934   Kentucky's "Ancient Buried City." *Wisconsin Archaeologist* 13:25–31.

Linn, Patti

1984   A Study of Discs and Discoidals at Wickliffe Mounds. Ms. on file, Wickliffe Mounds Research Center.

Loughridge, R. H.

1888   *Report on the Geological and Economic Features of the Jackson Purchase Region.* Kentucky Geological Survey, Frankfort.

Lutz, Edwin

1995   Typological Analysis of Projectile Points in the King Collection. Notes on file, Wickliffe Mounds Research Center, Wickliffe, Kentucky.

Lyon, Edwin A.

1996   *A New Deal for Southeastern Archaeology.* University of Alabama Press, Tuscaloosa.

McKern, W. C.

1939   The Midwestern Taxonomic Method as an Aid to Archaeological Culture Study. *American Antiquity* 3(4): 301–14.

Mainfort, Robert C., Jr.

1996   Late Period Chronology in the Central Mississippi Valley: A Western Tennessee Perspective. *Southeastern Archaeology* 15(2): 172–81.

Matternes, Hugh B.

1993   Post-Formative Cultural Representation in Cemetery Remains: A Modern-Prehistoric Example. *Ohio Valley Historical Archaeology* 10:31–38.

1994   Demographic Features of Wickliffe's Mound C Cemetery: A Model Defining the Presence of Post-Classic Mississippian Peoples in Western Kentucky. Wickliffe Mounds Research Center Report No. 5. Wickliffe, Kentucky.

1999a   An Evaluation of Radiocarbon Data from Mound C, Wickliffe Mound Group (15BA4). Paper presented at the Southeastern Archaeological Conference, Pensacola, Florida, 11 November 1999.

1999b   Radiometric Analysis of the Mound C Cemetery; Wickliffe Mound Group (15BA4), Wickliffe, Kentucky. Wickliffe Mounds Research Center Report No. 7. Wickliffe, Kentucky.

Maxwell, Moreau S.

1952   The Archaeology of the Lower Mississippi Valley. In *Archaeology of Eastern United States,* edited by J. B. Griffin, pp. 176–89. University of Chicago Press, Chicago.

Mehrer, Mark W.

1995   *Cahokia's Countryside: Household Archaeology, Settlement Patterns, and Social Power.* Northern Illinois University Press, DeKalb.

Milner, George R.

1984   Social and Temporal Indications of Variation among American Bottom Mississippian Cemeteries. *American Antiquity* 49(3): 468–88.

1986   Mississippian Period Population Density in a Segment of the Central Mississippi Valley. *American Antiquity* 51(2): 227–38.

1998   *The Cahokia Chiefdom: The Archaeology of a Mississippian Society.* Smithsonian Institution Press, Washington, D.C.

Moore, Clarence B.

1916   Additional Investigations on Mississippi River. *Journal of the Academy of Natural Sciences of Philadelphia* 16:492–511.

Morse, Dan F.

1990   The Nodena Phase. In *Towns and Temples along the Mississippi,* edited by D. H. Dye and C. A. Cox, pp. 69–97. University of Alabama Press, Tuscaloosa.

Morse, Dan F., and Phyllis A. Morse

1983   *Archaeology of the Central Mississippi Valley.* Academic Press, New York.

1990   The Zebree Site: An Emerged Early Mississippian Expression in Northeast Arkansas. In *The Mississippian Emergence,* edited by B. D. Smith, pp. 51–66. Smithsonian Institution Press, Washington, D.C.

Morse, Dan F., and Phyllis A. Morse, eds.

1998   *The Lower Mississippi Valley Expeditions of Clarence Bloomfield Moore.* University of Alabama Press, Tuscaloosa.

Muller, Jon

1966   An Experimental Theory of Stylistic Analysis. Ph.D. dissertation, Department of Anthropology, Harvard University.

1978   The Kincaid System: Mississippian Settlement in the Environs of a Large Site. In *Mississippian Settlement Patterns,* edited by B. D. Smith, pp. 269–92. Academic Press, New York.

1986   *Archaeology of the Lower Ohio River Valley.* Academic Press, New York.

1989   The Southern Cult. In *The Southeastern Ceremonial Complex: Artifacts and Analysis,* edited by P. Galloway, pp. 11–26. University of Nebraska Press, Lincoln.

1993   Lower Ohio Valley Mississippian Revisited: An Autocritique of the "Kincaid System." In *Archaeology of Eastern North America: Papers in Honor of Stephen Williams,* edited by J. B. Stoltman, pp. 127–42. Archaeological Report No. 25, Mississippi Department of Archives and History. Jackson.

1997   *Mississippian Political Economy.* Plenum Press, New York.

Muller, Jon, and Jeanette E. Stephens

1991   Mississippian Sociocultural Adaptation. In *Cahokia and the Hinterlands,* edited by T. E. Emerson and R. B. Lewis, pp. 297–310. University of Illinois Press, Urbana.

NAIRCA

1936   Lost City, Lewisburg, Kentucky. *North American Indian Relic Collectors Association Official Bulletin* 1(10).

National Research Council

1932   Conference on Southern Pre-History. Reprinted 1976 by the Archeological Survey of Cobb-Fulton Counties for the Southeastern Archaeological Conference, Tuscaloosa, Alabama.

Noel Hume, Audrey

1963   Clay Tobacco Pipe Dating in the Light of Recent Excavations. *Archaeological Society of Virginia Quarterly Bulletin* 18(2): 22–25.

Noel Hume, Ivor

1970   *A Guide to Artifacts of Colonial America.* Alfred A. Knopf, New York.

Olive, Wilds W.

1974   *Geologic Map of the Wickliffe Quadrangle, Kentucky-Missouri, and the Part of the Wyatt Quadrangle in Kentucky.* United States Geological Survey, Washington, D.C.

Orser, Charles E., Jr.

1989   On Plantations and Patterns. *Historical Archaeology* 23(2): 28–40.

Ortmann, Arnold Edward

1924   The Naiad-Fauna of the Duck River in Tennessee. *American Midland Naturalist* 9:3–47.

Pauketat, Timothy C.

1987   A Functional Consideration of a Mississippian Domestic Vessel Assemblage. *Southeastern Archaeology* 6(1): 1–15.

1994   *The Ascent of Chiefs: Cahokia and Mississippian Politics in Native North America.* University of Alabama Press, Tuscaloosa.

1997   Specialization, Political Symbols, and the Crafty Elite at Cahokia. *Southeastern Archaeology* 16(1): 1–15.

Pauketat, Timothy C., and Thomas E. Emerson

1991   The Ideology of Authority and the Power of the Pot. *American Anthropologist* 93:919–41.

Peebles, Christopher S., and Susan M. Kus

1977   Some Archaeological Correlates of Ranked Societies. *American Antiquity* 42(3): 421–48.

Phillips, James L.

2000   Architectural Remains at Wickliffe: A Middle Mississippian Pit House in Western Kentucky. M.A. thesis, Department of Sociology and Anthropology, University of Mississippi, Oxford.

Phillips, Philip
1939 Introduction to the Archaeology of the Mississippi Valley. Ph.D. dissertation, Department of Anthropology, Harvard University.
1970 *Archaeological Survey in the Lower Yazoo Basin, Mississippi, 1947–1955,* 2 vols. Peabody Museum of Archaeology and Ethnology Papers 60. Harvard University, Cambridge, Massachusetts.

Phillips, Philip, and James A. Brown
1978 *Pre-Columbian Shell Engravings from the Craig Mound at Spiro, Oklahoma,* 2 vols. Peabody Museum of Archaeology and Ethnology, Harvard University, Cambridge, Massachusetts.

Phillips, Philip, James A. Ford, and James B. Griffin
1951 *Archaeological Survey in the Lower Mississippi Alluvial Valley, 1940–1947.* Papers of the Peabody Museum 25. Harvard University, Cambridge, Massachusetts.

Pollack, David, and Jimmy A. Railey
1987 *Chambers (15Ml109): An Upland Mississippian Village in Western Kentucky.* Kentucky Heritage Council, Frankfort.

Price, James E., and James B. Griffin
1979 *The Snodgrass Site of the Powers Phase of Southeast Missouri.* Museum of Anthropology, University of Michigan, Anthropological Papers No. 66. Ann Arbor.

Price, James E., and Cynthia R. Price
1984 Phase II Testing of the Shell Lake Site, 23WE-627, near Wappapello Dam, Wayne County, Missouri, 1984. U.S. Army Corps of Engineers, St. Louis District Cultural Resources Management Report No. 11.

Price, James E., and Stephen Williams
1985 The Varney Tradition: and Other Mysteries Revealed. Paper presented at the Mid-South Conference, Starkville, Mississippi, June 8–9.

Putnam, F. W.
1878 Archaeological Explorations in Tennessee. *Eleventh Annual Report of the Peabody Museum* 2(2): 305–60.

Rafinesque, Constantine S.
1824 *Ancient Annals of Kentucky and Antiquities of the State of Kentucky.* Constantine S. Rafinesque, Frankfort.

Reinburg, Kathleen M. S.
1987 An Analysis of the Faunal Material from a Middle Mississippian Site at Wickliffe Mounds, Kentucky. M.A. thesis, George Washington University, Washington, D.C.

Riordan, Robert V.
1975 Ceramics and Chronology: Mississippian Settlement in the Black Bottom, Southern Illinois. Ph.D. dissertation, Southern Illinois University, Carbondale.

Scarry, John F.

1990   The Rise, Transformation, and Fall of Apalachee: A Case Study of Political
        Change in a Chiefly Society. In *Lamar Archaeology: Mississippian Chiefdoms
        in the Deep South,* edited by M. Williams and G. Shapiro, pp. 175–86.
        University of Alabama Press, Tuscaloosa.

Sears, William H.

1958   The Wilbanks Site (9CK-5), Georgia. *Bulletin of the Bureau of American
        Ethnology* 169:129–94. Smithsonian Institution, Washington, D.C.

Simpson, Charles T.

1895   The Classification and Geographical Distribution of the Pearly Freshwater
        Mussels. *The United States National Museum, Proceedings* 18(1068): 295–
        343.

Smith, Bruce D.

1975   *Middle Mississippi Exploitation of Animal Populations.* Anthropological Pa-
        pers No. 57. University of Michigan, Ann Arbor.

1978a   *Prehistoric Patterns of Human Behavior: A Case Study in the Mississippi Valley.*
        Academic Press, New York.

1978b   Variation in Mississippian Settlement Patterns. In *Mississippian Settlement
        Patterns,* edited by B. D. Smith, pp. 480–503. Academic Press, New York.

1984   Mississippian Expansion: Tracing the Historical Development of an Ex-
        planatory Model. *Southeastern Archaeology* 3(1): 13–32.

1985   Mississippian Subsistence and Settlement. In *Alabama and the Borderlands,
        from Prehistory to Statehood,* edited by R. R. Badger and L. A. Clayton, pp.
        64–79. University of Alabama Press, Tuscaloosa.

Smith, Marvin T., and David J. Hally

1992   Chiefly Behavior: Evidence from Sixteenth-Century Spanish Accounts. In
        Lords of the Southeast: Social Inequality and the Native Elites of North America,
        edited by A. W. Barker and T. R. Pauketat, pp. 99–109. American Anthro-
        pological Society, Archaeological Papers No. 3. Washington, D.C.

South, Stanley

1977   *Method and Theory in Historical Archaeology.* Academic Press, New York.

1988   Whither Pattern? *Historical Archaeology* 22(1): 25–28.

Stoltman, James B.

1973   The Southeastern United States. In *The Development of North American
        Archaeology,* edited by J. E. Fitting, pp. 117–50. Anchor Books, New York.

Stout, Charles B.

1985   *The Adams Site: A Spatial Analysis.* Department of Anthropology, University
        of Illinois, Western Kentucky Project, Report No. 2. Urbana.

1987   *Surface Distribution Patterns at the Adams Site, a Mississippian Town in
        Fulton County, Kentucky.* Department of Anthropology, University of Illinois,
        Western Kentucky Project, Report No. 6. Urbana.

1989   The Spatial Patterning of the Adams Site, a Mississippian Town in Western
        Kentucky. Ph.D. dissertation, Department of Anthropology, University of
        Illinois, Urbana-Champaign.

Stuiver, Minze, and B. Becker

1993   High-Precision Decadal Calibration of the Radiocarbon Time Scale, A.D. 1950–6000 B.C. *Radiocarbon* 35:35–65.

Stuiver, Minze, and Paula J. Reimer

1993   Extended 14C Data Base and Revised CALIB 3.0 14C Age Calibration Program. *Radiocarbon* 35:215–30.

Sussenbach, Tom

1993   Agricultural Intensification and Mississippian Developments in the Confluence Region of the Mississippi River Valley. Ph.D. dissertation, Department of Anthropology, University of Illinois, Urbana-Champaign.

Sussenbach, Tom, and R. Barry Lewis

1987   *Archaeological Investigations in Carlisle, Hickman, and Fulton Counties, Kentucky: Site Survey and Excavations.* Department of Anthropology, University of Illinois, Western Kentucky Project, Report No. 4. Urbana.

Thomas, Cyrus

1894   *Report on Mound Exploration of the Bureau of Ethnology.* Bureau of American Ethnology, 12th Annual Report. Washington, D.C.

Thruston, Gates P.

1890   *The Antiquities of Tennessee and the Adjacent States.* Robert Clarke, Cincinnati.

Trigger, Bruce G.

1978   *Time and Tradition: Essays in Archaeological Interpretation.* Columbia University Press, New York.

van der Schalie, Henry, and Annette van der Schalie

1950   The Mussels of the Mississippi River. *American Midland Naturalist* 44:448–66.

Vogel, Joseph O.

1975   Trends in Cahokia Ceramics—Preliminary Study of the Collections from Tracts 15A and 15B. In *Perspectives in Cahokia Archaeology*, pp. 32–125. Illinois Archaeological Survey Bulletin No. 10. Urbana.

Wauchope, Robert

1966   *Archaeological Survey of Northern Georgia with a Test of Some Cultural Hypotheses.* Memoirs of the Society for American Archaeology No. 21. Salt Lake City.

Webb, William S.

1952   *The Jonathan Creek Village, Site 4, Marshall County, Kentucky.* University of Kentucky Reports in Anthropology and Archaeology 8(1). Lexington.

Webb, William S., and W. D. Funkhouser

1931   *The Tolu Site in Crittenden County, Kentucky.* University of Kentucky Reports in Anthropology and Archaeology 1(5). Lexington.

1933   *The McLeod Bluff Site in Hickman County, Kentucky.* University of Kentucky Reports in Anthropology and Archaeology 3(1). Lexington.

Weinland, Marcia K., and Thomas W. Gatus

1979   *A Reconnaissance and Evaluation of Archaeological Sites in Ballard County, Kentucky.* Kentucky Heritage Commission, Frankfort.

Wesler, Kit W.

1984   Posthole Testing and Pattern Recognition at the Whitehaven Mansion, 15McN65. *Tennessee Anthropologist* 9(1): 32–47.

1985   Archaeological Excavations at Wickliffe Mounds, 15Ba4: Mound A, 1984. Wickliffe Mounds Research Center Report No. 1. Wickliffe, Kentucky.

1987   Posthole Testing and Pattern Recognition Revisited: The Moore House, Ballard County, Kentucky. *Proceedings of the Symposium on Ohio Valley Urban and Historic Archaeology* 5:30–31. Louisville.

1988   The King Project at Wickliffe Mounds: A Private Excavation in the New Deal Era. In *New Deal Era Archaeology and Current Research in Kentucky,* edited by D. Pollack and M. L. Powell, pp. 83–96. Kentucky Heritage Council, Frankfort.

1989   Archaeological Excavations at Wickliffe Mounds, 15Ba4: Mound D, 1987. Wickliffe Mounds Research Center Report No. 3. Wickliffe, Kentucky.

1990   The 1990 Excavation at Wickliffe Mounds: As Many Questions as Answers. Paper for the Midwest Archaeological Conference, Evanston, Illinois, October 5–6.

1991a Archaeological Excavations at Wickliffe Mounds, 15Ba4: North Village and Cemetery, 1988–1989. Wickliffe Mounds Research Center Report No. 4. Wickliffe, Kentucky.

1991b Aspects of Settlement Patterning at Wickliffe (15Ba4). In *The Human Landscape in Kentucky's Past: Site Structure and Settlement Patterns,* edited by C. B. Stout and C. K. Hensley, pp. 106–27. Kentucky Heritage Council, Frankfort.

1991c Ceramics, Chronology and Horizon Markers at Wickliffe Mounds. *American Antiquity* 56(2): 278–90.

1991d On the Analytical Utility of Disturbed Deposits: Moundfill and Backfill at Wickliffe Mounds. In *Studies in Kentucky Archaeology,* edited by C. D. Hockensmith, pp. 119–31. Kentucky Heritage Council, Frankfort.

1991e Uktena's Crest. *Dragon Magazine* 175 (November): 48–55.

1992a Chronological and Spatial Perspectives on Ceramic Vessel Form at Wickliffe Mounds (15BA4). In *Current Archaeological Research in Kentucky: Volume Two,* edited by D. Pollack and A. G. Henderson, pp. 119–38. Kentucky Heritage Council, Frankfort.

1992b Further Excavations in the Wickliffe Mounds Cemetery. Paper for the Southeastern Archaeological Conference, Little Rock Arkansas, October 21–24, 1992.

1992c The Wickliffe Mounds Cemetery: Educating the Public in a Changing Exhibit. Paper for the symposium Public Education at Archaeological Parks: Doing It Every Day, at the 57th Annual Meeting of the Society for American Archaeology, Pittsburgh, Pennsylvania, April 10.

1994   Historical Archaeology and Prehistory: Experimenting with Dating Formu-
        las for Mississippi Period Ceramics. *Midcontinental Journal of Archaeology*
        19(2): 260–90.

1996a   An Elite Burial Mound at Wickliffe? In *Mounds, Embankments, and Ceremo-
        nialism: Proceedings of the 11th Annual Mid-South Archaeological Conference,
        1990,* edited by R. C. Mainfort, Jr., and R. Walling. Arkansas Archaeological
        Survey, Fayetteville.

1996b   A New Look at the Mississippian Landscape at Wickliffe Mounds. In *Current
        Archaeological Research in Kentucky, Volume 4,* edited by T. N. Sanders,
        S. Sanders, and C. B. Stout, pp. 280–96. Kentucky Heritage Council,
        Frankfort.

1996c   *Wickliffe Mounds Research Center Laboratory Manual.* Wickliffe Mounds
        Research Center, Wickliffe, Kentucky.

1997   The Wickliffe Mounds Project: Implications for Late Mississippi Period
        Chronology, Settlement and Mortuary Patterns in Western Kentucky. *Pro-
        ceedings of the Prehistoric Society* 63:261–83.

1998   Cross-Cultural Archaeology: Nigerian Perspectives on North American Re-
        search Problems. In *Historical Archaeology in Nigeria,* edited by K. W. Wesler,
        pp. 311–52. Africa World Press, Lawrenceville, New Jersey.

Wesler, Kit W., and Hugh B. Matternes

1991   The Wickliffe Mounds Cemetery: More Complex than We Thought. Pa-
        per for the Southeastern Archaeological Conference, Jackson, Mississippi,
        November 8.

Wesler, Kit W., and Sarah W. Neusius

1987   Archaeological Excavations at Wickliffe Mounds, 15Ba4: Mound F, Mound
        A Addendum, and Mitigation for the Great River Road Project, 1985 and
        1986. Wickliffe Mounds Research Center Report No. 2. Wickliffe, Kentucky.

Wharton, Mary E., and Roger W. Barbour

1973   *Trees and Shrubs of Kentucky.* University Press of Kentucky, Lexington.

Willey, Gordon R.

1966   *An Introduction to American Archaeology.* Vol. 1, *North and Middle America.*
        Prentice-Hall, Englewood Cliffs, New Jersey.

Willey, Gordon R., and Phillips, Philip

1958   *Method and Theory in American Archaeology.* University of Chicago Press,
        Chicago.

Williams, J. Raymond

1974   The Baytown Phases in the Cairo Lowland of Southeast Missouri. *Missouri
        Archaeologist* 36.

Williams, Mark, and Gary Shapiro, eds.

1990   *Lamar Archaeology: Mississippian Chiefdoms in the Deep South.* University of
        Alabama Press, Tuscaloosa.

Williams, Stephen

1954   An Archaeological Study of the Mississippian Culture in Southeast Missouri.

Ph.D. dissertation, Yale University. University Microfilms, Ann Arbor, Michigan.

1980   Armorel: A Very Late Phase in the Lower Mississippi Valley. *Southeastern Archaeological Conference Bulletin* 22:105–10.

1983   Some Ruminations on the Current Strategy of Research in the Southeast. *Southeastern Archaeological Conference Bulletin* 21:72–81.

1990   The Vacant Quarter and Other Late Events in the Lower Valley. In *Towns and Temples along the Mississippi,* edited by D. H. Dye and C. A. Cox, pp. 170–80. University of Alabama Press, Tuscaloosa.

Williams, Stephen, and Jeffrey P. Brain

1983   *Excavations at the Lake George Site, Yazoo County, Mississippi, 1958–1960.* Peabody Museum of Archaeology and Ethnology, Harvard University, Cambridge, Massachusetts.

Wolforth, Lynne Mackin

1987   *Jonathan Creek Revisited: The House Basin Structures and Their Ceramics.* Department of Anthropology, University of Illinois, Western Kentucky Project, Report No. 5. Urbana.

Wright, Henry T.

1984   Prestate Political Formations. In *On the Evolution of Complex Societies: Essays in Honor of Harry Hoijer 1982,* edited by T. K. Earle, pp. 41–77. Undena Publications, Malibu, California.

Contributors

Kristin Brown, Mid-America Remote Sensing Center, Murray State University, Murray, Kentucky.

Philip J. Carr, Department of Anthropology and Sociology, University of South Alabama, Mobile, Alabama.

Penelope B. Drooker, Anthropological Survey, New York State Museum, Albany, New York.

Richard B. Edging, Columbia, Missouri.

Rebecca L. Fye, John Wornall House Museum, Kansas City, Missouri.

Brad T. Koldehoff, Department of Anthropology, University of Illinois, Urbana, Illinois.

Paul P. Kreisa, Public Service Archaeology Program, Department of Anthropology, University of Illinois, Urbana, Illinois.

Jenna T. Kuttruff, Department of Human Ecology, Louisiana State University, Baton Rouge, Louisiana.

Jacqueline M. McDowell, Department of Anthropology, University of Illinois, Urbana, Illinois.

Hugh B. Matternes, Department of Anthropology, University of Tennessee, Knoxville, Tennessee.

John Pafford, Archaeology Laboratory, Murray State University, Murray, Kentucky.

James M. Phillips, Arkansas Archaeological Survey, University of Arkansas, Monticello, Arkansas.

Margaret J. Schoeninger, Department of Anthropology, University of Wisconsin, Madison, Wisconsin.

Mark R. Schurr, Department of Anthropology, University of Notre Dame, Notre Dame, Indiana.

Kit W. Wesler, Wickliffe Mounds Research Center, Murray State University, Wickliffe, Kentucky.

Index